SATAN IN THE
CELLULOID

100 SATANIC AND OCCULT HORROR
MOVIES OF THE 1970S

Satan in the Celluloid: Satanic and Occult Horror Movies of the 1970s
By P. J. Thorndyke

https://pjthorndyke.wordpress.com/

CONTENTS

A VULGAR DISPLAY OF POWER: POSSESSION . 155

SEASON OF THE WITCH: BLACK MAGIC 255

INTRODUCTION: A SHORT HISTORY OF THE OCCULT AND OCCULT FICTION

"I feel quite guilty every time I hear of someone's having spent valuable time looking up the Necronomicon at public libraries." – H. P. Lovecraft in a letter to James Blish and William Miller

'Occult' is a slippery term, the definition of which has encompassed many things and has changed often throughout history. The word stems from the Latin *occultus* meaning 'hidden' or 'secret' and generally refers to the study of things that fall outside of science or religion. It has been used over the centuries to refer to anything from astrology to alchemy to paganism to devil worship.

In the ancient world, the division between magical rituals and religious rituals was not clearly defined but a general understanding seems to have been that magical rituals were for personal gain rather than worship. Zoroaster, Hermes Trismegistus, and Solomon and Moses of the Old Testament were all credited with possessing 'hidden knowledge' giving them command of the supernatural. Curse tablets and protective amulets were common in the ancient world and magical papyri from Graeco-Roman Egypt contain recipes and formulae as well as spells for social advancement and the summoning of gods and demons.

Hidden knowledge has often meant 'forbidden' knowledge and all too often the accused are members of a religious minority. Knowledge and practices that go against the prevailing worldview are vulnerable to prejudice, persecution and scapegoating which has

1

given the occult a dark and sometimes morally questionable aura. Zoroastrian priests (known as 'magi') were accused by the Greek philosopher Heraclitus of having 'impious rites and rituals' and Emperor Augustus ordered two-thousand magical scrolls to be burned. This preceded the book burning at Ephesus recorded in the Acts of the Apostles, where Christian converts burned their books of magic as they cast off their old faiths. When Christianity gained a foothold as the dominant religion in Europe, it wasn't long before followers of older paths began to be persecuted for forbidden practices.

The word 'pagan' comes from the Latin word *paganus* which originally meant 'of the countryside' which indicates a division between the urban and the rural. Christianity was an organized religion of the towns while those in the countryside, whose livelihoods were dependent on the agricultural cycle of the year, preferred to stick to the older ways. Over time, pagan festivals were gradually assimilated into the Christian calendar and even some of its deities became Christianized as saints. Old customs and rituals continued to a certain extent while their original meanings became obscured, and the various horned gods of the pagan past became the demons of the new religion.

Pagans or 'heathens' (from the Anglo-Saxon word *hæðen*, possibly meaning 'people of the heath', further suggesting that it was the rural folk who were slower to adopt the new religion) were targets of persecution and forced conversion in Europe as were the Jews at whom the baseless myth of 'blood libel' was levelled. Accusations of abducting Christian children, sacrificing them in cabbalistic rituals and using their blood to make unleavened bread to be consumed during Passover led to murderous persecutions which reached horrific levels in the Middle Ages.

As the division between church and state became increasingly blurred, even fellow Christians were not safe from accusations of occult practices and heresy. Stemming from the Ancient Greek word *haíresis* meaning 'to make a choice', heresy became a label to brand all those who interpreted the Bible in ways that differed from those approved by the church authorities.

Various Gnostic sects such as the Cathars as well as Arians, Pelagians, and Waldensians were all accused of heresy at some point or another and even the Knights Templar who had so ruthlessly waged war on the Muslim 'infidels' during the crusades, were wiped out in the 14th century on the orders of King Philip I of France. Accusations of sodomy, spitting on the cross and, most infamously, worshiping a deity called Baphomet resulted in dozens of Templars, including their Grand Master to be burned at the stake.

The truth behind these alarming claims has been debated for centuries but the Templars' position at the head of an international banking system meant that many (King Philip of France included) were deeply in their debt, suggesting a more material motivation for the accusations.

Like many since, the Templars were accused of *maleficium.* often translated as 'sorcery' or 'harmful magic' sometimes known as witchcraft. A word as tricky to define as 'occult', witchcraft stems from the Anglo-Saxon word *wicce* and usually refers to practices that have existed under other names since the dawn of humanity like soothsaying, folk medicine and spells such as the Norse practice of *seiðr* or the prophecies of the sibyls of Ancient Greece.

Despite references in the Old Testament forbidding the practices of casting spells and speaking to the dead, it wasn't until the 14th century that Christian authorities readily admitted that witchcraft even existed, belief in

3

supernatural powers being considered nothing more than delusions caused by the devil in Medieval texts such as the *Canon Episcopi*. Pope John XXII's paranoia of magical assault and assassination resulted in his 1326 papal bull which officially declared witchcraft as heresy and could be investigated under the Inquisition. The winds were changing and, in 1390, a French woman called Jehane de Brigue was tried and executed for witchcraft, the first such secular trial of its kind.

The Protestant Reformation reinterpreted the idea of witchcraft with books like Heinrich Kramer's *Malleus Maleficarum* associating it specifically with the devil. These books were essentially witch hunting manuals that led to a puritanical and misogyny-fueled crusade resulting in the torture, burning and hanging of thousands of women (and occasionally men) across Europe and in its colonies, most famously in Salem, Massachusetts.

Despite the witch hunts of the Reformation, the era also interpreted aspects of the occult which could be considered valid areas of science compatible with Christianity. Alchemy goes back to the Ancient Egyptians and Babylonians who experimented with creating dyes and metals. In the melting pot of the 8th and 9th century Islamic world, Greek, Chinese and Indian theories were drawn upon and great advances were made in astronomy, natural philosophy and medicine. Europe's Scientific Revolution in the second half of the Renaissance translated many Arabic texts into Latin and divided magic into two categories; 'sorcery' which involved spirits and enchantments and was inherently bad, and 'natural magic' which was concerned with the study of all natural things and therefore acceptable.

Alchemy, astrology, divination and even demonology all came under the scope of natural magic practiced by pious Christian occultists like Nostradamus and John

Dee who took care to avoid accusations of witchcraft and heresy. One such alchemist, Johan Georg Faust, gave his name to a body of legends concerning the sacrifice of spiritual values for hidden knowledge. By the 16th century, chapbooks were widely circulated in Germany concerning the legend of 'Doctor Faust' who made a deal with the devil, Mephistopheles. Whether the real-life Faust made any such deals with the devil or not, his name gave us the adjective 'Faustian' pertaining to deals that trade the soul for material benefit.

The occult has been part of stories for as long as people have been telling them, the enchantresses Circe in *The Odyssey* and Morgan le Fay in Arthurian legend are two examples along with the three witches in *Macbeth*. In the Faust tales, we have an early example of occult fiction in the modern age of the printing press and similar demonic deals appeared in the gothic fiction of the late 18th century. William Beckford's 1782 novel *Vathek, an Arabian Tale* is the story of the Caliph Vathek who, in his quest to master the secrets of the cosmos, engages in human sacrifice and sorcery, damning his own soul in the process. In Matthew Lewis's 1796 novel *The Monk*, Ambrosio sells his soul to the devil to escape the Inquisition while the titular character in Charles Maturin's *Melmoth the Wanderer* (1820) makes a similar deal with Satan in exchange for extended life. The German playwright Johann Wolfgang von Goethe penned the definitive version of *Faust* as a play in the early 19th century and the Promethean quest for hidden knowledge is the backbone of Mary Shelly's 1818 novel *Frankenstein; or, The Modern Prometheus*, one of horror's most celebrated classics.

Elements of the occult appear in the novels of Walter Scott whose 1830 study *Letters on Demonology and Witchcraft* was an important influence on Victorian supernatural literature. His contemporary, Edward

Bulwer-Lytton, had a strong interest in the occult which manifests in the incantation-casting sorcerers of his novels *Zanoni* (1842) and *A Strange Story* (1862). Bulwer-Lytton knew the French occultist Éliphas Lévi, the most prominent figure in the French esoteric circles at the time who was largely responsible for the 19th century's increased interest in the occult.

The religious skepticism ushered in by the Age of Enlightenment had led many people to seek out other interpretations of the world around them in an age that saw rapid technological and theological change. The late 19th century was the age of Charles Darwin, Sigmund Freud and Pierre and Marie Curie but also Helena Blavatsky, the Russian mystic who co-founded the Theosophical Society and her renegade pupil, Rudolf Steiner who sought to find a synthesis between science and spirituality. The founding of The Society for Psychical Research in 1882, was a symptom of the Victorians' fascination with mesmerism and telepathy while the séances and mediums of the Spiritualist movement claimed contact with the dead; an 'occult' practice explicitly forbidden in the Bible. Just as the occult sciences of the Renaissance were considered compatible with Christianity, by the 19th century, the study of magic and the supernatural strove to be compatible with science.

The occult fiction of the late 19th century often explored the possibilities of the human mind and its untapped secrets. Edgar Allan Poe's story *The Facts in the Case of M. Valdemar* which tells of a man placed in a hypnotic state for seven months at the point of his death was published in 1845 in two journals without claiming to be fictional, resulting in many readers assuming it was a scientific report. In Robert Louis Stevenson's *Strange Case of Dr Jekyll and Mr Hyde* (1886), Jekyll attempts to separate the evil side of his personality by consuming a special potion while Oscar Wilde's *The Portrait of Dorian Gray* (1891) concerns a painting which takes on the duty of aging leaving its subject free to pursue a life of debauchery. As with *Faust* and *Frankenstein*, these stories hint at the terrible consequences of manipulating the natural world for material gain and remind us that dabbling in the occult usually comes with a high price.

But the arcane rituals of the past still fascinated 19th century authors as much as the wonders of the new age. A plethora of esoteric orders sprang up in smoky gentleman's clubs across Europe and America, chief of them The Hermetic Order of the Golden Dawn. Born of the masonic tradition, the order was unusual in that it admitted women. Dedicated to magic, mysticism and the pursuit of power and enlightenment, it was a strong influence on the western concept of the occult and authors of occult fiction.

Robert W. Chambers's 1895 quartet of short stories *The King in Yellow* contains several mentions of a mysterious occult symbol called 'the yellow sign' the mere sight of which can drive a person mad. Borrowing place names from the haunting stories of Ambrose Bierce, Chambers instigated a mythology of evil cults and long dead cities, beginning a tradition which was continued by H. P. Lovecraft. Similarly, an evil cult is at the center of Arthur Machen's collection of linked short stories *The Three Imposters* (1895) in the form of three mysterious strangers who are after a rare gold coin minted to commemorate one of Emperor Tiberius's infamous orgies.

Another story by Machen which did not see print until 1904 is *The White People* in which the diary of a young girl is found recounting her initiation into rituals of black magic by her nurse. But by far the most well-known of Machen's work is his 1894 novella *The Great*

God Pan which tells of a botched surgical procedure by a scientist investigating the heightening of spiritual powers ("seeing the god Pan") resulting in the subject's madness and the terrifying consequences which span generations.

The figure of Pan, the Greek goat-legged god of shepherds, became something of an obsession for the Victorians and Edwardians. While he represents pastoral innocence in *The Wind in the Willows* (1908) and rambunctious childhood in J. M. Barrie's character of Peter Pan, he was also something of a figurehead for the Decadent movement as a highly sexual encapsulation of our pagan past championed by Oscar Wilde and Lord Dunsany. He rears his horned head in stories by E. M. Forster and E. F. Benson as a representation of the longing for our pre-industrial and pre-Christian past; free, wild, dangerous and seductive. It is no coincidence that representations of the devil often show him with horns and cloven feet.

It wasn't just European paganism that influenced western writers of occult fiction in the Victorian era. Europe's colonial expansions of the period brought home whispers of foreign customs and terrors that fed the exoticism of occult fiction. In Rudyard Kipling's *The Mark of the Beast* (1890) a policeman's colonial arrogance results in him being bewitched by a mysterious leper when he desecrates an image of Hanuman, a Hindu god. Egypt, with its long history of alchemy and hermetic lore, was a ripe subject for occult fiction in the Egyptology craze of the late 19th century. *The Mummy's Foot* (1840) by Théophile Gautier tells of a dream encounter with an Egyptian princess after its protagonist buys a mummified foot from an antique dealer and Arthur Conan Doyle (who was heavily into the Spiritualist movement) wrote two stories; *The Ring of Thoth* (1890) and *Lot No. 249* (1892) which involve the resurrection of Ancient Egyptian mummies and in so doing gave the horror genre one of its most iconic monsters. In 1903, *Dracula* author Bram Stoker wrote his own novel about the reanimated mummy of an Egyptian queen in *Jewel of Seven Stars*.

There was a deal of overlap between Egyptology and the study of the paranormal in the late 19th and early 20th centuries. The Hermetic Order of the Golden Dawn was heavily influenced by Egyptian mysticism and imagery and none more so than Florence Farr who became leader of its English lodges in 1897. In her focus on Egypt, Farr created a splinter group in its Isis-Urania lodge called 'The Sphere' which contributed to the order's mounting internal quarrels and eventual dissolution in 1903. At the center of these quarrels was a man who would come to embody the occult in the early 20th century and remain a powerful influence on occult fiction to this day.

Aleister Crowley, mountaineer, author, painter, philosopher and occultist was born in 1875 and led a libertine lifestyle of sex, drugs and occultism. He joined the Hermetic Order of the Golden Dawn in 1898 and was a favorite of one of its founders, Samuel Liddell MacGregor Mathers but was unpopular with other members for his bisexuality and enormous ego.

After the order's collapse, Crowley pursued his own occult philosophy called 'Thelema', of which he was its prophet, destined to usher in the 'Æon of Horus'. Dubbing himself 'The Beast 666', in 1904 he penned *The Book of the Law*; the first of fifteen books which outlined his teachings, much of which revolved around sex. Needless to say, scandal followed Crowley wherever he went, and the British press dubbed him 'the wickedest man in the world'. All of this has made Crowley an attractive figurehead for early 20th century occultism, and he remains the embodiment of the occult in pop culture.

It is unknown if Crowley and the antiquarian and author M. R. James knew each other during their time at Cambridge or that James based his character of Karswell on Crowley but that has not stopped a persistent theory to that effect. James's classic occult story *Casting the Runes* (1911) concerns a vindictive occultist who attempts to bring misfortune upon those who slight him by tricking them into accepting a slip of paper with runes written on it, the possession of which causes them to be pursued by a terrible demon.

As an antiquary and a medievalist, M. R. James was able to imbue his rather misnomered 'ghost stories' with a degree of authenticity, namedropping apocryphal texts and biblical history. A staunch Christian, his tales inevitably serve as warnings against delving too deep into things that should be left well alone. The archetypal 'Jamesian' protagonist is a stuffy professor who uncovers some sort of artefact, the disturbance of which unleashes some spectral guardian most notably in *Oh, Whistle and I'll Come to You My Lad* (1904) and *A Warning to the Curious* (1925).

The occult is delved into with more deliberateness in other tales featuring aristocratic alchemists in the well-stocked libraries of their stately homes. In *Count Magnus*, the titular count is revealed to have undertaken the 'black pilgrimage' to the ruined city of Chorazin (named in the 7th century *Apocalypse of Pseudo-Methodius* as the birthplace of the antichrist) while Mr. Abney plans to murder and consume the heart of his young nephew in his pursuit to achieve immortality in *Lost Hearts*.

Aleister Crowley exerts a clearer influence on two stories by another English son of a clergyman. H. Russel Wakefield's *He Cometh and He Passeth By* (1928) involves a murderous sorcerer called Oscar Clinton while an older, more sympathetic allusion to Crowley is the figure of Apuleius Charlton in his 1951 tale *A Black Solitude* which appeared in the pulp magazine *Weird Tales*.

The occult was a staple of the inter-war era pulp magazines in which lurid tales of cults, sacrifice and cosmic horror thrilled its readers. H. P. Lovecraft in particular made a name for himself by writing about esoteric practices, forbidden knowledge and forgotten gods who care not a jot for humanity. His contributions to dark fantasy and science fiction include the witch-haunted town of Arkham with its Miskatonic University and its famed library containing one of the few copies of *The Necronomicon*; the granddaddy of all fictional occult grimoires which has popped up in everything from video games to the *Evil Dead* movies.

Speaking of movies, this is a good point to take a look at the occult in cinema for by the time Lovecraft was creating his 'Cthulhu Mythos', the silver screen had been delivering tales of the occult to shocked audiences for a couple of decades. In the early 1900s, Georges Méliès, a founding father of cinema, directed three short movies based on the Faust legend (with himself playing Mephistopheles) that were seen more as magic tricks complete with floating heads, vanishing women, pyrotechnics and superimpositions. Faust was popular with early filmmakers and there were many variations of the legend in the years of silent cinema.

Also emerging at this time were three movies by German director Paul Wegener based on the 'golem' of Jewish folklore, an artificial being animated by magic, loosely adapting Gustav Meyrink's 1915 novel *The Golem*. The surrealist angles and deep shadows of German Expressionism was well suited to occult themes and a shining example is *The Cabinet of Dr. Caligari* (1920); the tale of a mesmerist who uses his subject to commit murders. A true classic of occult cinema came out of Scandinavia in 1922. *Häxan* (also known as *Witchcraft through the Ages*) takes its cue from *Malleus Maleficarum* and poses as a documentary showing the history of witchcraft from the Middle Ages to the modern day.

The advent of sound gave voice to tales of the occult and one studio in particular led the way in the development of the horror movie. Universal Pictures had early success in 1931 with *Dracula* and *Frankenstein*, redefining these characters of gothic literature for moviegoing audiences but they also contributed original stories which happily sit alongside Stoker's and Shelly's creations to this day.

The Mummy (1932) featured *Frankenstein* star Boris Karloff as the mummified priest Imhotep, who, once resurrected pursues the reincarnation of his beloved princess. *The Mummy* owes an obvious debt to Conan Doyle's story *The Ring of Thoth* but the more famous image of the shambling, bandaged mummy under the control of an evil cult did not appear until Universal began churning out sequels in the 1940s, this time drawing influence from Conan Doyle's other mummy story, *Lot No. 249*.

Universal united Karloff and *Dracula* star Bela Lugosi in 1934's *The Black Cat*, with Karloff playing a devil-worshipping architect who has stolen the corpse of Lugosi's wife for nefarious purposes. It was unusual for Karloff to play the villain and Lugosi as a (somewhat) sympathetic character. The Hungarian star of *Dracula* was in many low-budget shockers of this period, usually typecast as the villain. One of these was *White Zombie* (1932); the first feature length zombie movie, in which Lugosi stars as a Haitian plantation owner who uses 'Voodoo' to create an army of servants.

As with Egypt's mummies, the zombie has permeated western pop culture to such a degree that its origins have been wholly obscured along with its equally misunderstood counterpart, the 'Voodoo doll' (which owes more to European concepts of witchcraft than African diaspora religions). Rather than being the result of radioactivity as in *Night of the Living Dead* (1968) or a virus outbreak in countless movies and TV shows of recent years, the zombies of the early 20th century were almost exclusively linked to Haitian Vodou, 'Vodou' being the preferred term as opposed to 'Voodoo' which has been used as a derogatory catch-all for African diaspora religions. Although there is such a religion as Louisiana Voodoo, it is considered separate from Haitian Vodou. I will be using the term 'Voodoo' in this book purely in the context of movies which present a generalized (and occasionally racist) view of African diaspora religions.

The concept of the zombie was popularized in the west by the 1929 travelogue *The Magic Island* by occultist William Seabrook who spent some time in Haiti. Race politics inevitably play their part in the assimilation of the zombie into western occult fiction. Similar to the old chestnut of the 'cursed Indian burial ground', the zombie is a (mis)interpretation of the folklore of an oppressed culture, potentially a manifestation of the white man's fear that he might just have it coming. This is expressed no better than in Robert E. Howard's classic 'weird tale' *Pigeons from Hell* (1938) which tells of a curse on a plantation family who were known to be excessively cruel to their slaves.

By the 1930s a British author had emerged who would dominate occult fiction in the mid-20th century. Dennis Wheatley's 1933 novel, *The Forbidden Territory*, introduced Duke de Richleau who would go on to feature in ten more novels, most famous of which is undoubtedly *The Devil Rides Out* which he wrote after having dinner with Aleister Crowley. Wheatley's novels marked a return to the cozy occult detective stories of the 19th century such as *In a Glass Darkly* (1872) by Sheridan le Fanu, with Sax Rohmer and Seabury Quinn carrying on the tradition. Even Aleister Crowley himself had a fictional occult detective called Simon Iff.

Between 1974 and 1977 (the year of Wheatley's death), British publisher Sphere put out 'The Dennis Wheatley Library of the Occult'; a forty-five-volume series which repackaged genuine classics of horror like *Dracula*, *Frankenstein* and *The Monk* as well as lesser-known titles like William Hope Hodgson's *Carnacki the Ghost Finder* and Aleister Crowley's *Moonchild*. Various non-fiction entries on the occult and collections of short stories were also included, all in the form of trashy-looking paperbacks with introductions written by Wheatley.

The Wheatley-endorsed Library of the Occult signi-fied the increased interest in occult fiction in the 1970s. The mainstream appetite for all things robes, runes and rituals reached a high point in the decade which gave us *The Exorcist* and *The Omen* along with their countless imitators. It was also the decade that saw a boom in a genre that would later be called 'folk horror', which focused on supernatural or occult goings on in rural settings with heavy emphasis on the folklore and traditions of the countryside. Rock music, which had dabbled with the occult in the late sixties became increasingly Satan-heavy with the emergence of heavy metal gleefully self-identifying as 'the devil's music' much to the outrage of conservative, Christian America which was also on the rise, keen to save the souls of the young by tackling the devil and all his works head on.

But what was it about the 1970s that resulted in this rise of interest in the occult and the satanic? To understand that we must look at the turbulent decade that preceded it.

INFLUENCES: THE DEATH OF THE '60S

"... in the last decades of every century, there is a sudden revival of interest in the paranormal." – Colin Wilson, author of *The Occult*(1)

By the mid-1960s, the baby boomer generation was reaching adulthood, and it was plain to see that something was happening. The relative affluence of the post-war period had allowed a larger than normal generation to focus on things other than the struggle to get food on their plates, leaving them free to probe the cracks in the American Dream as no other generation had done before.

A rejection of the Norman Rockwell portrait of America with its nuclear family and the military mentality left over from World War II began to develop. A rebellion against materialism, conformity, nuclear armament, racial inequality and the Vietnam war bred a 'hippie' movement which came to a head in 1967 when thousands of people converged on San Francisco's hippie mecca of Haight-Ashbury for a 'Summer of Love'. And it wasn't just an American phenomenon. Nothing encapsulated the cultural change in the West more than the Beatles' transformation from a mop-haired, suited British pop band to long-haired hippies whose music and image, amid trips to India and dropping acid, became increasingly psychedelic, making them both agents and models of societal change.

The cultural shift wasn't just political but spiritual too. Disillusionment with Christianity and conservative values went hand in hand with peace marches and sexual liberation. The philosophies of Aleister Crowley (who appeared on the cover of The Beatles' 1967 album *Sgt. Pepper's Lonely Hearts Club Band*) gained a second

15

wind with his maxim of 'Do what thou wilt' and fetishization of sex and drugs an easy fit for the hippie revolution. Amid a general revival of Victoriana, the late sixties saw a resurgent interest in astrology, tarot readings and parapsychology including telepathy, precognition and clairvoyance as the new generation explored alternative spiritual beliefs and dabbled with eastern mysticism.

These practices often got lumped together under the heading 'occult' (after all, the Bible rules against practices like soothsaying) and magazines like *The Occult Trade Journal* and *Psychic World and the Occult Magazine* appeared on newsstands while occult bookshops did good business in tarot card sets and classes in astral projection and Transcendental Meditation. Just as the Victorians reached into the unknown for some meaning to their lives, the 'flower children' of the 1960s were even keener to expand their horizons.

In Britain the term 'Wicca' had begun to be used for the neo-pagan movement that had emerged in the early decades of the 20th century. The amateur anthropologist, Gerald Gardner, championed the religion in the 1950s, believing in a now debunked 'witch cult theory' which claimed that those accused of witchcraft in the Early Modern period were in fact followers of a pagan faith and not, as history indicates, innocent people forced to confess under torture.

The death of Gardner in 1964 did nothing to halt the increasing interest in 'the Craft' and new flavors of Wicca sprang up in Britain and America, most notably that of Alexander Sanders and his wife Maxine whose brand of Alexandrian Wicca (as opposed to Gardnerian Wicca) placed greater emphasis on ceremonial magic.

While neo-paganism cherrypicked aspects of pre-Christian religions, other groups delved into the darker realms of Judeo-Christian mythology, eager to reinvent

Satan as the good guy. The Our Lady of Endor Coven, founded in Ohio by Herbert Arthur Sloane and the Brotherhood of the Ram which operated out of a Los Angeles bookstore are two low-key examples. More famously, The Process Church of the Final Judgement was founded in 1966 by British Scientology dropouts Mary Ann MacLean and Robert de Grimston. Believing in four 'Great Gods of the Universe' - Jehovah, Lucifer, Satan, and Christ – the Process saw none of these as evil nor literal deities but rather, personality aspects to be manifested with the aid of meditation and psychotherapy. The Process owned coffee shops (like Satan's Cavern in London), put out a magazine and dressed in black robes with goat's head medallions, making them one of the more visible 'satanic' cults of the 1960s.

But the Process failed to impress one Anton Szander LaVey, who despised the hordes of hippies who infested his home of San Francisco. Born in 1930, LaVey had worked as a carny hustler and burlesque show organ player, and allegedly, as a crime scene photographer for the San Francisco Police Department as well as a psychic investigator taking '800 calls' dealing with unexplained phenomena. By the early sixties, LaVey had become something of an occult consultant, writing columns in newspapers and giving seminars on all things macabre and paranormal. He held court over a magic circle of likeminded individuals called the Order of the Trapezoid, and this became the basis of his burgeoning religious movement.

LaVey held Satan up not as a deity to be worshipped, but rather as a metaphor for man's primal nature. Based on indulgence over abstinence, LaVeyan Satanism is a rejection of Christianity's so-called sins in favor of satanic virtues which lead to physical, emotional or mental gratification.

On 30 April 1966 (Walpurgisnacht), Anton LaVey

declared himself High Priest of the Church of Satan, officially founding a new religious organization. Media reaction was a mixture of horror and titillation as reports of satanic weddings and baptisms emerged, leading the press to dub LaVey 'The Black Pope'. LaVey appeared on talk shows dressed in red and black robes, every bit the vaudevillian showman while the Church of Satan put out a recording of a black mass on LP in 1968 and the following year LaVey's *The Satanic Bible* was published as a mass market paperback. While some conservatives were horrified, most people seemed to get the joke; Satanism was now mainstream.

Playful flirtation with the devil became part and parcel of the era. The list of rumored members of the Church of Satan included Jayne Mansfield and Sammy Davis Jr. while rock stars were keen to strut some satanic chic. None more so than the Rolling Stones, starting with their psychedelic 1967 album *Their Satanic Majesties Request* and continuing with their follow-up *Beggar's Banquet* which kicks off with the classic track 'Sympathy for the Devil'.

It was during this period that the Stones began associating with avant-garde filmmaker Kenneth Anger, a Thelemite and early associate of Anton LaVey. Anger wanted Mick Jagger for the title role of his next project; *Lucifer Rising*. Jagger declined and Anger settled on another pretty-boy musician called Bobby Beausoleil with whom he was infatuated and took to calling 'Cupid'. After a catastrophic falling out (in which Anger claimed Beausoleil absconded with much of the footage for *Lucifer Rising*), Anger conceived a new project; *The Invocation of my Demon Brother*, shot in Haight-Ashbury and featuring Anton LaVey as 'His Satanic Majesty' and what little footage Anger had left of Beausoleil as Lucifer. Mick Jagger provided the noise music on a Moog synthesizer.

After the Summer of Love faded, the scene began to get pretty sordid in the Haight. The free sex and drugs so associated with the time and place began to be controlled by pimps and pushers as biker gangs muscled in to make a profit. Medical clinics were overloaded as venereal diseases skyrocketed, drugs grew harder and cruder and some of the self-appointed mystics and gurus were downright exploitative.

Into this sulfurous melting pot of drugs, exploitation and occultism stepped a thirty-three-year-old career criminal who had spent most of his youth in prisons and reform schools. When Charles Manson had last been a free man, the year had been 1960. As he gazed around at the sights of Haight-Ashbury, he could see that the world had changed drastically, and he wanted a piece of it.

Playing the guitar wasn't the only thing Manson had learned in prison. His interests ranged from Scientology to Dale Carnegie's self-help book *How to Win Friends and Influence People* all of which contributed to his growing philosophy that also included the fire and brimstone Christianity of his upbringing and old-fashioned racism. Manson was a master manipulator who gathered stoners and teenage runaways to him such as Susan Atkins, a former dancer in Anton LaVey's Topless Witches Revue.

With the scene in the Haight growing ever more dangerous, Manson and his groupies (who came to be known as 'the Family') headed for L.A. where they bummed around in Topanga Canyon, dumpster diving for food. It was at this point that Bobby Beausoleil resurfaced after his spat with Kenneth Anger and joined the Family. Manson also made the acquaintance of Beach Boys drummer Dennis Wilson whom he convinced could help him secure his big break in the music industry.

When record deals and stardom were not forth-coming, things took a turn for the worse. A vengeful Manson relocated his cult to a rundown Western movie set called Spahn Ranch and his preaching became ever more apocalyptic. The civil rights movement and the riots following the murder of Martin Luther King Jr. had Manson frantic that the black population would rise up and slaughter the whites. After a botched drug deal resulted in Manson shooting black drug dealer Bernard "Lotsapoppa" Crowe, mistaking him for a member of the Black Panthers, Spahn Ranch became a fortified stronghold with talk of surviving the coming apocalypse and emerging from the desert to rule over the blacks as 'the chosen ones'.

But in the meantime, the Family needed money and, upon hearing that their associate, Gary Hinman had recently come into a large inheritance, Manson sent three of his acolytes including Susan Atkins and Bobby Beausoleil to Hinman's house where they tortured him for two days in an attempt to get him to hand over the money. When it appeared that there was no inheritance after all, Manson told Beausoleil over the phone that he knew what he needed to do. Beausoleil hung up and stabbed Hinman to death, using his blood to write 'political piggy' on the wall along with a pawprint to suggest that it was the work of the Black Panthers. This was either to avert the blame or kickstart the inevitable race war Manson had envisioned.

Beausoleil, not exactly a criminal mastermind, kept Hinman's car for himself and was arrested less than two weeks later after falling asleep in it, the bloodied murder weapon stored in the tire well. Distressed by Beausoleil's arrest, the Manson Family began to discuss further murders that would match Hinman's and therefore prove that Beausoleil was innocent while placing the blame on the Black Panthers.

On the morning of August 10, 1969, a gruesome discovery was made at 10050 Cielo Drive in Benedict Canyon. Five bodies were found, horrifically butchered. The victims were rising movie star Sharon Tate and her friends Jay Sebring (celebrity hairstylist), Wojciech Frykowski and Abigail Folger (heiress to the Folger coffee fortune) along with Steven Parent; an eighteen-year-old who was on his way out after visiting his friend in the guesthouse. The word 'Pig' had been written on the door in the blood of Sharon Tate who had been eight months pregnant.

Hollywood was paralyzed with terror. The ritualistic nature of the murders fed theories that it was somehow connected to Sharon Tate's husband Roman Polanski who was in London at the time of the murders. The year before, Polanski had directed *Rosemary's Baby*, a terrifying story of a young woman impregnated by the devil in a ritual orchestrated by the satanic cult living next door.

The following night more murders were committed, and the bodies of grocery store chain owner Leno LaBianca and his wife Rosemary were found at 3301 Waverly Drive, both of them stabbed to death. The words 'Rise', 'Death to pigs' and 'Healter (sic) Skelter' were smeared on the walls in their blood.

In October, several members of the Family were arrested for auto theft, one of whom implicated Susan Atkins in the Hinman murder. While in custody, Atkins started bragging about her involvement in the Tate and LaBianca murders. More arrests followed in December and the world watched in horror as a picture emerged of a hippie cult led by a charismatic Svengali who ordered his followers to kill.

That very month, a free concert at the Altamont Speedway in California featuring the Rolling Stones descended into carnage due to bad drugs and overzealous security in the form of Hells Angels paid for in beer. Four people were killed including Meredith Hunter, a young black man who pulled a gun on the bikers and was stabbed to death. It might not have been the apocalyptic race war Charles Manson had predicted but any hope that Altamont would be a West Coast answer to the Woodstock festival held just four months earlier, evaporated. The vibe had changed, the mood had soured and the 1960s were over.

The senseless, drug-fueled insanity of the Manson clan may have rendered the connection between their victims and *Rosemary's Baby* nothing more than a coincidence, but both played their part in the growing unease over the cults and occult dabbling of the late-sixties. Suddenly the spiritual experimentations of the counterculture were laced with danger.

Ira Levin's novel of a satanic cult operating in modern-day New York City and Roman Polanski's near perfect movie adaptation marked a change in horror from the gothic castles of the past to the tenement blocks of the modern world. Similar novels followed such as *The Possession of Joel Delaney* by Ramona Stewart in 1970 and *The Other* by Thomas Tryon in 1971. Themes of cults, possessions and black magic took over from mad science, vampires and other stock monsters of the previous decades. Colin Wilson's academic book *The Occult* in 1971 fed the interest and helped define the occult for a new generation.

The cover of the June 1972 issue of *Time* Magazine featured a hooded member of the Church of Satan and its cover story *The Occult Revival: A Substitute Faith* claimed that black masses were being performed in middle-class households across America. The same article noted that William Peter Blatty's novel *The Exorcist* had been on the bestseller list for 52 weeks. When the movie came out the following year amid rumors of vomit bags being issued by theatres and women miscarrying during showings, sales of Ouija boards skyrocketed. The occult was now big business and it was clear to all that Satan sold. *Rosemary's Baby* may have been an early symptom, but *The Exorcist* fed a full-blown pandemic.

BURNT OFFERINGS: EVIL CULTS

*"I think Rowan Morrison was murdered, under circum-
stances of Pagan barbarity, which I can scarcely bring
myself to believe is taking place in the 20th century."* –
Sergeant Howie, *The Wicker Man*

In 1969, director of B-grade schlock, Al Adamson, made
two movies at Spahn Ranch while the Manson Family
were actually living there and were such a pain in the
ass by all accounts that Adamson personally kicked
them off his set(2). *The Female Bunch* (1971) is about a
gang of women who smuggle drugs into the US from
their ranch in Mexico while *Satan's Sadists* (1969) is one
of the plethora of biker gang movies of the late sixties
inaugurated by Roger Corman's *The Wild Angels* (1966).

The biker movie craze had begun to wind down by
1970 with the actions of the Manson Family making the
boozy, destructive antics of leather-clad motorcycle
enthusiasts seem playful in comparison. Hollywood had
already embarked on what could be termed the
'hippiesploitation' genre with movies like *The Trip*
(1967) and *Psych-Out* (1968) using psychedelic filmmaking techniques to depict the experience of drugs and,
more often than not, poked a little fun at the Haight-
Ashbury crowd. But as the Manson Family trial unfold-
ed, the image of the long-haired peacenik transformed
into something much more sinister. Hippies weren't just
an untidy nuisance anymore. Now they might break into
your house and kill you.

I Drink Your Blood (1971) was shot while the Family
were still on trial and stars Indian folk dancer, artist and
actor Bhaskar Roy Chowdhury as the Manson-esque
leader of a hippie cult who descend on a small town,
their minds bent on rape and murder. A local boy gets

revenge by extracting blood from a rabid dog and injecting it into meat pies which the cult then consume, making them even more dangerous.

While there is nothing occult about *I Drink Your Blood*, the effect of the Manson Family is obvious and can be seen again in *The Night God Screamed* (1971), *Last House on the Left* (1972) and *Snuff* (1976). One movie which took the dangerous hippie guru into supernatural territory was *Deathmaster* (1972), in which Robert Quarry played the second vampire in his career (after Count Yorga) as he worms his way into a hippie enclave in Topanga Canyon. As the decade wore on, the isolation of the American wilderness provided cover for cannibalistic hillbillies and mutants who prey on unsuspecting travelers in *The Texas Chainsaw Massacre* (1974) and *The Hills Have Eyes* (1977), demonstrating the unease felt about communes of people with different belief systems living beyond society, occult or otherwise.

The rise of the Wicca movement signified the em-powering aspects of the occult through the lens of the feminist movement and several witchy movies of the 1970s depicted immortal or reincarnated witches who were both vengeful and powerful. *Queens of Evil* (1970) and *Blood Sabbath* (1972) both deal with covens of witches surviving in the wilderness to lure young men into their dark ceremonies while *Daughters of Satan* (1972) concerns the reincarnation of a trio of witches seeking revenge on the descendant of the man who executed them.

'Folk horror' is a term that has become more and more popular in recent years to describe stories that deal with nasty goings on in rural communities with a focus on folklore, isolation and landscape. *Witchfinder General* (1968), an early example of the subgenre, inspired a cottage industry in movies about bloodthirsty religious zealotry served up with bared breasts and the brutalization of women for titillated audiences. These included *The Bloody Judge* (1970), the German-made *Mark of the Devil* (1970) and its sequel, *Mark of the Devil II* (1973). Even Hammer Productions gave it a shot with Peter Cushing playing a puritanical witch hunter in *Twins of Evil* (1971).

Most of these movies had nothing supernatural about them or even dealt with the occult other than spurious accusations of witchcraft but two such movies turned puritan superstitions into supernatural horror by making the satanic powers of the witches they feared real. *Cry of the Banshee* (1970) and *Blood on Satan's Claw* (1971) almost side with the religious authorities as they present the witchcraft of old England as a genuine threat.

The term folk horror was first applied to *Blood on Satan's Claw* during its filming by reviewer Rod Cooper in a 1970 issue of the magazine *Kine Weekly*. The term was used again by its director, Piers Haggard, in an interview in *Fangoria* in 2004. Writer and actor Mark Gatiss popularized the term further in his 2010 documentary *A History of Horror* in which he grouped *Witchfinder General*, *Blood on Satan's Claw* and *The Wicker Man* (1973) together as folk horror classics, united in their focus on the British landscape, its folklore and its superstitions.

The Wicker Man managed to blend the contemporary fear of Manson-esque cults with the age-old fear of paganism and witchcraft and remains the quintessential folk horror movie from a decade which seemed determined to conjure a darker interpretation of our pagan past. Possibly the disillusionment with the return-to-nature hippie optimism of the late sixties bears some of the responsibility for the folk horror boom, along with the souring of the counterculture by the actions of the Manson Family which suggested something darker behind the flower power and dancing in stone circles.

Sometimes the cultists of 1970s horror movies had more supernatural origins. As well as the aforementioned *Deathmaster*, Count Dracula himself was given a cult to do his dirty work in *The Satanic Rites of Dracula* (1973). In addition to this, *Invasion of the Blood Farmers* (1972), *The Reincarnation of Isabel* (1973), *Legacy of Satan* (1974), and *The Devil's Wedding Night* (1973) all hint at vampirism, taking old stock horror characters and giving them new purpose as evil cultists. Sometimes it was hard to tell if the cultists were vampires or zombies as in *Night of the Sorcerers* (1974) by director Amando de Ossorio. De Ossorio's 'Blind Dead tetralogy' focused on an evil cult of Templar knights who are resurrected (by different means in each movie) to either feast on innocent victims or sacrifice them to their heathen gods. While looking and acting like zombies, the first movie in the series, *Tombs of the Blind Dead* (1972), suggests that these undead revenants are in fact vampires by the way one of their victims is found drained of blood.

But the effect of *Rosemary's Baby* (1968) still held sway over much of the occult output of the 1970s. Many cults were so frightening due to their ability to masquerade as ordinary people. They could be friendly couples met on vacation as in *Race with the Devil* (1975), elderly relatives in *Satan's Slave* (1976) or old school friends in *Satan's Blood* (1978). The paranoia of not knowing whom to trust permeated these movies and tapped into the disillusionment of the post-Watergate era while the varied stomping grounds of these devil cults made them seem as if they might pop up anywhere. The anonymity of living in the big city was frightening enough in *Rosemary's Baby* but movies like *The Brotherhood of Satan* (1971) and *Necromancy* (1972) showed that small towns with their close-knit communities could be just as intimidating to the outsider. Several had a curious Western feel to them such as *Enter the Devil* (1972) and *The Devil's Rain* (1975).

While a lot of these cults were little more than hedonistic orgies in honor of Satan, many continued the tradition of *Rosemary's Baby* in focusing their attentions on the conception, delivery and raising of a child which was either the offspring of Satan or the antichrist. Both *Obscene Desire* (1978) and *Satan's Blood* (1978) featured pregnant women who were unknowingly safe-guarded by satanic cults. While a TV sequel to *Rosemary's Baby*, titled *What Rosemary's Baby Did Next*, was broadcast in 1976, many other movies pondered the idea of what exactly the devil's offspring might get up to. *The Omen* (1976) set the standard for the demonic child trope with *Holocaust 2000* (1977) conflating the apocalypse with Cold War era fears of nuclear annihilation. *Ring of Darkness* (1979) focused on the coming-of-age of a child born to a satanic cultist who had given her body to Satan.

The tradition of aristocratic Satanists meeting in country mansions of the Dennis Wheatley school of occult fiction remained in vogue. *All the Colors of the Dark* (1972) has a traumatized woman seek help (and sexual fulfilment) from a satanic cult who meet at a rambling country estate while *Virgin Witch* (1971) and *Satan's Slave* both see unsuspecting victims wind up at similar locations where occult rituals are screened by the pomp and grandeur of England's old ruling class.

The cultists of the 1970s came in many forms but the general idea seemed to follow a pattern. Whether they were hippies, vampires, witches, friendly neighbors or wealthy aristocrats, the universal motifs of robes candles, pentagrams and the invocation of demonic forces showed that the occult craze of the era could find limitless avenues and incarnations.

CRY OF THE BANSHEE (1970)
Director: Gordon Hessler
Writers: Tim Kelly and Christopher Wicking

American International Pictures (AIP) had a real hit in 1968 when they distributed Tigon British Film Productions' folk horror classic, *Witchfinder General*. It presented a heavily fictionalized account of the real-life Matthew Hopkins, the self-appointed witchfinder whose reign of terror went unchecked during the English Civil War. The movie was controversial but turned a healthy profit in the US where it was retitled *The Conqueror Worm* and tacked on to AIP's Edgar Allan Poe cycle (inaugurated by 1960's *House of Usher*) despite having nothing to do with Poe.

AIP was keen to expand on what they hoped would be a second cycle of Poe movies and its British subsidiary production company turned out *The Oblong Box* in 1969 which starred several of *Witchfinder General*'s cast including Vincent Price and originally, its director Michael Reeves too. Gordon Hessler was brought in to replace Reeves after he fell ill (and died several months later). The success of *The Oblong Box* led to Hessler directing the next 'Poe' installment, which was a clear attempt to mimic *Witchfinder General*, titled *Cry of the Banshee*.

Starting with a random quote from Poe purely to link *Cry of the Banshee* to previous Poe entries, the credits appear over some amusing animations courtesy of Monty Python's Terry Gilliam. We are introduced to Lord Whitman (Vincent Price), a 16th century magistrate and a thoroughly unlikeable brute who persecutes accused witches with zeal and allows his loutish son, Sean (Stephan Chase) to rape the local women without impunity.

Various side characters are introduced; Lady Whitman (Swedish actress Essy Persson), Lord Whitman's daughter Maureen (Hilary Dwyer, who had starred with Price in both *Witchfinder General* and *The Oblong Box*) and her childhood companion, Roderick (Patrick Mower) who seems to be of gypsy descent and was found by Maureen as an orphan. In addition to this, Lord Whitman's other son, Harry (Carl Rigg) returns from his education at Cambridge along with the priest, Father Tom (Marshall Jones), suggesting that this is taking place before Henry the VIII's break with the Catholic Church which is unusual for a witch-hunting storyline.

The real meat of the plot concerns the witch Oona (the British-Austrian stage actress, Elisabeth Bergner) and the curse she places on the Whitman family after Lord Whitman's sons break up one of her pagan rituals and murder several of her coven. And this is how *Cry of the Banshee* differs from *Witchfinder General* and many of its ilk in that its horror isn't purely the result of bigotry and religious zealots but instead embraces the supernatural as a real threat. As a result, it's hard to know who to root for (other than the poor saps caught in the middle) as Oona is more than happy to murder the whole family when her beef should be limited to Lord Whitman and his sons.

There's lots of chanting around candles and a chalk pentagram but once Oona's demoniacal tool of revenge starts stalking members of the Whitman family (aided by Oona sticking pins into dolls) we don't see a whole lot of it or really understand what it is. Perhaps that's for the best, given the quality of make-up that we do see. Despite the title, no banshees are involved (a banshee being a female creature from Irish folklore who heralds death by wailing) although there is a degree of wolf howling and the appearance of a mad dog which sets everybody on edge.

One gets the feeling that the mythological elements of the script (originally penned by Tim Kelly before being overhauled by Hammer regular Christopher Wicking) got buried at some point by the various attempts at family drama that are never explored in detail. Things are confused further by an overabundance of side characters who all look somewhat similar and feel superfluous.

Vincent Price is doing his best, but his character can't seem to decide if he believes in witchcraft or not. He's happy to persecute women accused of witchcraft but refuses to humor the superstitions of his tenants as he tries to downplay the existence of demonic powers. There is also some confusion around the character of Roderick who seems somehow connected to Oona's curse and wears a mysterious medallion found on him when he was a child which is never explained.

The English countryside is beautifully shot however, and the movie benefits from many scenes shot at the historic house at Grim's Dyke in northwest London. Hessler creates a moody, autumnal backdrop peopled by dim-witted yokels played by colorful character actors who add a level of camp to the proceedings. There's a good punch-up in a torture chamber and the movie's surprise climax almost makes up for its convoluted plot and muddled character motivations.

BLOOD ON SATAN'S CLAW (1970)

Director: Piers Haggard
Writers: Robert Wynne-Simmons and Piers Haggard

While AIP tried to follow up the success of *Witchfinder General* (1968) with *The Oblong Box* (1969) and *Cry of the Banshee*, Tigon British Film Productions (who had made *Witchfinder General*) were planning their own follow up. They asked Robert Wynne-Simmons to pen a portmanteau of separate stories the way rival horror studio Amicus had done with their movies *Dr. Terror's House of Horrors* (1965) and *Torture Garden* (1967).

Wynne-Simmons crafted three interconnected stories about devilish doings in a Victorian village but felt that a single full-length story would work better. The studio eventually agreed but changed the setting to the early 18th century as they felt that the Victorian period had been exhausted, particularly by the output of rival studio Hammer Film Productions. Wynne-Simmons's script (originally titled 'The Devil's Skin') is an unsettling story of nasty goings on in a simple farming community and of its children who become increasingly murderous.

While America was still reeling from the appalling crimes of the Manson Family, the UK had its own true horror story in the form of eleven-year-old Mary Bell who, in 1968, strangled two toddlers in an impoverished area of Newcastle. That the cherub-faced Mary Bell showed neither motive nor remorse for the killings was particularly chilling and was a partial inspiration for Wynne-Simmons.

The discovery of a deformed skull in a field by a local ploughman sets off a series of disturbing events at the center of *Blood on Satan's Claw*. Believing the remains to be some sort of demon, the ploughman's tale is met with skepticism by the judge (Patrick Wymark who played Cromwell in *Witchfinder General*). The judge is staying with Widow Banham whose nephew (Simon Williams) has also come to visit, bringing with him his betrothed, Rosalind (Tamara Ustinov). Rosalind suffers some sort of fit during the night and is carted off to Bedlam, sporting a nasty-looking claw where her hand used to be.

Then there is the case of Angel Blake (Linda Hayden) who has found a claw in the field and seemingly succumbs to its power, drawing in the local children who start skipping scripture lessons for games in a ruined church in the woods. Things take a turn for the seriously nasty when they start sprouting patches of scaly, hairy skin on their bodies as they continue to follow the increasingly deranged Angel with all the fanaticism of a murderous cult. Linda Hayden's performance bears an uncomfortable similarity to Mary Bell while the woodland frolics of her followers and their war on the adult establishment recalls Manson's crazies, making the movie timely in some of its most horrifying aspects.

The low camera shots make the viewer feel literally closer to the earth from which the evil seeps and one can practically smell the mud that is caked on boots and cartwheels all to the perfectly eerie musical score by Marc Wilkinson. That the movie's most shocking scenes happen in broad daylight is a testament to its commitment to a new kind of horror. The gothic cliches of dark forests and moonlit graveyards are dumped in favor of sunlit lanes and clearings where the evil feels all the more sinister when it does rear its head.

Much of the horror is corporeal and, despite the makeup effects of 'the devil's skin' not being particularly convincing, the surgical removal in one scene is suggestive enough to make the average audience member squirm. In another surprisingly gruesome scene, Widow Banham's nephew suffers a similar trauma to that of his ex-fiancé when he is attacked in bed by a clawed hand. After cutting the demonic hand off with a knife, he is distraught to discover that the hand was in fact, his own.

There are problems, however. The movie's original incarnation as a portmanteau of separate stories is occasionally apparent, its tight shooting schedule meaning that there wasn't time to fully rework the script into a cohesive narrative. Characters disappear without explanation and the plot feels a little disjointed and episodic. Then there is the rape and murder of the teenaged Cathy (Wendy Padbury) by her fellow adolescents on the orders of Angel; an infamous scene which was and is considered a little too strong bordering on gratuitous. As with *Witchfinder General*, it's an incredibly uncomfortable movie to watch, but then, maybe that's the point.

Originally released in late 1970 as *Satan's Skin*, *Blood on Satan's Claw* did little business until it was retitled and rereleased as a double bill with another Tigon shocker; *The Beast in the Cellar* the following year. Never as popular as some of its counterparts, *Blood on Satan's Claw* was more or less forgotten until recent years in which it has enjoyed a revival as a pioneering example of folk horror.

LA REGINE/QUEENS OF EVIL (1970)

Director: Tonino Cervi
Writers: Tonino Cervi, Benedetto Benedetti and Antonio Troiso

Italian writer and director Tonino Cervi made his debut with the Spaghetti Western *Today We Kill, Tomorrow We Die!* (1968) which he co-wrote with Dario Argento. While Argento would eventually immerse himself in the occult and direct the classic witchy movie *Suspiria*, Cervi served up an equally enthralling tale of a witches' coven in his 1970 follow-up; a strange, dreamlike fantasy movie that, like *Suspiria*, delivers on the horror while being a visually stunning piece of arthouse cinema.

Hippie biker, David (Ray Lovelock, who also provided the title song) is riding through the mountains, the wind in his hair. As darkness descends, he stops to help a suited man of the establishment fix a flat tire. The man (Gianni Santuccio) is less than graceful, giving David a lecture on his long hair and presumed unconventional attitudes towards sex. The man praises conservative values such as monogamy (even if "an occasional peccadillo does no harm").

Worse than this, David finds that the man has stuck a nail in the tire of his motorcycle. He chases after the man who crashes into a tree and is apparently killed. David tries to flag down help, but nobody wants to stop for a dirty hippy.

David splits the scene and, in one of many fairy-tale moments, meets a literal and moral fork in the road. Hand himself in to the police whose flashing lights can be seen in the distance or take the creepy route through the woods? He chooses the latter and winds up spending the night in somebody's wood store. He awakes the next day to find himself on the property of three astonishingly beautiful women; Liv (Haydee Politoff), Samantha (Silvia Monti) and Bibiana (Ida Galli).

Invited to stay with them, David enters what seems to be a paradise scenario that plays out against the interesting juxtaposition of an old farmhouse on the outside and ultra-seventies love pad inside. These women eat cake for breakfast, lounge about in sheer negligees and have no qualms about sharing a lover. They promise they won't get jealous if he sleeps with them all so, naturally, he does.

Starting out, *Queens of Evil* feels like another existential commentary on the plight of longhairs against the establishment. An extension of the previous year's *Easy Rider* with the addition of a witchy, supernatural element. But, as this weird fairytale progresses, we find a much more intriguing message at the center that at once embraces the counterculture of the late sixties and wags its finger at it.

As if the title wasn't enough of a clue, the titular *Queens of Evil* aren't quite what they seem. They perform pagan rituals in the woods and seem to possess supernatural powers. There's an old castle nearby owned by an eccentric man that the trio have a deep connection with. As the weirdness starts to pile up, David begins to wonder if he should really be sticking around.

Queens of Evil is brimming with neopagan elements, the most prominent of which is the maiden, mother and crone motif popularized by Robert Graves (although Ida Galli, the eldest of the trio and apparent leader of the coven, is anything but a 'crone'). The significance of apple trees and lakes is reminiscent of the medieval romances of King Arthur which, despite their Christian gloss, are chock-full of pre-Christian Celtic motifs.

It's unusual for a movie of this period (or any period) to have the evil satanic cultists represent conservatism in opposition to the free love of the hippie revolution but, through a series of enlightening discussions, we are told that the hippie utopia of unfettered liberty would destroy the concept of sin. The devil isn't on board with hippies, fearing that he'd be out of a job if they managed to infect the world with their ideas on freedom. As one of the bourgeois guests at the party in the castle towards the end says; "at what point does liberty become anarchy?" Sinners deviating from a world of rules is what the devil wants, not hippie orgies in a hedonistic paradise where there are *no* rules.

Given its preoccupation with sex, *Queens of Evil* feels on the verge of descending into Euro-sleaze at any moment but it's surprisingly restrained, with even the sex scenes showing only the barest glimpses of skin. There isn't a whole lot of gore either until the movie's brutal climax so those expecting a conventional horror movie will most likely be disappointed. However, approaching *Queens of Evil* with an open mind and an understanding of the context in which it was made, is very rewarding. It's a stylish, sexy and thought-provoking movie that ultimately delivers the goods with some non-conventional discussions on the devil and the counterculture that seemingly so embraced him.

THE BROTHERHOOD OF SATAN (1971)

Director: Bernard McEveety
Writers: L.Q. Jones, Sean MacGregor and William Welch

The effect *Rosemary's Baby* (1968) had on the horror genre cannot be understated. It shooed away the stock monsters of previous decades and ushered in a terror of satanic cults operating in our midst, with many movies taking the formula from its urban environment and trying it out in other settings. One such variant was *The Brotherhood of Satan*, part of a run of movies about satanic goings on in dusty, desert towns that continued with *Enter the Devil*, *The Devil's Rain* and *Race with the Devil*.

These movies had more than a touch of the Western about them and *The Brotherhood of Satan* boasted an impressive cast and crew of Western veterans. Director Bernard McEveety had helmed a slew of TV Westerns including fifty-two episodes of *Gunsmoke* while character actors Strother Martin and L. Q. Jones (who also produced and co-wrote the movie) were both alumni of *The Wild Bunch* (1969) as well as several other Sam Peckinpah movies.

The Brotherhood of Satan opens with an effective sequence that juxtaposes children playing with a toy tank and a pair of adults being crushed to death in their car by the caterpillar tracks of a real tank. Right from the get-go, we can tell that whatever is going to happen in this movie, it will involve children.

Ben Holden (prolific TV actor Charles Bateman), his new girlfriend Nicky (Ahna Capri) and Ben's nine-year old daughter from a previous marriage, K.T. (Geri Reischl) are driving through the area when they come across the mangled and blood-spattered wreckage. They head into the nearby town of Hillsboro, noting on their way in that the radio cuts out. Ben and his family receive a frosty reception. Something strange is going on in Hillsboro. Several adults have been killed and their children have gone missing.

Isolated at the best of times, Hillsboro seems completely cut off with no mail or delivery vans coming through. Only Ben and his family seem to have been let in through some cosmic barrier, and for a dark and macabre reason. Ben joins forces with Sheriff Pete (L. Q. Jones), Deputy Tobey (Alvy Moore), Doc Duncan (Strother Martin) and the local priest (Charles Robinson) to find out what's going on in a mystery plot that gets deeper and darker as it progresses.

It's not giving too much away, considering the movie's promotional material, to say that a coven of elderly Satanists are abducting children with the aim of placing their souls within them, thus rejuvenating themselves. In a particularly chilling touch, the coven members greet each other like old friends having not seen each other for decades, which not only suggests that these old coots have come from all over the country but have been doing this rejuvenation ritual for generations.

Like its protagonists, the viewer is in the dark for most of the movie's runtime with little in the way of exposition to tell us what the hell is going on until the end while the main characters, Ben and Nicky, are sidelined somewhat, not doing a whole lot to move the plot forward other than hang around listening to the others. This and the occasional lags in pacing make *The Brotherhood of Satan* a frustrating and tedious watch in parts.

Even by the climax's final kicker, there are questions left unanswered such as how the adults are being killed by toys. As well as the tank in the opening scene, there's a baby doll which appears to kill a man via telekinesis while yet another unfortunate parent is decapitated by a knight on horseback moments after a toy knight is seen onscreen.

The confusing plot and odd pacing nearly derail the movie but are made up for by some startling imagery. The set decoration for the satanic temple is fabulous. The cobweb-cloaked shadows put Universal to shame while the red light, gothic arches and bubbling cauldron are more vibrant than anything from Hammer or AIP. Bernard McEveety defies his TV background with some excellent shots and camera angles, in one scene, managing to fit all five characters in the sheriff's office with an impressive wide shot that shows each of them doing something different. The brutal beating to death of a member of the coven who secretly had her baby baptized is shocking in its POV angle as the fists of the elderly congregation rain down and Nicky's nightmarish dream sequence is almost arthouse in its surreal imagery.

The Brotherhood of Satan takes some obvious cues from *Rosemary's Baby* but mixes things up enough to be more than a cheap knock-off. The supernatural elements, while a little undefined, add something new and, while it's slow and confusing in parts, the frantically grim ending and lurid visuals make up for it.

WEREWOLVES ON WHEELS (1971)

Director: Michel Levesque
Writers: David M. Kaufman and Michel Levesque

As well as producing *Simon, King of the Witches* (which was double billed with *Werewolves on Wheels*), Joe Solomon put out several biker flicks in the late-sixties and early seventies, curiously reusing the fictional biker gang The Devil's Advocates again and again. *In Run, Angel, Run* (1969) the gang pursues a renegade member who spills the beans in a magazine article while in *The Losers* (1970) they take their armored bikes on a CIA-sanctioned mission into Cambodia. They can't seem to catch a break because a year later, they're pitted against the supernatural.

In the promisingly titled *Werewolves on Wheels*, we catch up with The Devil's Advocates as they're cruising around California, causing trouble and generally being the bullying louts the heyday of the biker movie usually depicts. Their leader, Alan, is played by Stephen Oliver, a veteran of biker flicks including Russ Meyer's *Motorpsycho* (1965) and the Joe Solomon-produced *Angels from Hell* (1968).

Also in The Devil's Advocates is the mystic Tarot (Deuce Barry) who reads fortunes and is generally a bit of a hippie despite the ridicule of his fellow gang members. At a roadside café, he reads the fortune of Alan's 'mama' Helen (D. J. Anderson) and predicts that she will come to a grisly end involving the devil.

Not long after, the gang stop overnight in the grounds of a church with a curious symbol atop its spire. The resident priests emerge dressed in hooded robes and offer the bikers bread and wine which they ungratefully wolf down. Low and behold, the wine is drugged and the bikers drift off into a slumber.

43

Helen is lured away by the priests and unwittingly becomes the central piece in a satanic ritual intended to make her the 'bride of Satan', dancing naked with a skull and a snake while the priests chant on. The rest of the bikers wake up and rumble the party, busting Helen out of there and taking to the road once more. But something has followed them as, the following night, two of their members are found with their throats torn out.

The title indicates what might be going on but the movie takes it sweet time in getting there and in the meantime veers off from exploitation genre flick to something approaching arthouse existentialism. Tarot wants out of the gang and spends some time meditating. Then, the gang vanish into the fug of a smoke machine and wind up lost in the dunes in some of the movie's more interesting shots, suggesting that there is something more cosmic afoot than the aftereffects of a werewolf bite.

The acid rock soundtrack and desert scenes are what the movie mostly has going for it. There's also a couple of fun appearances from former child actor Billy Gray (*Father Knows Best* and *The Day the Earth Stood Still*) and 'Eve of Destruction' singer Barry McGuire as members of The Devil's Advocates. That said, there's a hell of a lot of padding in this ninety-minute romp. Endless shots of the gang riding down desert highways (albeit with the real-life biker extras showing off their fancy tricks) will test the patience of most and the satanic ritual scenes go on for far too long.

The werewolf effects, when we finally get to them, aren't too bad considering the caliber of the movie but they are far too little too late. What promised to be a werewolf movie with biker elements is almost entirely a biker movie largely indistinguishable from the horde of similar titles in the wake of Roger Corman's *The Wild Angels* (1966). With a title this cool, there really should have been more werewolves riding motorcycles.

TUTTI I COLORI DEL BUIO/ALL THE COLORS OF THE DARK (1972)

Director: Sergio Martino
Writers: Santiago Moncada, Ernesto Gastaldi and Sauro Scavolini

Between 1971 and 1975 an Italian genre of mystery thriller movies emerged that influenced a generation of horror filmmakers. Known as 'giallo' (literally meaning 'yellow' in reference to the lurid covers of a series of pulpy Italian crime novels of the early 20th century), these movies were laden with suspense, eroticism and violence. They were vibrant and often surreal, with the visual trademarks of the killer's POV, black gloves and paint-red blood all to the keyboard bop of a funky soundtrack. Often featuring a disguised killer, grisly murders and a scantily clad female protagonist, the giallo movie had a strong influence on the American slasher genre of the late seventies and early eighties kickstarted by John Carpenter's giallo-esque *Halloween* (1978).

Director Sergio Martino would go on to be a major player in the genre with movies like *Your Vice Is a Locked Room and Only I Have the Key* (1972) and *Torso* (1973), often working with giallo stalwarts, Edwige Fenech and George Hilton. This early entry sees Martino blend the conventions of the giallo genre with the post-*Rosemary's Baby* infatuation with demonic cults, relying more on psychological terror rather than the usual whodunit featuring a black gloved killer.

Set in London, Jane Harrison (Edwige Fenech) is the typical fragile woman we see all too often in horror movies, especially gialli, but Jane has good reason to carry a little mental baggage. Not only is she recovering from a miscarriage caused by a near-fatal car crash, we also learn that she saw her mother murdered when she was five years old. She is currently suffering from nightmares of a sinister man (Ivan Rassimov) sporting blue contact lenses (which don't look too convincing in his many closeups) and her nightmares quickly become waking delusions as he starts to pursue her in broad daylight.

Entirely bossed about by those around her. Jane's big pharma boyfriend Richard (George Hilton) keeps pushing weird blue pills on her while her sister, Barbara (Nieves Navarro), is insistent that she continues to see the psychiatrist she works for (George Rigaud). Jane makes friends with her new neighbor, Mary (Marina Malfatti) who has an unorthodox solution to her problems. Take part in a black mass!

At her wits' end, Jane accompanies Mary to a large mansion where a satanic cult holds their rituals. There's no gently easing her into things and, before a word is spoken, the cult sacrifices a dog and forces Jane to drink its blood before the high priest (Julian Ugarte) has his wicked way with her on the altar. While a dose of Satanism seems to revive Jane's sex drive (much to boyfriend Richard's joy), her delusions only worsen until neither she, nor the audience, can tell what's real and what isn't.

All the Colors of the Dark is one of those movies that bombards its audience with dreamy sequences, placing us in the mind of Jane as we struggle to know what or whom to trust. It's an interesting departure from the giallo formula but the dream scenes do get repetitive, especially the shots of Rassimov jerking a dagger at the camera while Fenech screams and cowers. Plot threads that are left unfulfilled also confuse things (presumably unintentionally). Are Richard and Barbara having an affair? Why does he own a book on witchcraft? And what did Jane's lawyer want to talk to her about? When you have a plot that is as trippy and delirious as the one Martino presents us with, it would have been better to leave out the red herrings.

It also struggles to find a conclusion with a repetitive sequence of false endings that turn out to be dreams which turn out to be premonitions as well as a silly attempt to explain the satanic cult as a front for a drug ring that doesn't quite add up. This is most likely an example of the movie trying to be both a traditional giallo as well as an occult movie with supernatural elements, but it really can't have it both ways. A shortened US cut under the title *They're Coming to Get You* trimmed off the disappointing ending but isn't any more coherent for it.

Failings aside, Martino manages to create a claustrophobic and paranoid thriller that is perhaps best seen as metaphorical. The plot is silly when taken at face value and few would believe that Jane, messed up though she is, would take part in animal sacrifice, blood drinking and ritualistic orgies as a cure for psychosis, let alone turn up for second helpings in which she murders somebody. But the feeling of being trapped in a web and haunted by the past is what Martino conveys so effectively. Shot in soft focus to enhance the dreamlike atmosphere, the gloomy backdrop of autumnal London heightens the bleakness of the movie.

VIRGIN WITCH (1972)

Director: Ray Austin
Writer: Hazel Adair

British stuntman Ray Austin appeared in several big Hollywood epics like *Spartacus* (1960) and *Cleopatra* (1963) before returning to Britain to coordinate TV stunts for *The Avengers* and *The Champions*. He worked his way up to director, helming several episodes of *The Saint* among others as well as moving into sleazy exploitation features with *1,000 Convicts and a Woman* (1971) and *Virgin Witch* which was a joint production by Univista and Tigon British Film Productions (who are remembered for far better occult movies).

Real-life sisters Ann and Vicki Michelle star as sisters Christine and Betty, teenage runaways who wear the shortest of short skirts that they may as well not bother. In fact, they don't bother for much of the movie as *Virgin Witch* is very much a sexploitation horror movie with emphasis on the former.

Hitching a ride to London from a man called Johnny (Keith Buckley), Christine and Betty have their hearts set on modelling careers. Ignoring Johnny's advice, Christine calls a number she finds on a noticeboard in a newsagent and ends up auditioning for a modelling agency run by the smooth-talking lesbian Sybil (Patricia Haines).

Impressed with Christine, Sybil invites both sisters to stay at a country house appropriately called Wychwood. While Christine is being photographed in various states of undress for a cider commercial, Betty explores the house, finding a cellar full of occult paraphernalia. It's not long before Sybil and her friend and owner of Wychwood, Gerald (Neil Hallett), readily admit that they're part of a coven of witches.

It's strange for the villains to reveal themselves so casually before the halfway mark in an occult horror movie. Usually, the unmasking of a satanic cult doesn't happen until the final act but there is an interesting dynamic between Gerald, an academic with an interest in witchcraft who refuses to get involved with 'black' magic and Sybil, a genuine witch whom Gerald has allowed to run her coven on his grounds. Sybil wants to get her hands dirty with the darker side of things while Gerald, under the pretense of being a 'white' magician, seems to only be in it for the orgies.

What neither Gerald nor Sybil count on is the machinations of Christine who, in stark contrast to her more wholesome sister, is more than eager to join the coven. She seduces her photographer, sleeps with Sybil, willingly takes part in the coven's sabbat and, after finding a book on black magic, starts making plans to replace Sybil as high priestess.

All this leaves Betty somewhat at a loose end and she spends most of the movie hanging about and complaining of headaches. Meanwhile, Johnny, who seems to think he's Betty's boyfriend now, is digging up the dirt on Sybil's modelling agency front and makes his way out to Wychwood to find out what's going on.

Virgin Witch doesn't have a whole lot to it other than absurdly frequent scenes of disrobing. Even the opening credits appear over freezeframes of naked breasts. The jiggle factor was no doubt what got the movie initially banned by the BBFC (British Board of Film Censors) in 1971 before they reluctantly gave it an X certificate the following year.

Vicki and Ann do a fine job and their characters are different enough to sustain momentum with Ann as the ambitious and conniving Christine and Vicki as the doe-eyed innocent younger sister. The movie looks good too, with the bright seventies fashions and scenes of occult rituals amid pastoral English life nicely shot. Another strong point is the location of Admiral's Walk, a mock-Tudor house in Surrey which was also used in *Satan's Slave*.

But calling *Virgin Witch* a horror movie is stretching the definition a bit. There is nothing remotely scary about two young women spending the weekend with some friendly white witches. Although Sybil talks about black magic, we don't see anything that could be considered 'evil' and the whole scene comes off as a bunch of horny English suburbanites getting their kicks by playing at being Satanists. Needless to say, there is no blood or anything much to suggest that the coven has any real powers except the burning of a photograph which seems to have an adverse effect on Sybil in a rather well-executed scene.

Virgin Witch, while failing to be at all scary or even drum up anything by way of atmosphere, certainly delivers on the ritual orgies. There's nudity aplenty, particularly in the sabbat scenes in which the congregation strip off their robes and dance frantically (and quite comically) before an image of the devil which, for some reason, is represented by a Japanese Hanya mask (of the type seen in Kaneto Shindô's 1964 horror movie *Onibaba*).

LA NOCHE DEL TERROR CIEGO/TOMBS OF THE BLIND DEAD (1972)
Director: Amando de Ossorio
Writer: Amando de Ossorio

When a movie is as successful as George A. Romero's *Night of the Living Dead* (1968), you can always count on cash ins. This goes double if the trendsetter is as cheap and easy to make as a zombie movie. The 1970s were filled with entries trying to ape the success of Romero's gamechanger, most of which are beyond the scope of this book as Romero had swapped out the zombie's occult origins for Cold War-era science. Some movies remained faithful to the genre's black magic heritage such as Spain's *Tombs of the Blind Dead* which came from the mind of Amando de Ossorio, a Spanish director who had entered his country's burgeoning horror boom with *Malenka, the Vampire's Niece* (1969). His follow up was popular enough to spawn three official sequels and a couple of similar but unrelated spinoffs.

The titular 'blind dead' are a sect of Templar knights who, in an exaggeration of the real-life accusations of heresy levelled against them, content themselves with sacrificing virgins and drinking their blood at some Spanish castle in the 12th century. Again, in a nod to real history, they are rounded up by church authorities and executed after which their eyes are pecked out by crows.

At a modern-day holiday resort, Virginia (María Elena Arpón) bumps into her old college friend, Betty (Lone Flemming, a stalwart of Spanish horror movies who we would later see in de Ossorio's *Demon Witch Child*). Virginia's boyfriend, Roger (César Burner) seems particularly overjoyed by the reunion and asks Betty if she'd like to accompany them on a camping trip.

Roger is a total ass who flirts and even manhandles Betty right in front of his girlfriend on the train journey the next day. Understandably irked, Virginia throws a massive hissy fit by jumping off the moving train and vanishing into the Spanish countryside. As night falls, she seeks refuge in a ruined castle but doesn't count on its undead occupants rising from the grave and chasing her about in one of the movie's most effective scenes.

Her body is found the next day drained of blood, suggesting (to the audience, at least) the work of vampires. Roger and Betty, now looking very much like a couple, do the detective thing and get the lowdown on the Templars from fusty old librarian (Francisco Sanz) whose son, it turns out, is the leader of a smuggling racket and the police's prime suspect in Virginia's murder.

There's a lot of characters for so simple a plot but it never gets convoluted, despite being a little unfocused at times. The smuggler (José Thelman) and his girl-friend, Nina (Verónica Llimerá) accompany Roger and Betty up to the castle to prove that the Templar specters are real and there are some sexual escapades including a rape scene which feels very superfluous. The movie takes its time in getting going but once it hits its gear, it's an atmospheric bit of fun with its crumbly castle and equally crumbly zombies who are almost camouflaged against the rough stonework and deep shadows.

The Templars are, without a doubt, the best part of the whole movie. Perfectly creepy and shrouded in moldering rags, they are blind and seek out their victims by sound, in one case, by the beating of a victim's heart. Shot mostly in slow motion, they are somewhat reminiscent of the Nazgûl from *The Lord of the Rings*, especially when they mount their horses (which mysteriously have also been brought back from the dead).

The plot is not without its tangents. There's a hint of a lesbian relationship between Virginia and Betty in a flashback to their college days which is never referred to again. Another pointless detour is Virginia's corpse coming back to life, murdering the obnoxious morgue attendant before heading to Betty's mannequin factory and chasing her business partner about. Naturally, if a mannequin factory is mentioned in a horror movie, then the filmmakers are obligated to utilize it, but the whole sequence confuses the lore of the Templar knights, adds nothing to the plot and feels like it came from another, more generic zombie movie.

Tombs of the Blind Dead has been hacked about by distributors more than usual for a Euro horror. The original US version released in 1973 was called *The Blind Dead* and, as well as stripping down some of the sex and gore, it removed the rape scene and moved the flashback of the Templars' sacrifice to the beginning, presumably to keep audiences in their seats for what was to come. A later cut tried to cash in on the Planet of the Apes series by pretending it was set in a postapocalyptic future in which man had wrestled control of Earth back from the apes. A narrated prologue explained that the Templars are, in fact, blind zombie apes out for revenge. This bizarre cut carried the ludicrous title of *Revenge from Planet Ape*.

DEATHMASTER (1972)

Director: Ray Danton
Writer: R. L. Grove

What if the Manson family were vampires? That's the basic premise behind *Deathmaster*, a movie that takes its title from the promotional material for the Robert Quarry-starring AIP vampire hit *Count Yorga, Vampire* (1970). Also starring Quarry (not to mention the same custom fangs), *Deathmaster* was an entirely unaffiliated venture co-financed by Quarry himself and the directorial debut of actor-turned producer and director Ray Danton. AIP executive Sam Arkoff was reportedly none too pleased at this rogue attempt to cash in and subsequently bought the distribution rights to *Deathmaster* before shelving the movie until Quarry had made his contractually obligated sequel, *The Return of Count Yorga* (1971).

On a lonely Californian beach, flute playing acolyte Barbado (LaSesne Hilton) lures a coffin ashore. This attracts the attention of a lone surfer who opens it and is promptly strangled by Barbado. The coffin contains a centuries-old vampire by the name of Khorda (Quarry) who quickly worms his way into the company of a group of Topanga Canyon hippies, his charisma and supernatural party tricks earning their respect. But Khorda has more planned than hanging out and philosophizing.

He soon whips the peaceniks into shape, getting them to clean up the house and start taking better care of their bodies. He demands that they eat only 'living things', scorning meat as a poison for the body. It seems an odd choice at first to have a bunch of vegan vampires, but it's possibly an allusion to the lifeforce-leeching nature of the vampire. Dead things simply won't do. In fact, *Deathmaster* plays around with the rules of the vampire genre in several interesting ways. These vampires can survive sunlight and require an 'incubation period' to turn fully vamp, giving our hero a chance to save them.

Our 'hero' is Pico played by Bill Ewing in a bad wig. Initially impressed by Khorda's schtick, he quickly begins to smell a rat, particularly as his girlfriend, Rona (Brenda Dickson) falls under his spell. As the hippie group gradually transforms into a cult of bloodsuckers, Pico turns to an unlikely Van Helsing; a middle-aged bookstore owner affectionately called 'Pop', played by John Fielder (perhaps best known as the voice of Disney's Piglet).

Despite looking nice, *Deathmaster* doesn't really have any teeth and is a bloodless entry in a genre even Hammer were struggling with by this point. The only thing stopping it from being entirely old hat is the hippie angle. Made while the Manson Family were still on trial, *Deathmaster* feels chillingly topical with Quarry's long-haired, goatee-sporting guru a dead ringer for Manson.

Khorda isn't just here to feed. He wants to recruit and this mingling of the vampire and the evil cult movie is what sets *Deathmaster* apart from other entries in the genre. In a speech reminiscent of the Rolling Stones' 'Sympathy for the Devil', Khorda claims to have seen the rise and fall of great civilizations, the crusades, Napoleon, Stalin and Hitler. There has always been a demonic subtext to the vampire genre but here, Khorda almost feels like a stand-in for the Stones' 'man of wealth and taste'. The movie's climax follows the trend of the era with a full-blown satanic ritual in which Rona is to be sacrificed for reasons that aren't made entirely clear but have something to do with immortality.

As with Manson, Khorda spouts torrents of mystical claptrap without actually saying very much and his endgame is really up for interpretation. Neither is it explained why he keeps a bowl of leeches in his tomb other than to provide Pico with a handy way to sap Khorda's strength by tossing the contents into the vampire's face in the final battle.

Released the same year as Hammer's *Dracula A.D. 1972*, and following a very similar template, *Deathmaster* presents a much more genuine representation of the late hippie youth. The banter certainly feels a little more authentic, silly though it sounds to modern ears. We're even treated to some musical numbers, one of which is performed by 'Monster Mash' singer Bobby Pickett who plays one of the hippies. Shots of Topanga Canyon and its long-haired residents are the real deal and make the movie a wonderful time capsule of an era which was just about to vanish forever.

INVASION OF THE BLOOD FARMERS (1972)

Director: Ed Adlum
Writer: Ed Adlum and Ed Kelleher

In the midst of the flower power revolution, a journalist and musician called Ed Adlum got involved in the indie movie business and wrote the softcore hippiesploitation flick *Blonde on a Bum Trip* (1968). After that, he decided to write, direct and produce his own movie resulting in this unbelievably low budget schlocker filmed in the woods of upstate New York.

Shot over three weekends, the movie had a budget of $24,000, little of which was spent on the cast of family and friends (who were largely paid in beer). As such, there aren't really any actors in the movie, just regular folk who'd been asked to give it a shot and boy, does it show.

The opening narration (by somebody doing his best James Mason impression) tells us of the 'Sangroid blood-eaters'; an offshoot of the druids of ancient Britain, who still exist in small pockets in the remote corners of the world, practicing blood sacrifice. One such place is a backwoods town in Westchester County, New York. The local drunk (whose name, amusingly, is Jim Carrey) stumbles into a roadside tavern, oozing bright pink blood of a saccharine shade which is a constant throughout the movie and promptly dies.

Local scientist, Roy Anderson (Norman Kelley) and his student Don Tucker (Bruce Detrick), analyze the blood from the deceased man and discover that it is replicating itself at an alarming rate, meaning that poor Jim Carrey "blew himself to pieces" (the budget didn't stretch to *that* kind of special effect, but never mind). Don is carrying on with the doc's daughter, Jenny (Tanna Huner), and is very much a man of his time.

When he isn't demanding coffee from his future bride, he's packing her off to bed in the middle of the afternoon whenever she gets distressed.

Jenny is important to the Sangroids who are led by the utterly unconvincing Creton (Paul Craig Jennings). The Sangroids are abducting locals and looking for the one with the right kind of blood for their ritual but trying to make sense of their plan involving draining blood with tubes and filtering out the wrong ones by forcing them to drink from the cup of Mennenon is probably not worth the effort.

Originally conceived as an alien invasion movie, the lack of budget for any cosmic horror meant that the alien Sangroids were switched for a coven of druids. This didn't stop much of the original script from carrying over as it is clear that the Sangroids consider themselves to be a race apart from humanity and their slow, monotone speech and general weirdness don't exactly make them passable as humans. Moreover, the mystery surrounding a metal key made from some strange alloy indicates an otherworldly origin, making *Invasion of the Blood Farmers* feel like a low-budget rip-off of *Invasion of the Body Snatchers* (1956).

On the other hand, we might be dealing with a vampire movie. The Sangroids' eventual plan is to revive the dormant Queen Onhorrid (Cynthia Fleming), who is kept in a glass coffin while one of the druids seems to drink the blood of any person (or dog) who comes across his path, earning him a rebuke from Creton for his gluttonous ways. Aliens, druids or vampires, it doesn't really matter as the deluge of expositional dialogue doesn't make much sense or even always gel with what we're seeing on screen.

Although the plot is about as thin as its pink blood, *Invasion of the Blood Farmers* manages to wind itself into a convoluted mess with many phone calls and conversations on the same stale sets making the viewer feel like they are going around in circles (or at least feel like checking their watch). There are no night scenes, or even day for night, despite the dialogue suggesting otherwise, the editing is all over the place while actors flub their lines and plow on regardless in this unintentionally hilarious example of Z-grade cinema.

Despite having little violence or nudity in it, *Invasion of the Blood Farmers* was yanked from shelves in the UK as a 'video nasty' in the conservative atmosphere of 1980s Britain. Most likely this was due to its title and cover art which depicted a farmer shoving a pitchfork through a woman's chest (which never happens in the movie). Somebody must have watched the damned thing at some point as it was eventually granted a PG rating.

Despite its ineptitude, there's a definite knowing wink at the audience whom Ed Adlum clearly hopes are as into the schlocky B movies of yesteryear as much as he is, but what might have been a comedic parody falls flat due to a level of incompetence that would have been bad even in the heyday of the monster movie. *Invasion of the Blood Farmers* is a fun curiosity and those who get a kick out of the Ed Wood level of gung-ho guerilla filmmaking will be pleased to know that Adlum penned and produced an equally dreadful follow up; *Shriek of the Mutilated* (1974) in which a group of college kids head off in search of bigfoot.

NECROMANCY (1972)

Director: Bert I. Gordon
Writers: Bert I. Gordon and Gail March

There are few better weathervanes of the shift in horror movies circa 1968 than the career of director Bert I. Gordon. His early movies were of the giant rampaging monster kind like *The Amazing Colossal Man* (1957), *The Cyclops* (1957) and *Earth vs The Spider* (1958). With such sci-fi fare swept aside by the success of *Rosemary's Baby* (1968), Gordon quickly changed tact and made *Necromancy*, a muddled satanic coven movie starring Orson Welles.

After their baby is stillborn, Lori (Pamela Franklin) and Frank (Michael Ontkean) leave Los Angeles for a more relaxing life in the town of Lilith. As if the town's name wasn't enough of a red flag, Lori has serious misgivings about the job Frank has been offered in the marketing department of a toy factory. His new boss, Mr. Cato (Orson Welles) has a strong interest in the occult and asked Frank some odd questions about his faith during his interview.

Their journey to Lilith only deepens Lori's concerns. After a near collision on the highway, the other vehicle involved careens off a cliff and explodes into a fireball. Lori finds a doll tossed from the wreckage and decides to keep it, even after finding fingernail clippings in one of its pockets. After running out of gas Frank heads off in search of a gas station while Lori witnesses a funeral on a nearby hillside which turns out to be her own. This is the first of many waking nightmares to come, utilizing the old 'delusional, post-natal mother' trope.

Frank is thoroughly unperturbed by all this, nor is he put off by the armed guard and barricade that blocks the town of Lilith which is apparently under the control of Mr. Cato who runs it like a cult messiah. Nobody over the age of thirty is allowed to live there and there are no children, a strict ban placed on reproduction. Naturally, Lori wants out, but Frank seems content to see how things will pan out.

Mr. Cato is totally open about his occult practices and so are the rest of the townsfolk who are eager to accept Lori into their coven. That's because Mr. Cato is desperate to bring his dead son back to life and believes that Lori is the one to do it, although that will mean her taking his place in death. Not good news for Lori and her desperation only increases as she starts seeing a ghostly little boy around the town along with visions of black masses and other nonsensical things.

The plot feels like somebody attempting an Ira Levin thriller, blending the cult of Satanists from *Rosemary's Baby* with the newcomers arriving in a strange town populated by docile weirdos from *The Stepford Wives* (a TV version of the movie was even titled *Rosemary's Disciples*). Unfortunately, the end result is nothing quite as interesting as those examples.

There's a lot wrong with *Necromancy*. There is little explanation as to why Lori is so special other than a brief reference to her being 'born with a veil' (according to folklore, babies born within the amniotic sack are gifted with occult powers) or why she keeps seeing the ghost of Mr. Cato's son around town, or why the ghost boy feeds her magic mushrooms in one of the more bizarre sequences. Neither Lori nor Frank react in any realistic way to anything that's happening and it's possible Frank knew all about Mr. Cato's plot before their arrival in Lilith but that never gets explored as he vanishes for almost all of the third act. The incomprehensible ending that suggests some or all of the events happened in a dream that is about to be repeated does nothing to help matters.

The editing is abysmal too. Scenes end abruptly and seem out of place and, in one instance, Lori asks Mr. Cato a question which he responds to in a completely different scene. The culprit for this exceptionally choppy movie may be the range of different versions it was hashed together as. Originally rated R, a bunch of nudity was removed for a second PG theatrical release followed by a 1983 home video version sporting the new title of *The Witching* which reinstated a lot of the nudity as well as brand new scenes that muddled the plot even further.

But whichever version you watch, it's an unimpressive and confusing slog. Orson Wells mumbles his way through it, putting on a strange accent and, while Pamela Franklin is the true star of the movie, she isn't given a whole lot to work with other than looking frightened and confused. With an impressive cast and some nice locations such as Lilith's ornate mansions and cluttered antique and occult stores, *Necromancy* really should have been a better movie.

ENTER THE DEVIL (1972)

Director: Frank Q. Dobbs
Writers : Frank Q. Dobbs and David S. Cass Sr.

Not to be confused with the 1974 Italian movie *L'Ossessa* which was released as *Enter the Devil* in the US, this Texan production seems to have been born of the TV Western tradition, much in the way *The Brotherhood of Satan* was. Director Frank Q. Dobbs had helmed a couple of episodes of *Gunsmoke*, a show in which David S. Cass Sr. also played bit parts after his stunt work in *McLintock!* (1963) earned him a favor from John Wayne. He went on to feature in many more Western TV shows as did *Enter the Devil*'s other star, Josua Bryant. It's a fitting heritage as *Enter the Devil* really feels like an occult Western set in the modern day.

Somewhere in southern Texas, people are being abducted and crucified by hooded cultists. The local sheriff (John Martin) dispatches state trooper Jase (David S. Cass Sr. who co-wrote the movie) to find out what's up. Jase tracks the latest missing person to Villa de la Mina, a hunting lodge up in the hills run by Glenn (Joshua Bryant) who lives with several Mexican employees.

A group of hunters show up at the lodge and set out on the trail of deer but come across the burned-out wreck of the missing man's car containing his crispy remains. The county coroner suspects murder, but the sheriff is up for reelection and doesn't want any of that talk. It's up to Jase to wrap things up nice and quietly but, the more he investigates, the more sinister it all seems.

One of the hunters, a particularly lecherous jerk who thinks a pretty woman who doesn't put out is guilty of false advertising, tries to rape Maria, one of Glenn's employees. Another of the Mexicans sends him packing and the very next day, the hunter is grabbed by cultists and tossed into a rattlesnake pit. We might be inclined to mumble something about just deserts in this case, but it does indicate early on that Glenn's hired help might be mixed up in all this.

The coroner stops by to drop off Dr. Leslie Culvert (Irene Kelly), an attractive anthropology professor who is researching a book about cults. Sparks fly between her and Glenn as they sit about on shag rugs, drinking wine while Jase tries to crack the case.

We spend much of the movie with two male protagonists and, if it's a good bet that only one of them will make it to the end credits, we can spend the duration guessing which one. It's a refreshing narrative choice but, with a runtime of only 83 minutes, it doesn't leave much room for the other characters. One who particularly suffers from such a large cast is Irene Kelly's professor who doesn't do much more than tag along and drop tidbits of knowledge before needing to be rescued in the movie's finale begging the question of why she was introduced in the first place.

That said, there's some interesting side plots for such a straightforward movie. Jase is having an ongoing affair with Juanita, a maid at the lodge and it's clear that her coworkers don't approve of her carrying on with a gringo, no matter how polite they are to them. The politics of living on the border permeate the movie with casual racism rearing its ugly head frequently.

The shots of the barren, rocky Texan landscape in the chill of November are well done and the choral singing as hooded figures move across darkened desert hills bearing torches are chillingly effective. *Enter the Devil* strikes a more serious tone than its cousins like *Race with the Devil* and *The Devil's Rain*. It's not campy nor particularly grotesque or gory. Its slow burn may test the patience of some but, on the whole, it's a decent and tight little thriller.

The cult is interesting in that they aren't a bunch of generic devil worshippers. Instead they are presented as a branch of Los Penitentes; a Christian sect that arose in New Mexico in the late 19th century who were flagellants and known for reenacting Christ's crucifixion on Good Friday (actually crucifying one of their members). The Penitentes still exist today but evidently aren't numerous or influential enough to level a case of slander at movies like *Enter the Devil*.

Enter the Devil languished on the edge of being a lost movie for many years. A British VHS was put out in 1983 but made it onto the UK's video nasty list and promptly vanished before a poor print emerged on video in 1996 dragging the movie into mild cult status.

DAUGHTERS OF SATAN (1972)

Director: Hollingsworth Morse
Writers: John C. Higgins and John A. Bushelman

By the 1970s, the Philippines had become a popular location for American movie directors, particularly of the exploitation variety, where cheap labor and exotic locales were readily available. Roger Corman produced several 'women-in-prison' movies there, featuring nubile female convicts who are subjected to sadism and sexual exploitation on jungle plantations. Another producer of drive-in fodder who was drawn to the Philippines was Aubrey Schenck who made a couple of horror flicks which were released together as a double bill in 1972. The first was *Superbeast*, a story of genetic experiments gone wrong in the jungle directed by his son George Schenck, and the other was *Daughters of Satan*.

Veteran TV director Hollingsworth Morse (*The Lone Ranger* and *Lassie*) was called upon to direct, this being one of only a handful of movies he helmed (another being the 1970 kid's movie *Pufnstuf*). Tom Sellick stars in one of his first movie roles along with Barra Grant as man and wife James and Chris who are living in the Philippines where James works as a museum curator. James purchases a painting in an antique store (run by Filippino exploitation regular Vic Diaz who also appeared in *Superbeast*) depicting three witches being burned at the stake by a bunch of conquistadors. Seeing a striking resemblance to his wife in the face of one of the witches, he brings this little curiosity home.

His wife, Chris, is naturally unnerved by the painting and with good reason as strange things start to happen. A dog vanishes from the painting only to turn up in the flesh and start hanging around the property.

67

Next, a woman turns up at the house claiming to be James and Chris's new housekeeper, Juana (star of Filipino cinema, Paraluman). But James and Chris never advertised for a housekeeper and, what's more, Juana is a dead ringer for one of the other witches in the painting who promptly disappears.

Juana is pretty pushy on being their housekeeper and even gives Chris a ceremonial dagger with mumbled words about her 'fulfilling her destiny'. The final witch in the painting turns up at the office of Dr. Dangal (Vic Silayan), a psychiatrist James is seeing, in the form of Kitty (Tani Guthrie). She rambles about being forced to do evil things. She's not kidding as we recognize her from the movie's prologue as the leader of a satanic coven who, while wearing a rather fetching purple leotard adorned with red crabs, whips and murders an unfortunate victim.

Soon Chris is acting strange and making attempts on James's life as she comes under the sway of ancient demonic forces. She is apparently the descendant of one of the witches, as are Juana and Kitty, although they seem to be much more onboard with the whole idea and we must wonder how long Kitty has been running her evil cult before James brought home that weird painting, precipitating Chris's sudden possession. They want James dead because (it is eventually revealed) he also has a doppelganger in a different version of the painting Kitty owns, as the very conquistador who burned their ancestors alive!

Stories about cursed paintings are fairly common, going all the way back to M. R, James's *The Mezzotint* which this movie feels somewhat akin to. It's a creepy plot device that is well utilized here but the movie is dragged down by too much silliness in other respects, mostly in the form of pointless foreshadowing. Why does Kitty reveal herself to James at Dr. Dangal's office?

Why does she show him her alternate painting and tell him about his cruel ancestor later in the movie, essentially giving him a heads up? And what is the purpose of the dog turning up with an address on his collar (the oh-so-subtle '666 Calle Revelacion') that sends James on a detective hunt that leads back to the antique store, other than to give him something to do while others plot his death?

The direction is of the plodding TV variety (no surprise given its director's resume) and, while most seventies horror movies shot in the Philippines are sordid and gory, there is little in *Daughters of Satan* to push it above a PG rating besides the flagellation scenes and a bit of nudity. The whippings have little impact on the plot and feel tacked on just so the movie could live up to its poster promising women-in-prison levels of kinky sadism.

Asylum of Satan (1972)

Director: William Girdler
Writers: William Girdler and J. Patrick Kelly III

William Girdler was in his early twenties when he founded Studio One with his brother-in-law J. Patrick Kelly. Fresh out of the air force, he had been doing odd jobs around the set of the TV show *The Wild Wild West* and had made enough contacts in Hollywood to head back to his hometown of Louisville, Kentucky to shoot this local effort. The measly budget of $50,000 came from local investors as did much of its talent with the main exception of Carla Borelli who, as well as bit parts in a few movies, had appeared in episodes of *The Wild Wild West* and *Ironside*.

Asylum of Satan is the plight of Lucina Martin (Borelli), a patient who is in hospital for undisclosed reasons although a 'break down' is later mentioned, suggesting the old trope of the unreliable narrator. While under sedation, she is transferred in the middle of the night to Pleasant Hill hospital which is some sort of clinic set up in an old money mansion.

Lucina awakens to find herself a prisoner. The hospital is run by Dr. Specter played by Charles Kissinger, familiar to Louisville audiences as horror host 'The Fearmonger' who presented the double feature TV program *Fright Night*. Kissinger would become close friends with Girdler who cast him in several of his movies. He plays multiple roles in *Asylum of Satan*, including donning a wig and a dress as the strict head nurse Martine who keeps Lucina confined to her room and gives her a bath.

With no explanation of why she has been transferred to this weird asylum, Lucina meets the other inmates including a blind woman, a mute man and an

70

elderly woman in a wheelchair. There is also a score of mysterious hooded inmates who only eat hardboiled eggs and have bloody hands.

Dr. Specter tries to convince Lucina that she has suffered a severe breakdown and is here for her own good, but Lucina knows something strange is afoot, especially as the other patients start being murdered in increasingly horrific ways.

Fortunately, Lucina has a fiancé in the form of a tubby, mustachioed man called Chris (Nick Jolley) who has a yellow Porsche and a penchant for plaid. Chris doesn't do a great job of convincing Lt. Walsh (Louis Bandy) down at the police station that there is something amiss and when he drags him out to Pleasant Hill, they find the place a derelict, suggesting that the asylum occupies two places in time. Suspecting the old janitor (Kissinger again) of being Dr. Specter, Chris roughs him up and gets himself tossed in jail overnight. But the old janitor isn't pressing charges, so Chris is back on the case the following day, determined to get to the bottom of the whole mess.

The movie is light on horror and scares but there are a couple of effective scenes. When Lucina starts sneaking around the asylum in the night, the disfigured face of one of the murdered inmates lurches out at her from the shadows. While the makeup isn't particularly effective, it's at least a good popcorn-tossing moment. Far better is the suspenseful murder of the blind woman who meets her end in the swimming pool when somebody dumps a load of poisonous snakes into the water.

Other sequences are more disappointing. When one inmate is killed by insects, closeups reveal that they are jiggly rubber things that look like they were bought in a joke shop. Equally awful is the rubber-masked devil who puts in an appearance in the movie's inexplicable finale while the dry ice machines go full pelt.

Yes, this is another devil cult movie with Dr. Specter eyeing up Lucina (who is "unblemished by sin") for a sacrifice in the final act. It's the usual prayers to demonic forces before a hooded congregation (a scene allegedly advised by Church of Satan member Michael Aquino) but it goes on for far too long. Plenty is left unexplained, such as whether all the hooded figures are patients or hospital staff (and why they only eat eggs?). The interesting notion that the asylum is a place out of time is never explored further either.

Problems aside, *Asylum of Satan* is a fairly solid thriller that keeps the tension taut throughout, occasionally let down by clumsy shots and bad effects as well as some incomprehensible nonsense at the end. But for a first attempt by a twenty-four-year-old director, it shows promise.

Girdler's next movie, shot that same year, was *Three on a Meathook*, inspired by the crimes of Ed Gein. Horror would be something of a commodity for Girdler whose biggest hits would be *Grizzly* (1976) and *The Manitou* (1978) but not before making the blaxploitation *Exorcist* knock-off *Abby*.

BLOOD SABBATH (1972)

Director: Brianne Murphy
Writer: William A. Bairn

It's not often that occult horror movies of the seventies tackle the war in Vietnam, despite it taking up half of the decade, dividing the nation and deepening the generation gap like nothing before. *Blood Sabbath* utilizes the archetype of the returning vet and, although it's a bargain basement softcore venture, it surprisingly has a few things to say underneath all the boobs, bad wigs and topless grooving to Les Baxter's psychedelic soundtrack.

Its director, Brianne Murphy, is remembered as a pioneer for women in the movie business, having been a cinematographer on several television series such as *Little House on the Prairie* and *Highway to Heaven* as well as being the first woman to join the American Society of Cinematographers. She was also the first female director of photography in a major studio feature film (1980's *Fatso*). Before all that, her early filmmaking career consisted of helping both of her Z-grade horror movie director husbands (Jerry Warren and Ralph Brooke) on their movies before she got her own shot with *Blood Sabbath*, one of only two movies she would direct.

Vietnam vet David (Anthony Geary before his long stint on *General Hospital*) is wandering through the wilderness of Southern California, guitar on his back, presumably in search of America. He is assaulted in his sleep by several naked hippie girls (one of whom is Uschi Digard of *Supervixens* fame) and, while running away, stumbles into a creek, knocking himself unconscious.

He is awakened by a water nymph called Yyala (Su-

73

san Damante) and the two immediately fall in love. The only problem is, Yyala can't be with a man who has a soul so David does the only sensible thing and searches for a way to lose it.

He finds his chance in a coven of witches who live nearby led by Alotta (Dyanne Thorne before she became the demented dominatrix of 1975's *Ilsa: She Wolf of the SS* and its sequels). These witches demand a monthly sacrifice from the local villagers in the form of a young girl whose soul they strip before raising her to be one of their own. David offers his own soul in place of the latest offering.

With such fairytale trappings, *Blood Sabbath* treads similar ground to *Queens of Evil* (whose shaggy-haired drifter was also called David) although with far less visual flair. Both movies take place in a surreal, secluded forest world where time seems irrelevant and both have some rather mixed messages on the counterculture of the era.

The rural community who relies on the harvest in *Blood Sabbath* is still infused with pagan customs, despite paying lip service to Catholicism in the form of the local priest (TV actor Steve Gravers). In an interesting compromise between Christianity and paganism, he puts up with their rituals as they always turn up in church on Sunday (although he changes his tune when he learns about the sacrifices). What might be the basis for a folk horror movie ala *The Wicker Man*, it is instead the outsider who sides with the cult, ignoring the priest's warnings in pursuit of his own lust. In this, *Blood Sabbath* makes some attempt to explore the worries of the era that the younger generation were abandoning traditional Christian values for new age occultism and pleasures of the flesh.

Another interesting note is David's flashbacks to Vietnam which usually pop up as a comparison to what he is faced with in the movie. When he hears about the sacrifice of children to ensure a good harvest, he is revisited by scenes of the butchery he witnessed in the war (casualties that are regularly dismissed as 'the price of freedom' and blood sacrifices in their own right).

But what does having no soul entail? Apparently, it means David can't resist taking part in the coven's next ritual the following blood sabbath, in which a young virgin really is sacrificed and they all drink her blood. Yyala is horrified at the price David has paid to be with her and ditches him. Knowing she has David by the short and curlies, Alotta offers to reunite him with his love if he can bring her the head of 'the padre' (i.e. the priest).

Brianne Murphy, despite being a rare female director in 1972, knew who her audience was and few movies pack in as much wall-to-wall female nudity as *Blood Sabbath*. Made on a shoestring budget, it's surprising how many recognizable faces are on show here but despite that and the interesting ideas in the script, it does little to make up for the movie's shortcomings. The settings of grottoes and woodland glades become repetitive, and the performances are lackluster with the exception of Dyanne Thorne who, as can be expected, makes a damn fine witch queen.

RITI, MAGIE NERE E SEGRETE ORGE NEL TRECEN-TO.../THE REINCARNATION OF ISABEL (1973)

Director: Renato Polselli
Writer: Renato Polselli

With a literal title like 'Rites, Black Magic and Secret Orgies in the Fourteenth Century' you know you're in for a good time or, at least not a boring one. Like most Italian filmmakers of the era, writer and director Renato Polselli's career consisted mostly of Spaghetti Westerns and gialli before the trend for cults and possessions began to exert its influence on his movies. But Polselli already had a few early horror movies under his belt, the most notable of which is *The Vampire and the Ballerina* (1960) which concerns a group of young dancers who stay at a creepy old castle inhabited by vampires.

The basic set up for *The Vampire and the Ballerina* is remarkably similar to Polselli's later erotic occult horror, titled *The Reincarnation of Isabel* in the US and the two movies were even shot in the same castle, Italy's Castello Piccolomini. The first ten minutes are taken up with a delirious human sacrifice in which a young woman's heart is ripped out by cultists in red leotards while a dead woman chained to the wall with a hole in her chest watches on.

The plot? Jack Nelson (Mickey Hargitay, former Mr. Universe-turned-Italian movie star, not to mention one-time hubby of Jayne Mansfield) has recently purchased the castle which has a reputation for being cursed. That's not going to stop him hosting an engagement party for his stepdaughter Laureen (Rita Calderoni) and her fiancé, Richard (William Darni).

At the gathering, the gruesome history of the castle is recounted by a character known only as 'the occultist'

(Raoul Lovecchio) who lives on the castle grounds along with his hunchbacked Igor servant. We are told, via flashbacks, that a witch called Isabel was staked and burned at the stake (yes, both) hundreds of years ago by an angry mob. It also seems apparent that nearly everybody gathered is a descendant of those present at the witch burning. Calderoni plays both Isabel and Laureen while Hargitay plays Jack and Isabel's distraught lover with several other faces filling out the rest.

It's a baffling and mostly futile exercise trying to figure out who's who and what they want as the movie seems to be a series of scenes tossed together like a salad. The general gist is that Jack is in fact a vampire (the English dub takes the liberty of claiming that he is Dracula himself) and he wants to resurrect his dead love, Isabel, by using his stepdaughter as a vessel. The sacrifice of seven virgins is needed which spells doom for the young female guests at the castle. All except one, the irritatingly daft Stefania Fassio who gets entangled in a bedroom farce with a man and another woman, thus stripping her of her virginity.

This is because *The Reincarnation of Isabel* also has the element of the sex comedy to it in the spirit of the then-popular 'decamerotic' genre of historical erotic comedies inaugurated by *The Decameron* (1971). The movie alternates between scenes of bloody sacrifice and the jovial threesome to plinky-plonk piano music which makes for a strange mix in an already utterly unhinged movie.

Time seems to have no meaning in the castle, with characters switching clothes and day switching to night and back within the same scenes. The confusion only deepens as the movie reaches its climax in which some of the girls fall afoul of a local mob, one of the girls becomes a vampire and others are chained up and tortured in the dungeon. Is it all a dream? Time travel?

Metaphor? Who knows?

Needless to say, the movie makes no sense and contradicts itself at every turn. Jack, swearing revenge on those who murdered Isabel, studied the occult and became the first ever vampire (except, Isabel was already executed for being a vampire, meaning that he can't have been the first).

It's probably best not to worry too much about the plot as this is one of those movies that demands to be 'experienced'. And to be fair, it's a lovely looking movie. The sumptuous castle surrounded by snow-capped mountains lends a grandness to the movie that defies its budget. Gorgeous women in vibrant seventies fashions complement the lurid cinematography which is especially impressive during the occult ritual scenes in which red, green and purple compete for they eye amid swirling smoke machines and flickering candles. In short, *The Reincarnation of Isabel* is all style over substance.

IL PLENILUNIO DELLE VERGINI/THE DEVIL'S WEDDING NIGHT (1973)
Directors: Luigi Batzella and Joe D'Amato
Writers: Mark Damon, Ian Danby and Ralph Zucker

Mark Damon, who had made his horror bones in Roger Corman's *House of Usher* (1960), had moved to Italy and became a stalwart in Spaghetti Westerns and Italian horror before ditching acting for producing in the mid-seventies. One of the last Italian movies he starred in was this gothic period piece which feels like every Hammer vampire movie wrapped up in the Italian brand of sultry noblewomen, satanic cults and bared breasts.

Damon plays twin brothers Karl and Franz. Karl is the bookish type, feverishly questing after the fabled Ring of the Nibelungs which he has traced, rather oddly, to Castle Dracula. His brother, Franz, is a caddish libertine with gambling debts. When he hears of his brother's find, he heads off to Transylvania ahead of him, his heart set on getting hold of the priceless ring and selling it.

The Devil's Wedding Night feels very aware of not only its horror heritage (namedropping Karnstein from Hammer's vampire movies) but also the change in the horror landscape as it blends vampires with Satanism and possession, even having Franz abscond with a protective amulet of the demon Pazuzu (*The Exorcist* would be released later that year but the book was already big news).

Franz arrives in Transylvania coincidentally just before the Night of the Virgin Moon which occurs every fifty years and sees five virgins from the village called to Castle Dracula (Castello Piccolomini which was also used in *The Reincarnation of Isabel*) by a mysterious force and are never seen again. Ignoring the usual warnings from the innkeeper's pretty daughter (Enza Sbordone), Franz heads up to the castle, foolishly leaving his protective amulet behind. There, he encounters the seductive Contessa Dolingen de Vries (Rosalba Neri, aka Sarah Bay, star of many erotic horror movies of the seventies) and winds up in bed with her where she alarmingly changes into a giant bat mid-coitus.

With Franz now a vampire, and a reincarnation of Count Dracula no less (whom the Contessa reveals was her late husband), it's up to brother Karl to follow in his footsteps and try to sort it all out. This middle section drags a little as Karl wanders around the castle, finding his brother slumbering in a coffin and battling the Contessa's hunchbacked lackey (Xiro Papas). Things warm up a little in the third act as the Contessa uses her magic glowing ring to summon the five virgins to the castle and the movie lives up to the literal translation of its Italian title; 'The Full Moon of the Virgins' but the swashbuckling finale is full of silliness. The glowing ring looks tacky and there are far too many fake-out endings. The Contessa's transformation into a giant bat is a clumsy rear projection of wildlife footage but most amusing of all, is Karl's slow-motion battle against the forces of darkness which looks remarkably like Tai Chi.

Porn director, Joe D'Amato, directed portions of the movie at producer Franco Gaudenzi's request and, judging by D'Amato's subsequent output, we can assume it was the sexual scenes. The Contessa's bathing in the blood of virgins bears his fingerprints in particular, inspired, no doubt, by Hammer's take on the story of Elizabeth Báthory, *Countess Dracula* (1971). Curiously, it takes the form of a flashback while Franz and the Contessa are drinking wine and laughing deliriously, their gaping mouths mirrored by the castle's gargoyles in a particularly striking sequence.

The Devil's Wedding Night is a gorgeously shot gothic romp short on plot but heavy on atmosphere. Rosalba Neri is entrancing as the formidable Contessa; an interesting spin on Count Dracula. As well as Xiro Papas, she also has a beautiful young 'zombie' servant played by Esmeralda Barros who isn't the rotting flesh type, but a more traditional mind-controlled puppet and lesbian lover to boot. The sacrificial rites (proclaimed as necessary to keep the Contessa young and beautiful, *ala* Countess Dracula) involves a cult of hooded Satanists who emerge from their tombs to cut the throats of the five virgins, giving us plenty of gratuitous shots of blood gushing over naked breasts. Sleazy exploitation elements aside, *The Devil's Wedding Night* is an interesting blend of ideas, and a point of transition between old and new. Even the Pazuzu amulet is a fresh take on the old crucifix (though why devil-worshiping vampires should be averse to a demon's talisman is anyone's guess).

EL MONTE DE LAS BRUJAS/THE WITCHES MOUNTAIN (1973)

Director: Raúl Artigot
Writers: Raúl Artigot, Juan Cortés and Félix Fernández

Only directing three movies in his career, Spanish-born Raúl Artigot was primarily a cinematographer working with some of Spain's most famous directors of horror including Jess Franco. He lensed Franco's *The Rites of Frankenstein* and *The Demons* the same year he as he made his directorial debut with this strange, witchy mood piece shot in Spain's Picos de Europa.

In one of the most confusing openings to any movie ever, a woman called Carla (Mónica Randall) returns home to find signs of Voodoo all over her house including a knife stuck into a wig and dolls with pins in them. She also finds her dead cat in her bed, courtesy of a young girl (possibly her daughter?) who runs off into the garage. Carla follows her and burns her to death with gasoline.

After the blazing inferno of the credits, we then see Carla alive and well and visiting her ultra-seventies macho man boyfriend, Mario (Cihangir Gaffari). She wants him to jet off with her to Brazil, but he's lost interest in her. In fact, their relationship seems pretty sour at this point (maybe he knows she just torched a kid). He calls up his boss and demands an immediate assignment. He's a photographer and takes a job in a remote mountainous region.

On his way up into the mountains, Mario stops to ogle sunbathing beauty Delia (Patty Shepard, star of many Spanish horror movies including Paul Naschy's fifth and most successful entry in his *Hombre Lobo* series, 1970's *The Werewolf vs. The Vampire Woman*).

After chatting her up, the two hit it off and take lunch together before Mario asks her if she wants to take a trip up into the mountains with him. While stopping off at her place, Mario suddenly starts hearing haunting choral music which Delia is oblivious to. She simply laughs it off when he tells her, and inexplicably still decides to go on a road trip with a stranger who admits that he hears voices.

The couple wind up at a rustic hovel of a hotel with a Peter Lorre-like host (Víctor Israel) who warns them against venturing too far up the mountain. Naturally, they ignore him and set out the next day, coming across an old village deserted by all but an ancient woman (Ana Farra) who puts them up for the night.

Mario goes out on his own to snap some shots of their surroundings and, in an interesting device, subliminal black and white shots of mysterious women are flashed every time he takes a picture which the audience sees, but Mario doesn't. Darkness falls and Mario stumbles across a procession of torch-bearing, hooded figures. He snaps off a few shots and the next day, he develops the film under his coat on the hood of his car, and then enlarges the photos back at the old woman's house.

As well as reminding us what a hassle taking pictures was before digital cameras, this whole sequence also confirms that Mario's camera did indeed capture images of eerie women around the village who aren't there. Conversely, of the strange cult procession, there is no evidence. The movie only gets weirder from this point on with Mario discovering a witch's den filled with occult junk before he is attacked by cat who transforms into a woman. Meanwhile, Delia is having dreams of being dressed up as a bride by the witches and given as a wife to a slave kept chained up in a grotto (played by Luis Barboo, who provided many a hulking henchman in Spanish and Italian movies including *Satan's Blood* and *The Demons*). The movie's baffling climax does little to explain any of this or its pointless opening scene which really feels like it came from another movie.

A grammatical error in a movie's title is never a good sign and *The Witches Mountain* (sic) is incoherent from a plot point of view, not helped by sloppy editing, a superfluous first ten minutes, long stretches where nothing much happens followed by too much crammed into a baffling ending. It manages to be atmospheric enough with the mountainous landscape deepening the feeling of isolation and Fernando García Morcillo's haunting score, which blends Gregorian chants and opera, adding to the eeriness. That the witch coven is never seen very much, and explained even less, is a refreshing take, creating an ominous presence.

The movie was banned in Spain after some members of the cast, allegedly over a dispute regarding pay, reported the filmmakers to the authorities, claiming that they were being forced to do nude scenes. Nudity was tightly regulated in Francoist Spain, resulting in a practice of cutting two versions of many movies; a 'clothed' one intended for domestic release and an 'unclothed' version for more liberated international markets. As a result, despite its many connections to Jess Franco, the movie is very tame on the nudity front, most likely due to the 'clothed' version being the one which made it to American television screens in 1975 while the more sexed-up alternate cut was lost to obscurity in the ensuing legal debacle.

THE SATANIC RITES OF DRACULA (1973)

Director: Alan Gibson
Writer: Don Houghton

With *The Satanic Rites of Dracula*, British studio Hammer Productions continued a mission they began with the previous year's *Dracula A.D. 1972*; namely to bring their stalwart characters of Dracula and Van Helsing into the present day. While *Dracula A.D. 1972* was a campy attempt to place the bloodsucking count in swinging London, an altogether different approach and tone was attempted for its follow-up.

Satanic Rites is a direct sequel and includes several characters who featured in the previous movie. Detective Inspector Murray (Michael Coles) is now helping the secret service investigate the Psychical Examination and Research Group (PERG); an organization who meet at an isolated country house and include high up government members. PERG is in fact a satanic cult who sacrifice chickens over naked women headed by the mysterious Chin Yang (Barbara Yu Ling).

Once again, Murray recruits the help of Lorrimer Van Helsing, a descendant of *the* Van Helsing who took care of Dracula back in the 1870s. Now an expert on the occult, Van Helsing visits his friend Julian Keeley (Freddie Jones), a member of PERG, and learns that he has been developing an accelerated form of bubonic plague. Dracula, resurrected by PERG, is now the head of a property development firm and has a secret plan to wipe out all humanity with a new strain of plague. Van Helsing's theories on why he would want to kill off his main source of sustenance as part of an elaborate suicide plan don't hold much water and neither do the continuing satanic shenanigans of the cult once he had been resurrected.

85

Also on the case is Van Helsing's granddaughter, Jessica, who is now played by Joanna Lumley. She joins forces with Inspector Murray and his associates and they snoop about country houses, running through the woods, dodging sniper bullets and henchmen (dressed in sleeveless Afghan jackets, for some reason), reminiscent of seventies British TV shows like *The Avengers*.

With all the espionage guff of hidden cameras, microfilm, motorcycle stunts and snipers, *Satanic Rites* also feels a little like a Bond movie and Dracula himself is every bit the Bond villain. He's ditched the gothic crypts for a fancy house equipped with switchboards and reel to reel computers and his meeting with Van Helsing happens in a plush office block built on the site of St. Bartolph's church where he was vanquished by Van Helsing in the previous movie. Incidentally, Lee, clearly sick to the fangs of playing Dracula, would play a real Bond villain the following year in *The Man with the Golden Gun*.

Alan Gibson directed both *Dracula A.D. 1972* and *Satanic Rites* and knew how to make a fast-paced thriller which rarely gets dull even if it does get silly. It's got a bit more of a bite than its predecessor, even if it does lean more into spy thriller territory than horror. There are plenty of gory shootings and stakings and the scene in which Jessica is trapped in the basement where Dracula keeps his undead victims chained up is particularly effective.

That said, the gothic atmosphere of Hammer's back catalogue is entirely absent now and we are left with a curious mishmash of genres that doesn't really feel like a Hammer movie. That might have been what they were going for, but it failed to connect with audiences at the time and is a strange swansong for the series that put Hammer on the horror map.

While previous entries in the series went to great

lengths to explain how Dracula comes back again and again, *Satanic Rites* dispenses with this with a hand wave. The evil cult resurrected him somehow and that's all we know. It's perhaps a sign that the whole engine had run out of steam and by the time we see Christopher Lee crumble to dust after being staked by Peter Cushing for the third time (fourth if you count the opening of *Dracula A.D. 1972*), it's hard to disagree.

Hammer was on its last legs by this point and Lee refused to do any more Draculas, leaving the role open for John Forbes-Robertson in Hammer's other bizarre attempt to mix things up by collaborating with Hong Kong's Shaw Brothers on *The Legend of the 7 Golden Vampires* (1974). It wasn't enough to bring the studio profits back up to snuff and Hammer fizzled out a couple of years later after their baffling adaptation of Dennis Wheatley's novel *To the Devil a Daughter*.

EL ATAQUE DE LOS MUERTOS SIN OJOS/RETURN OF THE EVIL DEAD (1973)

Director: Amando de Ossorio
Writer: Amando de Ossorio

Amando de Ossorio knew he was onto a good thing with the success of his zombie Templar movie *Tombs of the Blind Dead*, quickly following it with a sequel that, at times feels slicker than its predecessor, but ultimately, is a different animal altogether.

The setting is the Portuguese town of Bouzano, apparently a different location to the first movie, despite some of it being shot in the same Monastery of Pelayos, near Madrid. The townsfolk are celebrating the 500th anniversary of the execution of the Templar sect by burning effigies and letting off fireworks. The latter are provided by Jack Marlow (Tony Kendall), a firework technician who is romantically involved with Vivian (Esperanza Roy), the fiancé of the town's corrupt and thuggish mayor (Fernando Sancho). There's another couple in the form of Monica (Loreta Tovar) and Juan (José Thelman who played the smuggler in *Tombs of the Blind Dead*).

As the festivities kick off, village idiot, Murdo (José Canalejas), who isn't quite as harmless as he seems, sneaks off to the local ruined monastery and, in a scene marred by cuts as to be almost indecipherable, sacrifices a woman he has captured in order to raise the blind dead from their tombs. This requirement of a sacrifice suggests that the resurrection of the Templars is a one-off opposed to the regular hauntings in the first movie.

When the Templars descend upon the town, butchering anybody in their path, a group of survivors (including Lone Flemming, who played a main character in *Tombs of the Blind Dead* and would latter appear in de Ossorio's *Demon Witch Child* alongside Fernando Sancho) take refuge in the local church. From that point on, we're solidly in *Night of the Living Dead* territory with a band of mismatched characters under siege. There's the little girl, the arguing over leadership and a botched attempt to get the car up and running due to the self-serving actions of the truly despicable mayor.

Return of the Evil Dead feels more like a remake than a sequel. As well as a different setting and reusing José Thelman and Lone Flemming as different characters, it alters the lore of the Templar legend, having them blinded by the mob rather than their eyes being plucked out by crows and requiring a blood sacrifice to emerge from their tombs (in footage mostly cribbed from the first movie).

While this second installment still has its problems (mainly its shoddy editing and continuity issues), it improves a little on its predecessor and its first act moves along at a brisker pace. Perhaps learning from its English cut, it kicks things off with a flashback to the dastardly Templars rather than saving it for later in the movie and, while there are a lot of characters and drama to be set up, the dead are resurrected soon enough to not lose the audience's patience.

Comparisons have been drawn to how *Aliens* (1986) upped the ante on *Alien* (1979) and that's a fair analogy. *Return of the Evil Dead* definitely relies more on action rather than the atmospheric tension of its predecessor. There are more Templars, more victims and more fight scenes but that does mean that the eeriness of the first movie is dampened somewhat. Far from the dreamlike slow movement of the Templars in the first movie, they now move with a speed that makes the fact that they are men in masks a little too apparent. Their blindness, however, is used more effectively in this installment with one particularly good scene towards the end that is reminiscent of Hitchcock's *The Birds*.

Literally meaning 'Attack of the Blind Dead' the movie was released in the US as *Return of the Evil Dead*, not to be confused with Sam Raimi's Evil Dead movies that started in the 1980s. Despite its leaning on better movies that preceded it, it must be remembered that it came before Romero's zombie classic *Dawn of the Dead* (1978) and John Carpenter's somewhat similar *The Fog* (1980), which makes it easy to understand its popularity (and the popularity of the Blind Dead series in general) in Spanish horror.

THE WICKER MAN (1973)

Director: Robin Hardy
Writer: Anthony Shaffer

Richard Pinner's 1967 novel *Ritual* was the result of a failed movie deal with director Michael Winner. Pinner's story treatment of an English police officer investigating the ritualistic murder of a child in an isolated Cornish village had interested Winner who had John Hurt in mind for the main role. The deal eventually fell through, and Pinner was advised by his agent to expand the treatment into a novel.

The novel caught the eye of screenwriter Anthony Shaffer and Christopher Lee who were looking to collaborate with director Robin Hardy on a movie about paganism that was less visceral and more cerebral than much of the Hammer fare Lee had starred in up to that point. They bought the rights to the novel from Pinner, but Shaffer quickly decided to pen an original screenplay that was only loosely based on the novel.

It's the story of the devoutly Christian police officer Sergeant Howie (Edward Woodward) who travels to the remote Scottish island of Summerisle to look for Rowan Morrison, a young girl who has been reported missing in an anonymous letter. The island, famed for its apples, is ruled over by the eccentric Lord Summerisle (Christopher Lee) and, much to Sergeant Howie's horror, its people have discarded Christianity for the 'old ways'.

Shaffer plundered the anthropologist James George Frazer's largely speculative 1890 study, *The Golden Bough* and *The Wicker Man* checkmarks just about every British custom known for its dubious pagan associations, from maypoles to green men to hobby horses and, of course, the titular woven basket figure. The only source for the notion that people were ever sacrificed in basketwork men comes from Julius Caesar no less, in his *Commentaries on the Gallic War*. When speaking of the sacrificial rites of the Gauls performed by their druids; "Others have figures of vast size, the limbs of which formed of osiers they fill with living men, which being set on fire, the men perish enveloped in the flames."

Sergeant Howie quickly realizes that he's being given the runaround, with the infuriatingly cheerful locals remaining tight-lipped on the whereabouts or even existence of Rowan Morrison while the landlord's daughter (Britt Ekland) attempts to seduce him by dancing nude and pounding on her bedroom walls in perhaps the movie's second most notorious scene. Howie's priggish puritanism meets its match in the slippery charm of Christopher Lee as he gives Howie the lowdown on pagan worship in one of his best performances, showing us exactly what he can do *sans* cape and fangs. Incidentally, Lee's fellow Hammer alumnus Ingrid Pitt also makes an appearance as the island's librarian.

Director Robin Hardy manages to create an ever-increasing sense of trepidation that builds throughout the movie. The carefree locals lose none of their sinister malevolence by frequently breaking out into folk songs and the movie feels a little like a dark musical at times. But it's when it dawns on Howie (and us) that he is being herded somewhere and may have been deliberately lured to the island for some sinister purpose, that the horror really kicks in.

The production studio (British Lion Films) was bought by EMI before *The Wicker Man*'s completion and the new owners had little faith in the movie, resulting in it being edited down and released to the drive-in market in the US and as a B movie to *Don't Look Now* (1973) in the UK. Attempts to restore the missing scenes and rerelease the movie later in the 1970s seemingly hit a brick wall when it became known that the original negatives had ended up in the concrete beneath the M3 motorway in England. Fortunately, Roger Corman (who had expressed an interest in distributing *The Wicker Man* but never did so) still owned a full print of the original cut and this has been used over the years to fill in the blanks, leading to both a director's cut and a 'final cut', both of which differ on how much extra footage is included.

Whichever version you watch, *The Wicker Man* is the quintessential folk horror story of the urban man who comes to a bad end in the bleak isolation of the countryside where they 'just do things differently' and its effect on the horror genre cannot be overstated. It encapsulates the battle between the arrogance of the 'civilized' world and the ancient horror of the land which is the backbone of folk horror from M. R. James to *Midsommar* (2019). Even a widely condemned 2006 American remake starring Nicholas Cage failed to tarnish *The Wicker Man*'s reputation as one of Britain's finest horror movies.

On the subject of follow ups, Shaffer's treatment for a direct sequel (called *The Loathsome Lambton Worm*) was never filmed but Robin Hardy wrote his own 'spiritual sequel' novel with the equally befuddling name of *Cowboys for Christ* which he filmed as *The Wicker Tree* in 2011, featuring a cameo by Christopher Lee. In 2014, Richard Pinner wrote *The Wicca Woman*, a sequel to his original novel *Ritual*.

LEGACY OF SATAN (1974)

Director: Gerard Damiano
Writer: Gerard Damiano

As with almost all things of a tightly regulated or outright illicit nature, pornography has often been controlled by organized crime. In the early 1970s, Anthony Peraino, a member of the Colombo crime family, was running peepshows in New York's Times Square, mostly with the aim of laundering money for the mob. His son, Louis "Butchie" Peraino, saw himself as something of a filmmaker, having written and produced 1962's *Night of Evil* about a cheerleader-turned-stripper who commits an armed robbery.

In 1972, Louis used $22,500 of his father's money to produce a movie directed by Gerard Damiano, who had made several 'loops' (short 8mm pornographic films) for the Peraino peep shows and had recently discovered a new talent by the name of Linda Lovelace. The result was *Deep Throat* starring Lovelace and Harry Reems, distributed by Bryanston Pictures which Louis Peraino and his uncle, Joseph, ran. *Deep Throat* was a porn movie which, due to a comparatively lavish budget and an actual storyline, entered the mainstream and became a cultural phenomenon not to mention a massive money earner for the Colombo family.

The controversy surrounding *Deep Throat* caught up with its makers in a slew of federal cases in 1976 which saw the Perainos and actor Harry Reems convicted for conspiracy to distribute obscenity across state lines. Bryanston Pictures subsequently filed for bankruptcy but not before it had distributed several notable non-pornographic horror movies such as *Dark Star* (1974), *The Texas Chainsaw Massacre* (1974), *The Devil's Rain* and *Legacy of Satan*.

94

Gerard Damiano had shot *Legacy of Satan* hot on the heels of *Deep Throat* in 1972 with Louis Peraino producing again. It was supposed to be another porn flick for Bryanston Pictures but somewhere along the line it was decided to remove the smut and make it a straight horror movie. How much hardcore stuff (if any) was shot isn't quite clear but what is clear is that Damiano didn't have much else to pad out the movie with, resulting in its paltry (but merciful) 70-minute runtime.

The plot is simplistic to the point of being a concept rather than an actual story. Married couple Maya (Lisa Christian) and George (Paul Barry) learn that their friend, Arthur (James Procter) is quitting his job as an architect to pursue a newfound interest in religion. But he's not about to run off to join a monastery. His interest leans more to God's opposite number.

Arthur is part of a cult who worship 'Lord Rakeesh' and are also vampires or at least, have a fetish for drinking blood. Their leader, Dr. Muldavo (John Francis), hints at being hundreds of years old and requires blood for sustenance. The cult wants Maya as its new queen and set about drawing her to them through black magic rituals. Quite why they need her when they already have a high priestess (Deborah Horlen) isn't really explained.

Maya starts acting weird. She sees blood dripping from a portrait's eyes and has a freakout in bed during which she claws George's chest to ribbons. Invited to a costume party at the cult's mansion, Maya and George turn up and are drugged with wine in preparation for the sacrificial rites. But there is trouble afoot as Dr. Muldavo's assistant, Aurelia (Anna Paul), has become jealous of Maya and sabotages the whole thing. George, dressed in silk pajamas, takes out the devilish congregation with a glowing sword like some kind of half-assed

Luke Skywalker. Maya wants to stick with the cult and the movie limps towards a non-climax, outstaying its welcome and wrapping nothing up, leaving audiences befuddled as to what the point of it all was.

The absolute worst part of the movie is the racket of a soundtrack which is an intrusive and irritating slew of sirens, buzzing and laser zaps which even makes some of the dialogue inaudible. Not that there's much to miss as what little plot there is, is nonsensical and dull. Even the sex scenes are boring and fully covered which is a surprising departure considering who was in the director's chair.

There are however, some nice shots of early 1970s New York and the scenes shot in the chic apartment of actress Christa Helm who stars in the movie with the unflattering credit of 'Blonde blood farm' (being one of the stable of attractive women kept on hand by the cult to feed their bloodthirsty appetites). Helm's character is later stabbed to death in the movie, something that would be tragically mirrored in real life when Helm was murdered in 1977 in a still unsolved case.

Bryanston Pictures apparently knew they had a stinker on their hands and sat on *Legacy of Satan* for a couple of years before tossing it onto drive-in screens in 1974, double billed with *Blood* (1973) and *The Texas Chainsaw Massacre* (1974).

EL BUQUE MALDITO/THE GHOST GALLEON (1974)

Director: Amando de Ossorio
Writer: Amando de Ossorio

The third entry in Amando de Ossorio's Blind Dead tetralogy cements the idea that none of these movies are connected and each one deals with a different group of satanic Templar zombies with different backstories.

This time, a couple of swimsuit models have been sent out to sea in a motorboat as part of a publicity stunt by sketchy sporting goods magnate, Howard Tucker (Jack Taylor). Things go awry when the couple get lost in the fog and encounter a ghostly 16th century galleon. Noemi (Bárbara Rey), the housemate and suggested lover of one of the girls, confronts her modelling agency manager, Lilian (Maria Perschy), demanding to know what happened to her friend. Lilian takes her to see Tucker who promptly kidnaps her to stop her running to the police while he tries to find out what happened to his models.

Alternating between the two models (Blanca Estrada and Margarita Merino) exploring the ghostly galleon and the plight of Noemi held captive in a basement is an interesting first act which unfortunately unravels once the group decide to head out to sea in search of the missing models. Tucker's villainous assistant, Sergio (Manuel de Blas) rapes Noemi, an incident which is then ignored for the rest of the movie (a frequent and troubling occurrence in de Ossorio's flicks) while Tucker recruits the help of Professor Grüber (Carlos Lemos), a scientist who has heard of the ghostly galleon and is all too eager to join them.

Once aboard the ship, very little else happens. It's

half an hour into the movie before the Templars make their first appearance while the audience watch characters wander around, fall asleep, wander some more, stop for a rest, etc. The Templars were spectral figures from a nightmare in the first movie but here they are reduced to slow moving stock zombies, so ineffectual that they require their victims to be seriously injured in order to catch them. One scene in particular, where a woman is dragged across the ship by the Templars, seems to take forever.

The new nautical setting however, is a nice change of scenery from the crumbling Iberian villages and ruins. The creepy old ghost ship is a great location well-utilized with sounds of creaking and clanking chains, although spoilt a little by a laughable shot at the end of what is clearly of a toy boat in a bathtub. But the atmosphere doesn't always gel with the dialogue (and abundance of bikinis on show) which suggests that the temperature is warm. There isn't a single bead of sweat to be seen, however, and the blue filters and thick mist makes you think they should all put on some warmer clothes.

The gore is severely toned down in comparison to the previous installments with only one victim being beheaded and feasted on. We never see what happens to the first two women who go missing which is part of why the movie is so slow. There are no grisly flashbacks this time around either, but Professor Grüber, who has been reading the ship's log, gives a garbled bit of backstory about a sect of heretical Templars being ferried from the holy land to Europe in the 16th century, the obvious anachronism explained by the Templars' ability to conquer mortality.

Grüber proves himself something of the Van Helsing of the group by banishing the Templars to the hold with an improvised exorcism which he performs by fashioning a cross from two belaying pins and lighting them on fire. Further supporting the idea that the Templars are more vampires than zombies, they cower from the crucifix, although it could be fire they're afraid of, as in the previous installment.

What started out as an interesting setup filled with promise, ultimately falls short perhaps due to overambition with a measly budget and just not enough of a pulse to the proceedings. As with many of de Ossorio's movies, there are a lot of characters with nobody coming forward to claim the role of protagonist, resulting in a messy movie that never really hits the same gear as its predecessors.

La noche de los brujos/Night of the Sorcerers (1974)

Director: Amando de Ossorio
Writer: Amando de Ossorio

Opening in the year 1910 in a fictional African county called Bumbasa, we are treated to a deranged prologue only an exploitation fan could appreciate. A missionary played by Bárbara Rey (star of de Ossorio's *The Ghost Galleon* released the same year) is tied between two trees by dancing natives and has her clothes literally whipped off her before she is forced to lie face-down on a stone altar and is decapitated. A group of colonial soldiers turn up and open fire on the demonic congregation while the head of the decapitated woman spins around and screams with glee, her mouth now filled with vampire fangs.

As you might surmise, this is the type of movie that could never be made today. Amando de Ossorio milks a few extra miles out of the motifs of his Blind Dead tetralogy by sticking them in an African setting with Voodoo and all the casual racism that entails. Connection between Voodoo and vampires had been done before in *Scream, Blacula, Scream*, which, although not entirely free from stereotypes, at least presented the good and bad sides of the religion as dependent on the person using it. There's no such nuance in *Night of the Sorcerers*, in which the practitioners of Voodoo are one-dimensional savages.

In the present day, an expedition arrives in Bumbasa led by Professor Jonathan Grant, played by Jack Taylor, who was in more exploitation movies than you can shake a stick at, including *The Ghost Galleon*, *The Mummy's Revenge*, *Exorcism* and *Devil's Exorcist*.

Accompanying him is his girlfriend, Tanika (Kali Hansa) along with tough guy Rod (Simón Andreu), photographer Carol (Loreta Tovar, from *Return of the Evil Dead*) and spoiled brat Liz, whose father is financing the whole shebang (María Kosty, who was in *Vengeance of the Zombies* and would also pop up in *Demon Witch Child*, and *Exorcism*).

Being an exploitation movie, everybody is horny and there is a secret love affair between Tanika and Rod not to mention jealousy from all quarters and an ugly rape scene later on (as per de Ossorio's movies). Upon arrival, the group is approached by a fur trader called Munga (José Thelman) who takes them to the sacred grove where the sinister altar still remains, surrounded by cairns denoting the graves of the massacred natives who were presumably buried where they fell. He warns them of a local legend which tells of sorcerers who rise from the grave at night and vicious leopard women who guard the spot.

While he's supposed to be on watch that night, Rod takes a romantic tumble with Tanika while Carol snaps a few sneaky photographs from the bushes. She then heads off to check out the sacred grove (perfectly dressed for the jungle in miniskirt and go-go boots) before being attacked by the missionary who is now a vampire-leopard woman who subjects her to the same whipping and decapitation she herself endured in the prologue. With two nubile leopard women on the loose, it's not long before the bodies start piling up amid jealous quarrels when Carol's camera is found and its film is developed.

Night of the Sorcerers is a fast-paced bit of nonsense in which de Ossorio hurls everything at the screen including vampires, Voodoo, zombies and sexploitation with plenty of gushing blood and decapitations to keep the gore hounds happy. There are some bad day-for-night shots but some good stuff too such as the mist slowly creeping out of the cairns in an effective shot which feels particularly lifted from *Tombs of the Blind Dead* as well as lots of slow-motion shots of the vampire women running through the jungle in their leopard skin bikinis.

There are the usual continuity issues such as the titular zombie sorcerers pushing their way out of their cairns in one scene and magically materializing on top of them in another. Also, it is established that bullets have no effect on them but that doesn't stop Rod from taking down a whole horde of them by tossing his gun magazine onto the campfire in the movie's climax.

Having vampires created by decapitation is a weird idea too as that's usually the way you kill them. The leopard women wear green ribbons around their necks to conceal their wounds and die when the ribbons are removed. This is an interesting nod to an old folktale which was popularized by Washington Irving and Alexander Dumas but will be more familiar to readers of a certain age via Alvin Schwartz's version *The Girl with the Green Ribbon* which traumatized a generation of schoolkids in his collection *In a Dark, Dark Room and Other Scary Stories*.

SVENGALI THE MAGICIAN/LUCIFER'S WOMEN (1974)

Director: *Paul Aratow*
Writers: *Paul Aratow and Cecil Brown*

This 1974 movie directed by Paul Aratow (responsible for the sexploitation romps *Bizarre Devices* and *China Girl*, 1973 and 1974 respectively) was originally titled *Svengali the Magician* for its brief festival release of that year. It was rereleased in 1977 as *Lucifer's Women* for a short run before sinking into obscurity. *Nurse Sherri* producer Samuel M. Sherman had bought the movie but struggled to distribute it. Together with his regular collaborator, Al Adamson, they reworked some of the footage into *Doctor Dracula* which didn't see the light of day until 1983 while the original cut of the movie was thought to be lost forever. It was discovered and released on DVD and Blu-ray by Vinegar Syndrome in 2018.

Lucifer's Women is a loose adaptation of the staggeringly antisemitic 1894 novel *Trilby* by George du Maurier (grandfather of Daphne du Maurier) which not only gave the world the name of the fashionable narrow-brimmed hat, but also the sinister figure of Svengali; a manipulative hypnotist who targets young women. In most movie and stage adaptations of *Trilby* (and there have been plenty), Svengali's Jewish heritage has been downplayed or removed altogether. In *Lucifer's Women* he is reincarnated as gloomy professor Dr. John Wainright (Larry Hankin), a mesmerist and magician who has published a book about reincarnation. Laughably, the movie's promotional material claims it is set in 1954, although the fashions and cars suggest that nobody was aware of this during shooting.

Wainright's publisher, Sir Stephen (Norman Pierce) is a satanist and is possibly the Sir Stephen from Anne Desclos's 1954 novel *The Story of O*, which could account for the attempt to set the movie in that year. Sir Stephen's occult powers are waning and the only way to renew his contract with the big, bad man downstairs, is to sacrifice a woman at the moment of orgasm, while simultaneously killing himself, at midnight on the dot. To make this unlikely task even trickier, the woman has to be pure of soul; a goddess in human form.

Fortunately, Wainright has recently stumbled across just such a woman; exotic dancer, Trilby (Jane Brunel-Cohen) and the two have embarked upon a relationship. The trouble is, Wainright has fallen for the young woman and begins to doubt his commitment to Sir Stephen's 'Society of the Bleeding Rose' cult. This leads to a battle with the spirit of Svengali which has possessed him and is keen to continue the reincarnation gig by keeping his alliance with Sir Stephen.

Lucifer's Women is little more than a softcore skin flick and the satanic ritual scenes are clearly more interested in the sex than the sacrifice. There's not much in the way of gore besides a 'sawing-in-half' trick gone wrong but the seedy street scenes of 1970s San Francisco together with the uncompromising depictions of drug taking and prostitution as well as the focus of a grubby sexual tryst with an older man, make *Lucifer's Women* decidedly more sordid than the average occult movie. The ritual scenes have a nastiness to them which surpass the usual robes and candles of its brethren (Anton LaVey was a technical consultant, though his actual contribution other than his name, is vague).

A couple of subplots bog the story down such as sleazy club owner Roland (Paul Thomas in his second movie after 1973's *Jesus Christ Superstar* before a long career in porn) trying to pressure Trilby into prostitution and Trilby's lesbian fling with housemate Barbara (Tween Morris) that goes nowhere.

Being based on a Victorian novel and with a focus on hypnotism and drawing room spiritualism, *Lucifer's Women* bridges the gap between the 19th century occult revival and its twin movement in the counterculture of the 20th century. It's hard not to see the influence of Charles Manson in a Svengali movie made in the early seventies. The bohemian runaways eking out a living in the dark underbelly of San Francisco who get sucked into Sir Stephen's satanic web wouldn't look out of place in the company of Susan Atkins and her pals and the descent of hippie free love and experimentation with the occult into a dark place of drugs and murder is very much the vibe of *Lucifer's Women*.

RACE WITH THE DEVIL (1975)
Director: Jack Starrett
Writer: Wes Bishop and Lee Frost

Whenever a genre starts to get a little stale, there will be the inevitable attempts to try and mix things up a little. In *Race with the Devil*, two defining genres of the 1970s collide; the occult thriller and the road movie and it couldn't have picked its stars better. Peter Fonda and Warren Oates had both starred in classic existentialist road movies of the counterculture period – *Easy Rider* (1969) and *Two Lane Blacktop* (1971) respectively – but there is no such naval-gazing or 'searching for America' in *Race with the Devil*. In fact, the movie makes a good analogy for the dropouts of the sixties dropping back into society as middle age approaches with its jobs, mortgages, marriages and recreational vehicles while the counterculture grows ever darker and more sinister in their absence.

That's the basic setup of *Race with the Devil*. No longer the counterculture icons of the outsider living on the edge, Fonda and Oates play two middle-class buddies who take their wives Alice (Loretta Swit) and Kelly (Lara Parker) on vacation in their sumptuous RV, complete with shag carpets, microwave and dirt bikes. On their way to Colorado, they stop for the night somewhere in rural Texas and the men observe what they think is some sort of hippie orgy only to find out that it is a human sacrifice to Satan. Spotted by the cultists, the gang flee for their lives but are pursued across the state by the evil cult resulting in not one, but two thrilling car chases in which Fonda and Oates take turns at the wheel while fending off cultists as they swarm the RV.

There are echoes of *Deliverance* (1972), *The Hills*

Have Eyes (1977) and *The Texas Chainsaw Massacre* (1974) in the oblivious city folk falling afoul of rural locals in the ass-end of nowhere. While not quite folk horror, *Race with the Devil* is still part of that seventies preoccupation of Middle America coming up against the horrors of isolated communities as well as tapping into the paranoia of the Watergate era. No matter how far they run, the four protagonists can never seem to outrun the cult which seems to have infected everyone, including local law enforcement.

Director Jack Starrett keeps the adrenaline pumping with regular action set pieces even before the movie's thrilling final chase. When things threaten to get too quiet, he tosses in a couple of rattlesnakes left in a cupboard by cult members, resulting in a frantic ski-pole-versus-snake fight in the confines of the RV. Even a narratively pointless dirt bike race is a fun diversion.

But it's the uneasy feeling of not knowing whom to trust that makes the movie so effective as a thriller. The characters encounter several colorful types on their journey, from the fatherly sheriff (R. G. Armstrong) to the overly cheerful couple at an RV park who invite them out for an evening of beer and live music. It's the *Rosemary's Baby* tactic of lacing amicable eccentricity with malevolence. When the cultists *are* seen, they take the form of a faceless mob reminiscent of the shadowy attackers in the following year's equally effective *Assault on Precinct 13*. The fact that we can't pick out any recognizable faces in the blood-crazed loonies only adds to the fear that we have no idea who they are.

It's really Fonda and Oates's movie and it's clear they had a blast filming it. They had previously worked together in Fonda's directorial debut *The Hired Hand* (1971) and the sense of camaraderie is palpable. Loretta Swit and Lara Parker are good as the dutiful wives but unfortunately lean a little towards the hysterical female trope. There's a *lot* of screaming from the sidelines while the men battle the forces of darkness, although there is a refreshing sequence in which the ladies head to a local library and pinch a book on witchcraft.

The occult isn't delved into with any seriousness. While the baddies are undoubtedly Satanists, we, like Fonda and Oates, only see their activities from a distance and by the time we're enjoying the high-octane final chase, they might as well be zombies or a biker gang. *Race with the Devil* is more of an action thriller than an occult horror but it's one of the better examples of mixing genres to keep things fresh and remains a favorite of the drive-in era.

THE DEVIL'S RAIN (1975)

Director: Robert Fuest
Writer: Gabe Essoe, James Ashton and Gerald Hopman

The Devil's Rain was another non-pornographic horror movie distributed by the mob-connected Bryanston Distribution Company which had made its bones with the first mainstream porno *Deep Throat* (1972) as well as putting out *Legacy of Satan* and *The Texas Chainsaw Massacre* (both 1974) before the company collapsed amid the fallout of *Deep Throat*'s legal woes. The level of talent behind this 1975 effort really should have resulted in something better. Directed by Robert Fuest who had helmed *And Soon the Darkness* (1970) and *The Abominable Dr. Phibes* (1971) and boasting an impressive cast including William Shatner, Ernest Borgnine, Ida Lupino and Tom Skerritt, *The Devil's Rain* is a dull bit of hokum occasionally punctuated with interesting visuals.

The convoluted mess of a plot is the real culprit. At the center of it is the Preston family who live on a ranch somewhere in the American Southwest. Eldest son Mark (William Shatner) and his mom (Ida Lupino) await the return of Mark's father amid a torrential downpour. When pop does turn up, he is missing his eyes and tells Mark to give a mysterious book to somebody called Corbis. He then promptly melts in the rain like an overheated waxwork while mumbling prayers to Satan.

Mom is all for giving the book (which the Preston family has kept hidden under the floorboards) over to Corbis but Mark is having none of it. He loads a pistol and sets out to finish Corbis but before he makes it out of the driveway, somebody ransacks the Preston home and abducts Mark's mother.

The following day, Mark sets out for Redstone, a deserted mining town. There he meets Corbis who reveals himself to be the head of a satanic order of eyeless cultists who now include Mark's mother in their number. In a battle of faiths, Mark pulls his gun and shoots one of them (who bleeds red and green goo for some reason) before he is overwhelmed by the cultists.

And that's pretty much all we get from William Shatner, billed as the star of the movie, until the final act. Instead we are introduced to his younger brother Tom, (Tom Skerritt) and his wife Julie (Joan Prather, who had starred with Skerritt and Shatner in the Roger Corman produced prohibition era sleaze fest *Big Bad Mama* the previous year).

Tom is a psychic researcher and Julie, subject of his experiments, seems to possess psychic powers. They head to Redstone to find out what happened to Tom's family where Julie experiences a flashback which reveals that Corbis has been knocking around since the 17th century and was betrayed by an ancestor of Mark Preston resulting in him being burnt at the stake. The book he is so keen on recovering contains the names of all his followers who have pledged themselves to Satan. After a run in with Corbis and his cult, Tom and Julie recruit Tom's research partner Dr. Richards (Eddie Albert) to help vanquish Corbis and save Tom's mother and brother. The titular 'devil's rain' is a glass vessel containing the souls of Corbis's followers, another MacGuffin which only confuses the plot further but by the time the vessel is shattered and the rain starts melting the cultists in an exceedingly long and self-indulgent special effects sequence, the audience probably won't care.

The Devil's Rain ladles on the atmosphere and looks pretty fine too, courtesy of Álex Phillips Jr.'s cinematography. The colors are vibrant and the set design of Corbis's satanic church is striking. The cast are giving it a good go, despite the nonsensical plot and Ernest

Borgnine in particular is having a blast, grinning maliciously throughout, and literally turning into a goaty demon in the third act, sporting a makeup job that has to be seen to be believed.

Unfortunately, for all its striking special effects and stellar cast, *The Devil's Rain* is just too convoluted to hold the viewer's attention. There are no real scares aside from the gooey special effects and Borgnine's alarming makeup.

Give yourself a pat on the back if you spot Anton LaVey as the gold-helmeted high priest (this was one of several movies of the period which boasted LaVey as a technical advisor). Similarly in a blink-and-you'll-miss-it role is a young John Travolta in his first movie (he pops up as a robed cultist who hands the book over to Corbis towards the end) and it was during the shoot that Joan Prather gave Travolta a copy of L. Ron Hubbard's book *Dianetics: The Modern Science of Mental Health*, thus kindling his relationship with Scientology.

Another interesting tidbit for horror fans is that the cast made of Shatner's face for his eyeless scenes in *The Devil's Rain* was the very same one Don Post Studios used to manufacture their 'Captain Kirk' masks that hit stores later that year. One such mask was purchased during the filming of *Halloween* (1978) and, after a few alterations and a white paint job, became the iconic face of serial killer Michael Myers.

SATAN'S CHILDREN (1975)

Director: Joe Wiezycki
Writers: Gary Garrett, Ron Levitt and Joe Wiezycki

Joe Wiezycki was a programming director for WTVT television in Tampa, Florida who tried his hand at a couple of bargain basement regional drive-in flicks, the first being the now-lost *Willy's Gone* (1972) and the second, this satanic hippie jaunt with the post-Manson vibe of *Deathmaster* which no doubt felt a little late to the party by 1975.

The limp protagonist is Bobby (Stephen White), a scrawny teenager who lives with his unpleasant stepdad (Eldon Mecham) and nasty stepsister, Janis (Joyce Molloy). Whatever happened to his mother isn't explained but Bobby's life is a miserable one of chores and constant beratement along with sexual teasing from Janis.

Eventually flipping his lid, Bobby hits the road and ends up in a bar where he is chatted up by an elderly gay man. It's left to a greaser called Jake (Bob Barbour) to rescue him and take him back to his place for beer and weed. Unfortunately, Jake invites his greaser buddies around and they drive about drinking beer and raping Bobby while he's jammed between the front seats before dumping him naked in the middle of nowhere.

A group of hippies pick him up and nurse him back to health on their commune. In another stroke of foul luck (Bobby really can't catch a break), the hippies turn out to be a weirdly homophobic cult of Satanists who worship a papier-mâché head of Baphomet. There is friction in the ranks as some don't want to let Bobby into their cult as he might be 'a queer'.

Viewers might notice a theme running through the movie by this point. It's unclear what its attitude towards homosexuality is, being populated by unpleasant characters who are either gay or gay hating (or both, in Jake's case) with only poor Bobby caught in the middle of them. On the one hand, *Satan's Children* feels like a dated fundamentalist educational video warning youngsters of the dangers of homosexuals. It would be a low but predictable blow to try and equate gayness with the devil, but no such message is borne out by the movie's baffling satanic cult who seem to hate homosexuality as much as the staunchest fundamentalists. Far from preaching 'do what thou wilt', these joyless puritans leave us wondering why any rebellious teen would ditch Christianity to join Lucifer's ranks.

The cult is under the control of Sherry (Kathleen Marie Archer) while its real leader, Simon, is away. Sherri berates one of her subordinates, Monica (Rosemary Orlando), for being a lesbian and has her scheduled for execution. Oh yes, this cult isn't just messing around with pentagrams and Sherry in fact postpones Monica's execution to hang three other members for objecting to her letting Bobby into the commune.

When the cigarillo-puffing Simon (Robert C. Ray II) does appear, he seems more of a disco stud than a Charles Manson. He's pissed that Sherry has been overstepping the mark during his absence and has her buried up to the neck in sand, coated with syrup and left to the ants. After taking an earful from Simon about how weak and unworthy of being a satanist he is, Bobby decides that enough is enough and makes a break for freedom.

For a movie that constantly seems to come down on gay people, it turns into absolute homoerotic tedium as Bobby flees through the swamps in his tighty-whities while being pursued by incompetent henchmen who get shocked by electric fences and stumble into quicksand.

It's unclear if the cult has any actual demonic powers but, in one scene, blood starts gushing from the mouth of Monica while she is being interrogated by Simon suggesting that he, at least, has some command of the occult.

The movie is slow and dull for the most part, punctuated by occasional flashes of insanity. The acting is abysmal with long pauses during dialogue as if the actors are trying to remember their lines. Bored viewers might cheer in the final ten minutes as Bobby gains some gumption and goes on the rampage against all those who have wronged him but it's all too little, too late and ultimately directionless.

It's clumsy directing and editing mean that *Satan's Children* has similar production (and unintentional humor) values as other regional stinkers like *Invasion of the Blood Farmers* and *Asylum of Satan*, the latter of which was paired with *Satan's Children* on a 2002 DVD release by Something Weird Video; a company which made a name for itself by rescuing forgotten exploitation titles from obscurity. Many viewers would agree that they probably should have thrown this one back.

LA NOCHE DE LAS GAVIOTAS/NIGHT OF THE SEAGULLS (1975)

Director: Amando de Ossorio
Writer: Amando de Ossorio

Amando de Ossorio's final entry in his Blind Dead tetralogy is unusual in that it has a fairly slim cast and some actual protagonists. It's the story of Dr. Henry Stein (Víctor Petit) and his wife Joan (María Kosty, who was something of a de Ossorio regular by this point) arriving in an isolated fishing village where Henry is to take over as the local doctor. The villagers are unwelcoming to say the least, even refusing to serve Joan in the grocery store. The only ones who don't treat the newcomers with absolute disdain are the village idiot, Teddy (José Antonio Calvo) and Lucy (Sandra Mozarowsky who tragically died two years later in mysterious circumstances, sparking conspiracy theories that she was carrying the child of King Juan Carlos of Spain).

Night of the Seagulls improves on its slow-moving predecessor, *The Ghost Galleon*, by delving into the Templars' backstory more, kicking off with a flashback to medieval times in which, as in the first two movies, they brutally sacrifice a young woman to their god, this time some sort of Lovecraftian frog deity. Exiled from France, the Templars took up residence in a nearby castle and emerge from their tombs every seven years to demand the sacrifice of seven virgins over seven consecutive nights.

Henry and Joan take Lucy in as a maid and soon realize that she is to be the next sacrificial victim. Determined to save her from a grisly fate, Henry and Joan decide to intervene but they have more than the undead Templars to deal with and this is what makes *Night of the Seagulls* the most interesting entry in the series. The fears of the locals have turned them into something of a cult themselves. It is the living humans who sacrifice virgins this time around, with the Templars filling in for the demonic deity. In switching things around and presenting rustic locals as the villains, de Ossorio created an intriguing folk horror along the lines of *The Wicker Man* and Shirley Jackson's *The Lottery*. There is also a similarity to Robert E. Howard's classic short horror story *Pigeons from Hell* in the idea that the ever-screeching seagulls who wheel over the village are the souls of the sacrificed girls.

Even when the movie reverts to type in the final act with the survivors boarding up windows in a house under siege, it feels earned instead of routine. Rather than lacking any motive other than feasting on the living, the Templars have been denied their sacrifice and are coming to claim what they were promised as the terrified villagers always feared.

The rustic coastal location of Spain's Tossa de Mar provides an eerie and isolated setting, and the Templars have a spiffy new temple for their base although, once again, footage is snatched from the first movie to depict their rising from the grave which anybody who's seen the previous installments must surely spot by now. The Blind Dead (who don't seem so blind in this movie) look better and more decrepit than ever and there seem to be a whole lot more of them too.

Night of the Seagulls is the most polished and tightly plotted of the series, even if it isn't as atmospheric as the first or as action heavy as the second. It's certainly better than the third while sharing its reliance on mood and tension rather than gore. Like *The Ghost Galleon*, there's very little blood apart from some silly and superfluous gushing from the Templars' eye sockets at the end which feels like it might have been included just to satisfy certain tastes. But de Ossorio proved that he could do more than generic zombie movies with this one and it's a shame the series never continued beyond this point other than in the form of unofficial spinoffs and short homages.

TO THE DEVIL A DAUGHTER (1976)

Director: Peter Sykes
Writer: Chris Wicking, John Peacock and Gerald
Vaughan-Hughes

By 1974, Hammer Film Productions, which had brought a splash of color (and blood) to the horror genre with their adaptations of *Dracula* and *Frankenstein* in the late 1950s, was in dire straits. Their heyday of the 1960s in which they enjoyed great success churning out gothic period horrors with lucrative distribution deals in the US was at an end. Financing from Hollywood had dried up and Hammer's attempts to modernize by amping up the blood and nudity as well as updating the setting of its final Dracula movies to swinging London, had failed to rejuvenate the studio.

It wasn't a story unique to Hammer. The British film industry all but died a sordid death in the 1970s, with audiences abandoning theatres for the ever more prevalent medium of television amid funding cuts from all quarters. In a somewhat 'if you can't beat them, join them' attitude, head of Hammer, Michael Carreras, began exploring an idea for a television series based on the works of Dennis Wheatley, taking its name from the occult writer's 1971 non-fiction title *The Devil and All His Works*.

Wheatley had been so pleased with Hammer's 1968 adaptation of his novel *The Devil Rides Out* that he had given the rights to his books to Christopher Lee and Hammer producer Anthony Nelson Keys, who had set up their own company, Charlemagne Productions, with the intention of adapting *The Haunting of Toby Jugg* and *To the Devil a Daughter*. Unfortunately, Charlemagne's one and only movie – *Nothing but the Night* (1973) – sank without a trace at the box office, obliterating their hopes for future products. The rights to Wheatley's novels passed to Hammer, something Wheatley would come to lament.

To the Devil a Daughter was to be the first episode of Hammer's conceived TV series but its movie potential was reevaluated after a preview screening of *The Exorcist*. Present at the screening was head of EMI Films, Nat Cohen, who agreed to finance half of the movie's budget, leaving Hammer to stump up the rest. Even that was a tall order for the cash-strapped Hammer, and they secured extra funding from German production company, Terra Filmkunst, necessitating some of the movie being shot in Bavaria.

In keeping with Hammer's attempts to modernize, the book's 1953 setting was updated to the 1970s. Much of the plot however, was heavily rewritten as to be almost unrecognizable. Veteran of films noir and war movies, Richard Widmark (an American actor was necessary to secure EMI funding) stars as occult writer John Verney who is asked by a stranger (Denholm Elliott) to pick up his daughter from the airport and keep her safe from a satanic cult. Sniffing a plot for his next bestseller, Verney agrees but soon finds himself in the sights of Father Michael Rayner (Christopher Lee); a defrocked priest who now heads a heretical order. The young girl, Catherine (Nastassja Kinski), was promised to Rayner as a vessel for the demon Astaroth upon her birth by her mother, a member of the order. With the help of his literary friends Anna Fountain (Honor Blackman) and David Kennedy (Anthony Valentine), Verney tries to save Catherine from her fate, ultimately racing towards a showdown with the sinister Father Rayner.

A difficult shoot caused by constant rewrites during filming led to a patchwork plot lacking in direction. The cobbled-together ending in which Christopher Lee is hit on the head by a rock and promptly vanishes and an utterly bizarre sequence involving a grotesque fetus-goblin crawling into Nastassja Kinski's womb seemed to baffle the movie's cast as much as it did its audiences.

Critics found the movie distasteful bordering on obscene while the gratuitous nude shots of the then-fourteen-year-old Nastassja Kinski have mired the movie in controversy ever since. None of this stopped *To the Devil a Daughter* being a massive success and Hammer's most profitable movie of the 1970s.

It was too little too late, however, as Hammer had shared the budget with other investors and didn't reap enough of the profits to embark on a follow-up. Even if they had, another Wheatley adaptation would have been out of the question as the author was so disgusted by *To the Devil a Daughter* that he forbade the studio from adapting any of his books ever again. It was to be Hammer's last horror movie until the studio was revived in the new millennium.

But it's not all bad. Being shot partly abroad gives the movie a more geographically sweeping feel compared to Hammer's almost exclusively England-bound productions which tended to reuse the same locations and sets over and over. It certainly feels different to Hammer's other entries, especially the studio's campier fare of the early seventies. Part of that might be the level of gore and downright nastiness as Hammer desperately tried to compete with the more visceral horror coming out of New Hollywood.

Lee gives it his all as the demonic priest and is so evil and driven in his performance that he is more frightening than Dracula (a creature merely compelled by its own hunger) or even the cheerful pagan overlord Summerisle. Widmark looks a little bored but presents a cynical version of Dennis Wheatley; an American author of trashier occult fiction to Wheatley's imperialist pomp.

Kinski holds her own in only her second movie role, alternating between doe-eyed vulnerability and murderous intent when she is occasionally possessed.

With such a cast and willingness to go beyond what Hammer had done before, the movie really had potential and it's a shame that its chaotic shoot turned it into such an incoherent mess. What should have been an enthralling confrontation between good and evil from the studio that had defined British horror for nearly two decades is instead a confusing, dull and sordid death whimper.

THE OMEN (1976)

Director: Richard Donner
Writer: David Seltzer

The early 1970s was a gloomy time in many ways. The optimism of the 1960s had collapsed with the escalating war in Vietnam and the Watergate scandal gradually eroding America's faith in itself along with the ongoing threat of nuclear war and rising environmental concerns about what was happening to the planet. People could be forgiven for thinking that the western world was in fast decline and that, with the approaching millennium, something big might be going down.

The rise of the Christian right and evangelicalism saw an increase in 'dispensational premillennialism'; a literal reading of the Book of Revelation identifying different stages (dispensations) in God's dealings with humanity with heavy focus on the rise and seven-year rule of the antichrist that precedes Christ's return. The idea was popularized in the 1970s by evangelical writer Hal Lindsey in his books *The Late, Great Planet Earth* (1970) and *Satan is Alive and Well on Planet Earth* (1972) which inspired a whole genre of 'apocalyptic pop prophecy' books.

Against this backdrop of the perceived end times, the idea for a new movie that capitalized on the devil trend of *The Exorcist* arose. Producer Harvey Bernhard, whose career up to that point included low-budget grindhouse fare like *Sixteen* (1972) and the blaxploitation flicks *The Mack* (1973) and *Thomasine and Bushrod* (1974) was inspired by a conversation with his born-again Christian friend Bob Munger concerning the Book of Revelation. Bernhard asked screenwriter Devid Seltzer to come up with a script based on the premise that the antichrist was already among us in the form of a little boy.

Seltzer used his own imagination as much as scripture, putting several things in the movie which have since been taken as 'gospel' by many. For instance, the Bible never claims that the antichrist is Satan's son. Seltzer also fabricated the famous quote "From the eternal sea he rises, creating armies on either shore, turning man against his brother 'til man exists no more."

The 'eternal sea' is taken to mean the world of politics and the movie centers around Robert Thorn, the American ambassador to the United Kingdom whose son dies in childbirth. In a desperate and misguided attempt to spare his wife's grief, Robert secretly adopts a baby whose mother has just died. With his wife none the wiser, the couple raise this boy as their own and name him Damien but by the time he is five, strange things start to happen.

Pitched as a psychological thriller rather than a horror movie, various big-name actors were considered for the role of Robert Thorn including Oliver Reed, Charlton Heston, Roy Scheider, Dick Van Dyke and Charles Bronson. Gregory Peck was eventually cast, familiar to Middle America for his wholesome leading man roles like Atticus Finch in *To Kill a Mockingbird* (1962). The casting of Peck helped give the movie a touch of class which convinced other actors to take a chance on a low-budget entry in a genre which, generally speaking, did not attract A-listers. As a result, the superb cast really makes the movie, including Lee Remick as Damien's loving but increasingly frantic mother Katherine, David Warner as a curious photographer who senses that there is something amiss surrounding the Thorn family, Patrick Troughton as a tormented priest desperate to avert the apocalypse and Billie Whitelaw as the satanic nanny who weasels her way into the Thorns' confidence in order to safeguard

His Satanic Majesty's offspring.

And then there is young Harvey Spencer Stevens as Damien who puts in an unnerving performance as the demonic six-year-old. Animals are terrified of him (apart from rottweilers who guard him with loyal ferocity) and there is an uncomfortable aura whenever he is on screen. Switching between silently staring with those piercing eyes, and full-on meltdown mode when threatened with being taken to church, he's enough to give any parents the heebie-jeebies. Evil kids had been done before (most notably in 1960's *Village of the Damned*) but *The Omen* helped create the 'devil child' trope which has been copied and parodied ever since.

Director Richard Donner wanted to play down the supernatural angle and leave it ambiguous as to whether Damien is in fact the antichrist. David Selzer and Harvey Bernhard pushed against this and eventually won out with the movie leaving no doubt that there is some demonic power surrounding the boy. That said, Donner was able to give the movie a feeling of credibility, reining in some of Seltzer's more outlandish ideas (such as caped creatures who leave cloven hoofprints in the Italian cemetery scene) leaving us with a movie that is so unnerving because it feels so grounded.

It is Peck's performance as Robert Thorn which anchors the audience in reality, making the movie all the more frightening. Things might initially be brushed off as freak accidents or signs of mental illness but Thorn, like the audience, is gradually forced to believe otherwise, resulting in a trip to Rome with photographer Jennings (David Warner) in which they learn about Damien's true origin and the satanic conspiracy surrounding him.

The Omen is best remembered for the brutality of several 'accidents' that befall people who stand in the way of Damien's destiny, namely impalement by a falling church spire and beheading by a sheet of plate glass. Despite being entirely bloodless, the scenes are still effective even half a century later, a testament to the movie's special effects and clever editing. In a movie that mostly works on a psychological level, the sudden violence of the scenes is rendered utterly shocking.

The Omen's promotional campaign cashed in on the zeitgeist of the time. Its taglines included "Today is the 6th Day of the 6th Month of 1976. You Have Been Warned" and "Good morning. You are one day closer to the end of the world." David Seltzer quickly churned out a novelization of his own script which hit paperback racks before the movie's release and became a bestseller, giving ticket sales an extra push. The movie was a massive success considering its 2.8 million budget. Audiences ignored the critics (several of whom unfavorably compared the movie to *The Exorcist* and snorted at the religious mumbo-jumbo of Seltzer's script) and flocked to theatres, making *The Omen* one of the highest-grossing movies of 1976. Jerry Goldsmith's terrifying score infused with Gregorian chants won an Oscar for Best Original Score with its theme song 'Ave Satani' nominated for Best Original Song.

The Omen (along with *The Exorcist* and *Rosemary's Baby*) forms part of that unholy trinity of occult movies which dragged the horror genre from the grindhouses of previous decades into a more respectable arena in the 1970s, attracting big name actors. It was part of the wave of 'new horror' which abandoned the gothic castles and period dress of the genre's roots and reinvented itself for the modern world in which horror was much closer to home, even as close as within our own children.

No doubt the grim sense of fatalism that permeates the movie helped it strike a chord with audiences in 1976. Unlike *The Exorcist*, no priest can successfully win out over the devil. In *The Omen*, the fate of the world is predetermined. Gruesome deaths are signaled in photographs and cannot be changed. The future is written and death, like the devil, cannot be cheated.

THE DEVIL'S MEN (1976)

Director: Kostas Karagiannis
Writer: Arthur Rowe

Released in a truncated form in the US to secure a PG rating with the less-diabolic sounding title *Land of the Minotaur*, this Greek movie was written by American TV writer Arthur Rowe who had penned occasional episodes for the likes of *Mission: Impossible, Gunsmoke* and *Kolchak: The Night Stalker*. The presence of British horror stalwarts Donald Plesance and Peter Cushing really gives the impression that this movie belongs to a higher caliber than it does. Directed by Kostas Karagiannis, a prolific Greek director of thrillers and comedies, *The Devil's Men* is a plodding and fairly silly low-budget occult caper, even if it does make good use of the Greek scenery and its ancient ruins.

Tourists have been disappearing around the ruins of an old Minoan temple. Donald Pleasence (sporting a rather inconsistent Irish accent) is on the case as the ex-pat priest Father Roche. He suspects murder and is treated as an old coot by the local police, forcing him to send to New York for help in the form of his friend, Milo, a silver-haired playboy private detective played by Greek actor Kostas Karagiorgis.

Before Milo's arrival, Father Roche is visited by his friend Beth (Vanna Reville) along with her boyfriend Ian (Bob Behling) and their new friend Tom (Nikos Verlekis). Against Roche's wishes, the three youngsters head off to visit the temple. While Beth is dispatched into town to pick up groceries, Ian and Tom poke around in the ruins and discover the bodies of some missing tourists before being given a fright by a speaking, fire-breathing statue of the Minotaur which rises up out of the ground.

Beth, searching for her missing friends, encounters the friendly Baron Corofax (Peter Cushing), before being abducted by robed cultists. She is reunited with Ian and Tom in the temple where the three of them are now captives at the hands of the cult which is under the control of Baron Corofax. This comes as no surprise to the audience as the movie opened with a robed Peter Cushing sacrificing a couple to the Minoan statue.

In fact, that's the main problem with the movie. The audience knows who the villain is right from the get-go and watching the rest of the cast gradually cotton on is a laborious process only occasionally relieved by points of mild interest. Tom's girlfriend, Laurie (Luan Peters, a veteran of British TV as well as bit parts in a couple of Hammer horrors) turns up around the same time as the American detective Milo, and it's only at the half-hour mark that our triumvirate of heroes are established. With a large Greek cast playing the locals including police chief, widow, shopkeeper and his daughter all contributing variously to the plot, it's a dizzying number of characters for such a straightfor-ward movie.

Detective Milo doesn't do much aside from act like a boorish chauvinist who doesn't believe anybody and even belts Laurie across the chops in one scene. It's not quite clear why he is needed in the movie other than to provide a more square-jawed protagonist than Donald Pleasance. Pleasance is reliable as ever playing the slightly doddering but fanatic crusader against the forces of darkness similar to what we would see two years later in *Halloween* (1978). Peter Cushing turns up for a paycheck as the exiled noble from Carpathia, a strange detail the only explanation for which is that Cushing didn't make a convincing Greek aristocrat.

There is a rather effective scene in which hooded cultists burst in on Laurie while she is taking a bath but, amusingly, it doesn't stop her from wanting another bath a couple of scenes later. The lair of the cultists is impressive enough for such low budget fare but the final battle in which Father Roche and Milo take on the cult is marked by silliness. Peter Cushing's sacrificial dagger looks more like a butter knife and the cultists inexplicably explode when their plan is foiled. Equally befuddling is why the stone statue of the Minotaur has guts inside it when it is smashed apart.

What could have been an interesting little folk horror is little more than a by-the-numbers occult movie which utilizes virtually nothing from Greek mythology. The Minotaur was simply chosen because the movie was shot in Greece and is used only as a stand in for the devil.

Much has been made of the odd fact that Brian Eno provided the score for the movie but it's little more than atmospheric humming that doesn't do much to rack up the tension. A more interesting musical contribution is the end credits song 'The Devil's Men' by blues rock musician Paul Williams which is far livelier than the movie deserves.

SATAN'S SLAVE (1976)

Director: Norman J. Warren
Writer: David McGillivray

With Hammer Productions on the rocks by the mid-seventies and Amicus going the same way, British horror seemed to have lost its bite along with its funding. Hammer had tried to get with the program by sexing things up a little and bringing Dracula into the 20th century, but it was too little too late. With *The Exorcist* and *The Texas Chainsaw Massacre* unleashing a new brand of visceral, nasty, gory horror on the other side of the Atlantic, the efforts of British studios seemed tame and old hat even when they were trying to be hip.

It fell to a new generation of British filmmakers to shake things up. Both Norman J. Warren and Pete Walker worked extensively in the sexploitation genre before switching to horror in the early seventies, forming a 'new wave' of British horror that was much grittier and gorier than anything that had preceded it. Walker was first off the mark with *House of Whipcord* and *Frightmare* (both 1974) while Warren was still struggling to break away from the skin flick genre in which he had made the notorious *Her Private Hell* (1967). Intent on making an independent horror movie, Warren teamed up with producers Les Young and Richard Crafter (who sold up assets and invested their own money) and shot *Satan's Slave* at the mock Tudor house, Admiral's Walk in Surry where *Virgin Witch* had been shot (Warren would return to it again in 1978 for *Terror*).

A talky satanic ritual muffled behind animal masks kicks off the proceedings in which a blonde woman is stripped naked and brutally sacrificed. A second shock-opener immediately follows with a young woman

(Gloria Walker) being sexually assaulted by her date (a super creepy Martin Potter) who ties her up, threatens her with a pair of scissors and then crushes her head in a door jamb when she tries to flee. At only twelve minutes in, we've already seen more nudity and gore than Hammer would ever have attempted.

The protagonist is nineteen-year-old Catherine (Candace Glendenning) who, with her parents, goes to visit a mysterious uncle she has never met. Their car crashes into a tree upon arrival at the uncle's estate and Catherine is the only survivor. Newly orphaned and in grief, Catherine is taken in by her uncle, Alexander (Michael Gough), but despite his pleasant warmth, there are two others in the house who make Catherine uneasy. Uncle Alexander's son, Stephen, is the murderous chap from the beginning and he develops an unhealthy interest in his cousin while the family secretary, Frances (Barbara Kellerman), looks on with jealousy. On top of this, Catherine starts having visions of a woman who was tortured and burned as a witch on the estate's grounds centuries ago.

The woman is, of course, Catherine's ancestor and her presence at Uncle Alexander's is to become to vessel for the reincarnation of the witch. Uncle Alex heads a satanic cult and even murdered his wife in a botched ritual years previously, a ritual witnessed by young Stephen which, understandably, had something of a poor effect on his mental health, turning him into a raging psychopath who likes to rape and murder women.

The basic plot is fairly by-the-numbers and a little plodding at times, even if there's a few diversions like the aforementioned homicidal son. A similar dead end (in the literal sense) is the plight of Catherine's boyfriend, John (Michael Craze) who, in any other movie, would be playing detective only to burst in on the coven in the final act. Here, any help from home is efficiently nipped in the bud via black magic which reveals that the cult really does have some supernatural powers.

Poor editing might be to blame for some nonsensical character moments. Catherine seems to quickly forget that her parents were recently consumed in a blazing car wreck and doesn't seem to kick up much of a fuss when cousin Stephen suggests a bit of incest, apparently also forgetting that she has a boyfriend. The slighted secretary Frances similarly displays a nonsensical devotion to Stephen, only to betray him on a dime, filling Catherine in on her uncle's plot and suggesting they escape together. More scenes might have been shot, but, in its final cut, the movie feels a little patchy which, in a way, only adds to the hazy dreamlike feel.

Despite the odd character choices and long lulls in which Catherine wanders about, looking almost as bored as the audience, *Satan's Slave* rescues itself from total tedium with some truly shocking violence. The real standouts being a man tumbling from a high-rise block with close ups of shattered bones and crushed skull and a nasty nailfile to the eyeball towards the movie's end. This and Warren's well-practiced nudie shots which don't shy away any more than the gore does, make for a startling and disturbing British horror movie that almost feels like an Italian entry in its lurid colors and nightmarish atmosphere.

SUSPIRIA (1977)

Director: Dario Argento
Writer: Dario Argento, Dario Nicolodi

Born in Rome to a film producer, Dario Argento began as a scriptwriter of low-budget Italian action movies until he helped Sergio Leone devise the story for his epic, all-star western *Once upon a Time in the West* (1968). His directorial debut came in 1970's *The Bird with the Crystal Plumage*, a movie that was immediately compared to the suspense thrillers of Alfred Hitchcock and was a first for the giallo genre as it drew critical and commercial acclaim. Argento perfected the form in *Deep Red* (1975) which is widely considered to be the pinnacle of the giallo movement.

But by the mid-seventies, gialli were growing tedious and cliché-ridden. Argento wanted to make something more in line with his growing interest in the occult and, after his talks with American producers to adapt an H. P. Lovecraft story fell through, he decided to make a supernatural horror movie of his own.

His relationship with Daria Nicolodi (the star of *Deep Red*) has often been cited as key to Argento's obsession with the occult. Nicolodi had some spooky tales of her own including one told to her by her grandmother of her time in a German academy, the faculty of which she was convinced was practicing black magic. Argento and Nicolodi took a tour of the region where the borders of Germany, France and Switzerland meet (also the area where the social reformer and occultist Rudolph Steiner founded the first Waldorf School as part of his anthroposophical society). Together they began working on the screenplay and came up with the simple but frightening tale of a young ballerina who travels from New York to a prestigious ballet school in Germany which she gradually comes to realize is run by a coven of witches.

Taking its name from the 1845 collection of essays *Suspiria de Profundis* (*Sighs from the Depths*) by English writer and drug fiend Thomas De Quincey, *Suspiria* is a nightmarish adult fairy tale that makes up for its basic plot with astounding visuals that have elevated the movie to art house status.

The rather disorientating opening flips between the arrival of Suzy Bannion (Jessica Harper) at the dance school and the abrupt departure of another student, Pat Hingle (Eva Axén). Pat flees the school in terror and makes for her friend's apartment only to be butchered by a demonic entity and left hanging by her neck through a shattered skylight while her friend is impaled by a falling shard of glass.

It's a hell of an opening and only hints at the delirious madness to come. Once admitted to the school, Suzy begins to suspect that Pat uncovered a dark secret about the school's instructors; Miss Tanner and Madame Blanc, played by veterans of Hollywood's golden era, Alida Valli and Joan Bennett. Horror set pieces ensue including maggots falling from the ceiling, a nasty pit full of razor wire and a final confrontation with the hidden leader of the coven; an ancient witch called Helena Markos (allegedly played by a ninety-year-old former prostitute Argento found on the streets of Rome).

Suspiria is an intoxicatingly vivid movie. The blood-red façade of Freiburg's famous Whale House was reconstructed on a soundstage in Rome and the interior sets intentionally eschew spatial logic. Velvet wallpaper, gossamer curtains and geometric stained glass create a surreal and claustrophobic world. The primary colors seem to seep out of the screen, an effect achieved by using Technicolor's 'dye-transfer' process on old Kodak film stock with the contrast dialed right up.

The adoption of an outdated Technicolor process was a deliberate nod to *Snow White and the Seven Dwarves* (1937), Technicolor's first feature length animated film, and the similarities don't end there. The tale of a young woman falling afoul of witchcraft in a gloomy forest is an obvious parallel, enhanced by the innocent doe-eyes of Jessica Harper and the childish dialogue of the students. Even the doorhandles on the sets were raised to make the students seem smaller and the screenplay originally called for a cast of eight to ten-year-olds, something that was vetoed by producers who were naturally concerned about a script that had kids being tossed into pits of razor wire.

As with *Deep Red*, Argento employed Italian prog-rock band Goblin (amusingly miscredited as 'The Goblins') in the movie and their eerie, eclectic score has become a favorite of the genre and a defining feature of *Suspiria*. The surrealist imagery overlaid by Goblin's ever-present gasping, sighing, drumming and moaning gives the movie the feel of a music video as well as a nightmare.

Argento explored *Suspiria*'s namesake further in its sequel, *Inferno* (1980), namely De Quincey's mentioning of three companions for the Roman goddess Levana. *Suspiria de Profundis* gives their names as Mater Lachrymarum (Our Lady of Tears), Mater Suspiriorum (Our Lady of Sighs) and Mater Tenebrarum (Our Lady of Darkness). Collectively known as 'Our Ladies of Sorrow', these figures draw upon the triple deity motif from European paganism, examples of which are the three fates of Ancient Greece or the Celtic 'Matrone' (mothers).

The triple goddess has become an important figure in Neopaganism, popularized by the mythographer Robert Graves in his book *The White Goddess*. Often associated with witchcraft, the triple goddess motif is the basis of *Inferno* which reveals that the defeated Helena Markos of *Suspiria* was but one of a trio of witches who are determined to rule the world through black magic. Mater Suspiriorum might be dead but Mater Lachrymarum and Mater Tenebrarum (living in Rome and New York respectively) are still at large. While *Suspiria*'s basic plot was given a dreamy patina, *Inferno*'s surreal dream questing has little rhyme or reason to it. Still visually stunning, its lack of coherence isn't for everyone and unfortunately was a sign of things to come.

After *Inferno* and his breakup with Nicolodi, the quality and success of Argento's work rapidly declined. It would be twenty-seven years before he would complete his 'Three Mothers' trilogy with 2007's *The Mother of Tears* a bafflingly disappointing movie that is disliked and derided even by Argento fans.

THE SENTINEL (1977)

Director: Michael Winner
Writers: Jeffrey Konvitz and Michael Winner

Producer Jeffrey Konvitz was working for MGM in the early seventies when he decided to pen and produce his own movie, the early slasher *Silent Night, Bloody Night* (1972). His follow-up pitch for an apartment-bound occult thriller in the vein of *Rosemary's Baby* (1968) didn't find any takers in Hollywood so he decided to turn it into a novel. The result was a smash hit in the cultural atmosphere following *The Exorcist*'s release and the rights to *The Sentinel* were purchased by Universal for $500,000.

Konvitz collaborated on the script with British director Michael Winner who had made a name for himself helming several American action thrillers starring Charles Bronson like *The Mechanic* (1972) and *Death Wish* (1974). Cristina Raines stars as the lead and had a minor part in one of Winner's Bronson actioners, *The Stone Killer* (1973). She was in a relationship with her *Hex* co-star Keith Carradine when Winner cast her in *The Sentinel* (alongside Carradine's father, John).

The rest of the cast is quite a talking point as the movie is filled to the brim with recognizable faces from golden age stalwarts, (Ava Garnder and José Ferrer), to familiar character actors (Eli Wallach and Burgess Meredith) to up-and-comers who would become big stars in later decades (Jeff Goldblum and Christopher Walken).

Raines plays fashion model Alison Parker who, despite the urgings of her hot-shot lawyer boyfriend Michael (Chris Sarandon), is holding out on marriage and is looking for her own apartment. Some serious baggage is hinted at with reference to two suicide attempts (one after her own father attacked her after she walked in on one of his orgies). Her relationship with Michael started as an affair when he was still married leading to his wife's suicide, resulting in a large degree of guilt. She is also a lapsed Catholic; a clumsy echo of Father Karras's plight in *The Exorcist* that isn't really gone into in any depth.

Moving into an ivy-clad brownstone in Brooklyn, Alison quickly learns that the other tenants are an eccentric bunch. There's an old man (Burgess Meredith) who throws birthday parties for his cat, a lesbian couple who seem to lack boundaries, and the top floor is occupied by an old blind priest called Father Halleran, who does nothing but stare out the window all day. Pretty soon, Alison starts feeling some ill effects such as blackouts and nightmares while noises emanate from the apartment above hers; an apartment which is supposed to be empty. The mystery deepens when Alison complains to the estate agent and is informed that, aside from her and the priest, the building is uninhabited.

Michael does some digging and finds out that the diocesan council of New York own the building and a cabal of priests have been covering up some sort of identity theft scheme for decades. That's because the brownstone was built over a portal to hell, requiring a sentinel to guard it at all times and Alison is next up for the job.

The scares are effectively done. Alison's nighttime exploration of the empty apartments and her encounter with its ghostly denizens (including the pasty specter of her recently deceased father) are as creepy as any haunted house movie but it's *The Sentinel*'s particularly nasty special effects which will remain with the viewer. Some feel like stop motion with sped-up violence and the makeup effects of flakey, decaying faces with pale, dead fish-eye stares are quite haunting.

There's a subplot in which detective Gatz (Eli Wallach) suspects that Michael's ex was in fact murdered by Michael while other evidence is dug up on the people Alison has seen in her building and they all appear to have been murderers. This all makes for a slightly overcrowded and confusing plot. There is also the question of taste in Winner's use of people with physical differences to play the demons of hell in the final scenes as they add little but carnivalesque spectacle and feel like a bit of a cheap shot.

The Sentinel tries to be *Rosemary's Baby* (1968) while simultaneously trying to top *The Exorcist* and *The Omen* in the gross-out visceral horror department. As a result, it lacks focus and never rivaled the members of the unholy trinity of satanic horror. It remains a bit of a cult movie, less known than its brethren, but certainly worth a look if only for the astonishing cast and creepy bits. Konvitz penned a sequel to *The Sentinel* – *The Guardian* – which hit shelves in 1979 but was never adapted.

HOLOCAUST 2000/THE CHOSEN (1977)

Director: Alberto De Martino
Writers: Sergio Donati, Alberto De Martino and Michael Robson

Director Alberto De Martino had previously dabbled in the devil trend with *The Antichrist*, a possession movie which attempted to ride on the coattails of *The Exorcist*. The title would have been more appropriate for his next demonic outing which took its cue from *The Omen*, beating its official sequel to screens (in Italy, at least) by nearly a year.

But it's unfair to label *Holocaust 2000* (released in the US as *The Chosen*) as another Italian rip off of a popular American movie. A joint British/Italian production, *Holocaust 2000* isn't the postapocalyptic sci-fi movie its title suggests. Nor is it a movie about evil cults, demonic possession or black magic, making its entry in this book tenuous were it not for its obvious reliance on the Gregory Peck-starring blockbuster. It's a movie about the devil and the Book of Revelation, wrapped up in the environmentalist concerns of the nuclear age and the rapidly approaching millennium.

Copying the formula *The Omen* initiated by putting a highly recognizable middle-aged American actor in a modestly-budgeted horror movie, *Holocaust 2000* stars Kirk Douglas as industrialist Robert Caine. Caine wants to install a nuclear powerplant that can generate the heat of the sun in an unspecified Middle Eastern country. A lot of people aren't happy about this, including throngs of anti-nuclear protestors and the unnamed country's new prime minister, Colonel Harbin (Spiros Focas). Also opposed to the idea is a religious nut (Massimo Foschi) who tries to murder Caine but, due to the intervention of his son, Angel (Simon Ward), ends up killing his wife instead.

Caine's wife (Virginia McKenna) also wasn't keen on his nuclear ambitions and, as controller of most of the company shares, had the power to stop him, which makes her death rather convenient. When Colonel Harbin is decapitated by a freak helicopter accident, Caine starts to notice a pattern of unfortunate ends to those who oppose the construction of the plant. On top of that, a lot of religious symbolism seems to be popping up. The company computer briefly goes haywire and spits out a seemingly nonsensical equation '2√231' which Caine discovers spells 'IESVS' (Jesus) backwards; the same word carved in a rock near where he wants to build his plant. Also, Caine's proposed plant has seven turbines, matching the seven heads of the beast.

Soon, Caine is having nightmares about his creation spelling doom for mankind and, as a helpful priest (Romolo Valli) points out, the antichrist is a 'second son' who will unleash the beast and bring about the end times. Not good, as the young journalist (Agostina Belli) with whom Caine has recently begun a relationship, has just announced that she is pregnant.

Like *The Omen*, *Holocaust 2000* adds its own bits and pieces to the biblical tale of the apocalypse such as the name Jesus spelled backwards being used throughout history as a symbol of the antichrist. It's a little contrived but still fun, interesting and well-made with well-executed death scenes that feel like they belong in the Omen series. The eventual twist as to the antichrist's true identity is signaled way too early and will surprise nobody and the lack of information as to how he came into being and exactly *what* he is, is just one of several gaps in the story that could have been explored further. Kirk Douglas gives it his all, not once tempted to phone it in and even bravely *bares all* at the age of sixty-one in a full-frontal nude nightmare scene. A great cast including classic British character actors Anthony Quayle and Geoffrey Keen rounds out the movie with an operatic score by Ennio Morricone.

Holocaust 2000 made its way to American shores in the spring of 1978 with the title *The Chosen* and an alternate ending which ditched the original (and rather bleakly open-ended one) in favor of Kirk Douglas taking down the antichrist armed with explosives. It reverted back to its original title when syndicated on TV but kept its American ending. The original European version was released on DVD in 2008, inexplicably retitled *Rain of Fire*.

DAMIEN: OMEN II (1978)

Director: Don Taylor
Writer: Stanley Mann and Mike Hodges

The massive success of the modestly-budgeted *The Omen* meant that a sequel was inevitable and indeed, the final shot of young Damien looking sinisterly over his shoulder at us at the funeral of his parents, while clutching the hand of the President of the United States, demanded one.

David Seltzer, the writer of the first movie wasn't interested in doing a sequel so producer Harvey Bernhard penned the story himself and handed it over to screenwriter Stanley Mann. Original director Richard Donner was busy making *Superman* (1978) so the director of *Get Carter* (1971), Mike Hodges was initially placed at the helm. Progress was slow however and Hodges was replaced with the reliable Don Taylor, no stranger to franchise sequels having directed *Escape from the Planet of the Apes* (1971).

Damien: Omen II takes place seven years after the original. Damien (now played by Jonathan Scott-Taylor) is thirteen and, instead of being nestled within the White House as suggested by the previous movie's ending, has been adopted by his uncle, Richard (brother to Gregory Peck's character) an exceedingly wealthy industrialist with a fancy house by a lake. Instead of politics, corporate America is the environment in which the young antichrist rises and it's an interesting premise.

As with the first movie, a high-caliber cast was sought. William Holden, one of many serious leading men who was in the running to play Damien's father, hadn't wanted to be in a horror movie about the devil back in 1976 but the massive success of *The Omen* apparently changed his mind and he plays Damien's uncle with Academy Award winner Lee Grant as his wife.

Damien and his adoptive brother, Mark (Lucas Donat) are shipped off to military school where, as we can expect, Damien takes a dim view on bullies. Jonathan Scott-Taylor does a good job of portraying angsty adolescence, but Damien's acceptance of his evil heritage is a little sudden. Seemingly all it takes is reading a few bible passages and finding '666' on his scalp for a nice kid to turn into a serial killer.

As with the first movie, satanic cult members are lurking about to protect Damien and pave his way to ultimate domination. Lance Henriksen puts in a turn as Damien's military instructor, telling him which passages of the Bible to read by way of easing him into his destiny and Robert Foxworth plays a manager of Thorn Industries who worms his way to the top to prepare the company for Damien's eventual takeover.

Of course, there are some outstanding deaths awaiting any and all who stand in the Dark Lord's way. One unfortunate falls through the frozen lake during a hockey game and is sucked under the ice by the current while another is sliced in half by a falling elevator. The slavering rottweilers of the original are replaced with a sinister raven who heralds death to those who see it, and even gets its beak bloody by pecking out the eyes of an inconvenient reporter.

There are some interesting ideas hinted at in *Omen II*. Foxworth's shady character wants Thorn Industries to focus on agriculture with the aim of controlling most of the world's food supply, thereby making famine a business and much of humanity slaves. Damien, rather than being a passive focal point for the evil around him, seems to have special powers of his own. He can cause bullies to freak out just using his eyes and can rattle off historical dates with such accuracy that you might think he had been there. He even has an unusual cell structure (his biological mother, you may remember, was impregnated by a jackal), the discovery of which leads to one of the movie's most memorable death scenes.

While *Omen II* certainly satisfies in the shock department, far surpassing the body count of the original, the movie lacks its predecessor's buildup of suspense. Entertaining enough, it feels a little like a retread determined to simply dial up the elaborate deaths to eleven rather than continuing the story in any meaningful way and is really just a steppingstone on Damien's path to conquest. Competently directed, it lacks the gothic menace of *The Omen* and, while we have to wait for the disappointing *Omen III: the Final Conflict* (1981) to see Damien's rein of terror, *Omen II* is a solid by-the-numbers horror movie in its own right.

ESCALOFRÍO/SATAN'S BLOOD (1978)

Directors: Carlos Puerto and Juan Piquer Simón
Writer: Carlos Puerto

This Spanish softcore satanic thriller was the second movie of Carlos Puerto, who had primarily been a TV writer in the early years of the decade before teaming up with Paul Naschy to write *El francotirador* (1977) which he also directed; a gritty drama about an attempt to assassinate Franco.

Escalofrío (literally meaning 'chill'), begins with an introduction by real Spanish parapsychologist, Fernando Jiménez del Oso, who was something of a pseudoscience celebrity in Spain, presenting programs and writing books on everything from UFOs to witchcraft to ancient civilizations. It's the usual Satanic Panic bunkum about black masses being practiced across the nation and evil cults performing blood sacrifices in every park after dark, but it does lend a novel framing device which gives an idea of the building unease about the occult.

The main characters are Andrés (José María Guillén) and Ana (Mariana Karr), a couple who live in Madrid with their dog and are expecting a baby. While out for a drive, they run into another couple, Bruno (Ángel Aranda) and Berta (Sandra Alberti). Bruno insists that he and Andrés went to school together, but Andrés has no memory of him and, what's more, some things about Bruno's story don't add up. He's much older than Andrés for a start, and mistakenly remembers the dean being one of their teachers. Also, the dog isn't having any of it, so the audience knows that something bad is afoot.

Nevertheless, they agree to go back to Andrés's and Berta's house for cheese and wine and find themselves being led miles out into the countryside to a grim-looking mansion. Soon, the two couples are getting along like old friends (smoking and drinking no big issue for pregnant women in the 1970s). A Ouija board session gets weird when old grudges and infidelities are referred to by the communicative spirits and the whole thing suddenly turns into an orgy and a black mass with Andrés and Ana going merrily along with it, seemingly in the thrall of something beyond their control (what was in that wine?).

Oversleeping the next day (again, the wine?) Andrés and Ana find themselves stranded at the weird mansion with what is rapidly looking like a couple of deranged Satanists. The dog goes missing and turns up dead, the car won't start, and Ana starts having nightmares about the creepy porcelain doll in the living room coming to life.

Satan's Blood draws heavily on *Rosemary's Baby* with the friendly neighborhood Satanists motif but Ana's pregnancy is almost forgotten about, playing no part in the satanic plot and was probably left over from an earlier version of the script in which it was somehow relevant. There's also an attempt to show some animalistic qualities to the Satanists that is never really developed. They eat raw meat from a dog bowl and Bruno makes snarling wolf sounds (which recall the noises Andrés and Ana hear in the night) while making love to Berta. The twist ending does reveal that there is something more supernatural going on other than a demonic sex cult but, ultimately, it's the usual surreal Spanish dream logic at work, tossing everything into the mix including the aforementioned doll which bleeds along with a random attempted rape by what is presumably a wayward cultist.

But it's a great looking movie with nice opening scenes in autumnal Madrid and the mansion offers some interesting sets from the cluttered living room with its occult knick-knacks to the chilly kitchen and chest freezer which feels altogether unhealthy. The occult scenes are some of the best and boldest in the genre with sex being a key ingredient to the movie, albeit presented in a sleazy, grindhouse way. The plot descends into utter surrealism at the end, but it almost makes sense once the twist is revealed and the first half of the movie is a great thriller about a likeable couple getting lured off the beaten track and end up in a situation they can't escape from.

L'OSCENO DESIDERIO/OBSCENE DESIRE (1978)

Director: Giulio Petroni
Writers: Joaquín Domínguez, Giulio Petroni and Piero Regnoli

Most famous as a director of Spaghetti Westerns (especially 1967's *Death Rides a Horse* starring Lee Van Cleef), Giulio Petroni began making more sex-oriented movies in the 1970s, be they comedies like *Do Not Commit Adultery* (1972) or giallo-infused drama like *Lips of Lurid Blue* (1975). His second-to-last movie was a sexually charged take on *Rosemary's Baby* meets *The Exorcist* with a touch of *The Omen* to boot.

Obscene Desire stars Marisa Mell and Chris Avram as newlywed couple, Amanda and Andrea who move into Andrea's family mansion. They arrive to find that the loyal butler Michaele, whom Andrea knew all his life, has recently died, leaving only the creepy old gardener (Víctor Israel who was something of a go-to man for creepy old men in Italian horror movies, popping up in *The Witches Mountain* and *Devil's Kiss*).

Married life isn't so easy to settle into however, as Andrea shows that he has problems in the sack while somebody is murdering local prostitutes, giving this occult thriller something of a giallo flair. Amanda makes the acquaintance of a fellow American in the village; an expert in folklore and mythology called Peter (Lou Castel) who turns out to be a plainclothes priest. Peter fills Amanda in on her husband's family. Centuries ago, his ancestor fell in love with a witch and, when his efforts to get her to abort their illegitimate child were unsuccessful, he outed her to the authorities and she died at the stake, cursing his family line.

Amanda is the pragmatic type and dismisses all this but what is the creepy gardener up to and why won't her husband allow her to see anybody except his two friends, Rachael (Laura Trotter) and her husband Fabio (Javier Escrivá)? As she begins to feel increasingly isolated in the gloomy old mansion, Amanda learns that she is pregnant and soon finds herself fawned over by the mysterious threesome who, she learns, are more than just friends.

While most Italian occult movies of the late seventies aped *The Exorcist*, *Obscene Desire* delves farther back and plunders *Rosemary's Baby*, right down to Marisa Mell's pixie haircut and rape by an evil entity (which might have just been a nightmare). Ten years is mighty long to cash in on a popular Hollywood movie, but Petroni tosses in an exorcism scene and an ominous ending *ala The Omen* for good measure, making this an Italian summation of the devil craze of the seventies in one movie. Peter even makes reference to Pope Paul VI's 1972 confirmation that the devil is real and not just a symbolic threat.

There's nothing particularly original in *Obscene Desire*, being a mixture of elements from far better movies, but it's a well-executed occult drama nonetheless. The gloom-haunted mansion and the plight of a female protagonist isolated and out of her element evokes the gothic and Mell (pushing forty at the time of filming) makes for a refreshing middle-aged lead in contrast to the sexy femme fatale roles of her early career.

There is some confusion around the prostitute murders which muddle an otherwise simple plot and were most likely put in to score high on the nudity and earn the movie's titillating title. Amanda and Andrea's character motivations are also unclear with the former apparently possessed towards the end, but not quite, and the latter involved in satanic shenanigans but also a staunch Catholic. It's not as surreal and incoherent as the movies of Bava or Argento, and feels a little slow in parts, lacking some visual flair, but it's a solid psychological thriller, low on scares but interesting and with enough twists to keep the viewer guessing.

UN'OMBRA NELL'OMBRA/RING OF DARKNESS (1979)
Director: Pier Carpi
Writer: Pier Carpi

Pier Carpi was an Italian writer who penned novels, non-fiction and comic books including the Italian versions of Mickey Mouse and Batman as well as the long-running Italian series *Diabolik* which was adapted in 1968 as Mario Bava's *Danger: Diabolik*.

As a member of the Theosophical Society, Carpi had a strong interest in the occult, writing books on everything from secret societies to magic to Rasputin to Cagliostro (about whom he penned the screenplay for the 1975 movie *Cagliostro*). His work in movies continued the following year with his directorial debut, *Povero Cristo*, based on his own novel of the same name about a private investigator charged with providing evidence for the existence of Jesus Christ. Carpi's directorial career wasn't exactly prolific, with only one other title to his name, 1977's *Ring of Darkness*, also based on a novel of his.

It's the story of a small satanic cult of middle-aged women who come to regret their pact with Satan, particularly as the daughter of one of them shows signs of being demonic in her own right. It begins with an occult ceremony that takes the form of a dance routine (a bit like Pan's People but with more full-frontal nudity) in which Carlotta (Anne Heywood), Elena (Valentina Cortese), Agatha (Marisa Mell from *Obscene Desire*) and Raffaella (Irene Papas) offer themselves to a rather suave Lucifer (Ezio Miani).

Several years later, things aren't going so well for the women. Raffaella has fallen into prostitution despite being rich, because apparently it's the only way she can 'recapture the semblance of human warmth', while Carlotta is having trouble with her teenage daughter, Daria (Lara Wendel). She might be acting up due to her parents' divorce compounded by the revelation that her father, Peter (West Buchanan) isn't her biological father. Or could there be something more sinister afoot?

Once Daria's powers have manifested to the point of burning her classmates by touching them and driving her teacher (Cortese) to take a swan dive from a high window by simply drawing an occult symbol on the chalkboard, it's pretty clear that she's the devil's spawn and she knows it too, doing her own research and finding out all about her mother's youthful indiscretions.

So far so *Omen*. But the movie heads into *Exorcist* territory in the third act when the surviving cult members recruit a conflicted priest (John Phillip Law) to help combat the apparent antichrist. This is the movie's most interesting aspect. It's a rare occult movie in which the Catholic Church joins forces with a satanic coven but that's exactly what happens here, as the women explain to the befuddled cleric that they are in fact against drinking blood and sacrificing children while the similarity of the cult's robes and the vestments of the priest feel like a deliberate parallel.

Ring of Darkness takes an interesting position on the God versus Satan motif. It never gives the impression that the cult is particularly evil, rather a LaVeyan group interested in spiritual and physical gratification. This philosophy is perhaps best exemplified by the character of 'the professor' (Ian Bannen) who, as well as commenting on the eternal battle between light and dark as symbolized by chess, is something of a libertine, philosophizing with prostitutes and championing indulgence over abstinence. This is no doubt a result of

Carpi's own feelings on the occult, but it does rather suck the horror out of a so-called horror movie.

Whatever interest is generated by these ruminations is spoiled by the movie's banality. The 'exorcism' ceremony is a lengthy, wordless ritual infused with Stelvio Cipriani's electronic score which seems to go on forever and ultimately fails in its purpose. This results in a mother versus daughter climax but why they need to be naked is a mystery, particularly in the case of Lara Wendel who was thirteen at the time (and already no stranger to controversy, having played the lead in the notorious 1977 movie, *Maladolescenza*), which makes for a pretty sordid and troubling finale.

Ring of Darkness is a bit of a hodge-podge of ideas, none of which are utilized to the full, likely due to its conflicted production. Cameras started rolling in 1977 but producer Piero Amati demanded reshoots to cash in on *The Exorcist* as well as dialing up the nudity. As a result, it tries to be a mixture of *The Exorcist* with a sprinkling of *The Omen* but didn't reach screens until 1979 when the fad was looking a little long in the tooth. Worst of all, the movie fails to deliver any scares or atmosphere, its impressive cast (which also includes Frank Finlay) deliver terrible dialogue in flat monotones with little visuals to catch the eye. Released on home video as *Circle of Fear* and, later, *Satan's Wife*, *Ring of Darkness* is full of interesting ideas that were unfortunately dully presented.

A Vulgar Display of Power: Possession

"I think the point is to make us despair. To see ourselves as ... animal and ugly. To make us reject the possibility that God could love us." - Father Merrin, *The Exorcist*

The idea that a person can become possessed by an evil spirit which might then control their actions appears in many cultures and religions dating back to antiquity. The Old Testament makes several references to incidents which might be interpreted as possessions and exorcisms while in the Gospels there are numerous instances of Jesus casting out evil spirits. The jinn (anglicized as 'genies') of pre-Islamic Arabia are creatures of fire and air and purported to be able to possess people. They are mentioned in the Quran as well as 'shayatin' (a word cognate with 'Satan'); invisible evil spirits who tempt humans into sin by whispering to them. Belief in spirit possession is also common in parts of Africa as well as in African diasporic religions such as Haitian Vodou.

The Catholic rite for a 'major exorcism' (as opposed to 'minor exorcisms' found in baptismal ceremonies) is found in Section 11 of the *Roman Ritual*, a liturgical text containing all the services priests and deacons can perform. It defines possession by four characteristics; manifestation of superhuman strength, speaking in tongues or languages the subject doesn't know, revelation of knowledge the victim doesn't know, and blasphemous rage or aversion to holy symbols.

Despite this, Christianity has always had a strange relationship with the rite of exorcism with many clerics being opposed to the practice, equating it with superstition and magic. The danger of misinterpreting mental illnesses and epileptic seizures as possession has made the Catholic Church tread cautiously when prescribing exorcisms. Only an ordained priest may perform an exorcism and only with the express permission of the local bishop after medical examination has eliminated the possibility of mental illness.

While the rite of exorcism survived in an abbreviated form in Protestantism after the Reformation, it generally fell out of favor in the following centuries. There was a small rise in exorcisms in the twentieth century as the evangelical movement reembraced the idea, but for most of the general public, the words 'possession' and 'exorcism' were obscure terms found in the more antiquated corners of theology, banished there by modern medicine and psychology.

That all changed with the publication of William Peter Blatty's *The Exorcist* and William Friedkin's 1973 movie adaptation. Suddenly possession was a hot topic and priests and psychologists were inundated with claims of possession. Its release was timely. The 1970s saw the rise of the 'charismatic movement' in both Protestant and Catholic churches with groups such as Pentecostalism focusing on the presence of the Holy Spirit (as well as demonic interference) in everyday life.

Possession had appeared in movies before *The Exorcist* shone a light on the phenomenon. *The Mephisto Waltz* (1971) and *The Possession of Joel Delaney* (1972) were both big budget, all-star movies that focused on possession, not by Satan or any of his minions, but by the spirits of the deceased. *J.D.'s Revenge* (1976), *Cathy's Curse* (1977) and *Jadu Tona* (1977) continued this tradition of corporeal 'hauntings' in which a person's body effectively played the part of the haunted house with a vengeful spirit of some criminal or disgruntled family member taking control until it can be effectively exorcised.

But the phenomenal popularity of *The Exorcist*

meant that most possession movies that followed it, fixated entirely on the religious battle between God and the devil. Most were low-budget retreads of the familiar, like *The Eerie Midnight Horror Show, Beyond the Door* and *The Antichrist*, all hitting screens in 1974 with *Demon Witch Child, Exorcism, Devil's Exorcist* and *The Return of the Exorcist* the year later, all hoping to cash-in on *The Exorcist*'s success. *Seytan* (1974) and *Jadu Tona* (1977) eschewed the Catholic trappings for Islamic and Hindu influences respectively, making up for their familiar plots with fresh cultural takes but, at their hearts, offered little variation on the green vomit and head twisting.

Most *Exorcist* cash ins were more focused on the titillating potential of possessed young women tearing their clothes off and performing vulgar and blasphemous acts. *Magdalena, Possessed by the Devil* (1974) and *Nurse Sherri* (1977) felt like particularly sleazy entries but at least they held on to some semblance of an occult plot. Many erotic movies like *Malabimba/The Malicious Whore* (1979) and *The Sexorcist* (1974) hopped onto the occult bandwagon but more or less ditched the horror aspect and, as such, are somewhat beyond the focus of this book, as their occult trappings are shallow excuses for hardcore pornography.

Sexuality has often been linked with demonic possession and several movies of the period seem to suggest that possession is the manifestation of sexual awakening and release from repression. *Devil's Exorcist* has a strictly brought up Catholic schoolgirl writhing and moaning as if in the throes of orgasm while simultaneously displaying a terror of men. The wholesome titular character in *Abby* (1974) masturbates in the shower after becoming possessed as a sure sign of demonic interference and there is the touch of the Freudian in *The Antichrist* and *Eerie Midnight Horror Show* in which possessed young women display incestuous feelings for their own fathers. *Return of the Exorcist* has some lesbian undertones (almost a prerequisite in many possession movies of the 1970s) in which a corrupted nobleman's daughter (with a pixie haircut and men's clothes) frolics in the woods with a demonic succubus.

The idea of purity being corrupted by the powers of darkness resulted in some crossover with the 'nunsploitation' genre. Ken Russell's *The Devils* (1971), about a real-life case of mass hysteria in a French convent in the 17th century, kick-started the trend of horny nuns being sadistically punished for indulging their natural urges. The 'possessions' in Russell's movie are undoubtedly all in the mind and borne of sexual repression which was enough of an excuse for most copycats to freely depict nuns engaging in lewd acts for titillated audiences while a minority introduced actual demonic possession. *Satanic Pandemonium* (1975) has a young, lesbian nun go on a murder spree within her convent, almost as an act of revenge against her tyrannical superiors while *Alucarda* (1977) heavily criticizes the church for its repression of sexuality as its nuns and priests associate lesbianism with demonic possession.

There were even movies about the possession of inanimate objects like *Death Bed: The Bed that Eats* (1977) and at least two movies about possessed cars, *Crash!* (1976) and *The Car* (1977). An inherently dangerous object in its own right, the car has often been given a mind of its own in books and movies, the idea of something in which we daily trust with our lives suddenly turning on us, clearly a potent image.

At the end of the day, it is the loss of control that is most horrifying in possession movies, whether it is objects or loved ones or even ourselves. When something evil takes root with the intent of corrupting innocence and reducing humans to mere puppets, the feeling is deeply unsettling. Most possession movies offer some sort of resolution in the form of a priest who has the strength to banish evil and the power of God to return things to the status quo. These movies often seem like recruitment commercials for religion, offering a literal *deus ex machina* and an ultimate triumph over evil. But there are the occasional possession movies in which no happy ending is forthcoming, when religion either fails or is irrelevant, leaving us with a bleak feeling of despair. And even those movies which depict a world ruled by a good and undefeatable God are still frightening as they also depict a world with dark shadows from which the devil might leap and possess any of us at any time.

MARK OF THE WITCH (1970)

Director: Tom Moore
Writers: Mary Davis, Martha Peters

This low budget drive-in schlocker begins three-hundred years ago with the hanging of a rather compliant witch who gleefully curses one McIntyre Stuart for betraying her coven and brands him with 'Satan's mark' which will haunt him for eternity. *Creak!* goes the trapdoor, *Snap!* goes the witch's neck and so roll the credits which are set to an acapella witch's rune.

At a present-day college campus, psychology professor 'Mac' Stuart is getting his insufferably chirpy students into Ouija boards and tarot cards as part of his psychology of superstition class. At a book dive, one of his students, Jill (Anitra Walsh), picks up a grimoire filled with spells.

Mac Stuart is, of course, a descendant of McIntyre Stuart (clear from the get-go as both are played by Robert Elston with the exact same haircut). This rather unprofessional professor holds a boozy party for his students at his pad where it's miniskirts and go-go boots ahoy. You can see that Mac is the 'cool' professor; he supplies the beer but "if you want the hard stuff, you'll have to bring your own". At the party, his students take a look at Jill's book and decide to try out the 'enchantment for the summoning forth of witches', just for kicks. Mac seems content to let them get on with it, suggesting that he doesn't take any of this particularly seriously.

The incantation doesn't seem to do anything but after the party, Jill's boyfriend, Alan (Darryl Wells) notices a change in her behavior. That's because Jill has been possessed by the spirit of the unnamed witch from the prologue. Ditching her boyfriend, Jill returns to Mac's apartment and convinces him that not only is she possessed by a witch but the curious birthmark on his wrist is proof that he is descended from McIntyre Stuart, as all members of the coven bear 'the devil's kiss'. Even Jill has one which suggests she is descended from the witch as well as being possessed by her which seems like a bit of a coincidence, but the movie never really goes into this.

Initially skeptical, Mac eventually believes her and realizes he can't do anything that will threaten the life and liberty of Jill (like calling the police and having her tossed in jail). He resigns himself to explaining some of the wonders of the modern world to her like telephones and coffee. When neither Mac nor Jill turn up for class the next day, Alan stops by and thinks he's caught the pair of them having an affair. It's much worse than that however and Jill gives an amusing demonstration of her powers by exploding Mac's pet bird in the movie's only real special effect.

Mac enlists Alan's help in exorcising the witch's spirit while Jill starts murdering their classmates in sensuous rituals in which she invokes the name of every biblical demon the scriptwriters could name. This is where the movie will test the patience of some as it is very talky considering its short runtime and the incantation scenes are especially long-winded right from the prologue. But, if you can put up with this, *Mark of the Witch* is a fun, silly little movie that oozes the bright colors and fashions of the late-60s and early-70s. Anitra Walsh does a fair job considering the amateurish production values and another standout is Marie Santell as the unnamed witch who gives it her all in the few scenes she has.

The movie is very much a local production from the Lone Star State. Director Tom Moore would go on to make an unofficial sequel to 1972's *The Legend of Boggy Creek* (the G-rated 'adventure for the entire family' flick, *Return to Boggy Creek*). Other than that, very few of the

people involved went on to do anything more than
occasional TV episodes.

THE MEPHISTO WALTZ (1971)

Director: Paul Wendkos
Writer: Ben Maddow

The old Faustian deal gets dusted off for this big-budget occult thriller based on the 1969 novel of the same name by pianist-turned author, Fred Mustard Stewart. Its title references the four waltzes composed by Franz Liszt in the late 19th century that took their narrative from Nikolaus Lenau's version of Faust. Stewart readily admitted that his tale of a husband seduced by a cult of old eccentrics leaving his wife to deal with the consequences, was a deliberate homage to *Rosemary's Baby* (1968). The then-struggling 20th Century Studios was clearly hoping to ride on Polanski's coattails, with legendary TV producer Quinn Martin purchasing the rights to Stewart's bestseller for a whopping $250,000 and handing the reins to reliable director of modest genre pictures and TV movies, Paul Wendkos.

A pre-*M*A*S*H* Alan Alda stars as Myles, a music journalist who interviews Duncan Ely (future Bond villain, Curd Jürgens), an aging piano virtuoso. When Ely becomes fascinated by Myles's hands, Myles reveals that he studied piano for four years but gave up on his dreams to be a concert pianist. But Ely has already been watching Myles, even calling his young daughter (Pamelyn Ferdin who would shortly be in the running to play Regan in *The Exorcist*). In a sinister subplot not fully explored, Myles's daughter is already painting giant bats like the taxidermized ones we later see in Ely's mansion.

Ely is clearly sizing Myles up for something, letting him into his inner circle of hideously pretentious artsy types and inviting him to swinging masked parties with nude dancers (though in a movie of this period, it is

163

sometimes hard to tell where the seventies end and the Satanism begins).

Myles's wife, Paula (Jaqueline Bisset) smells a rat. For a start, Duncan Ely's stunningly attractive daughter Roxanne (Barbara Parkins) shows a strong interest in Myles. At an orgiastic party, Paula spots Ely making out with his own daughter. Repulsed, she sneaks upstairs and discovers a library of occult knick-knacks including a wall of plaster face masks and a bottle of blue liquid.

Alda and Bisset aren't particularly believable as parents. We neither see nor hear from their kid unless her presence is strictly necessary and when she is eventually snuffed out, Mom and Dad don't seem all that upset. Paula is more concerned about Myles's sudden increased piano skills while Myles isn't exactly himself by this point.

That's because *The Mephisto Waltz* is less about a cult than it is about possession. Ely is dying from leukemia. He wants something from Myles and a blood transfusion is just the start of it. By using the aforementioned bottle of blue gunk and a plaster cast of Myles's face, Roxanne is able to transfer the spirit of her father/lover to Myles's body upon Ely's death. And, as we saw a cast of Ely's face in Roxanne's library, we are left to wonder how many lives this chap has led, which would go some way in explaining their apparently incestuous relationship as he might not be her actual father.

Although *The Mephisto Waltz* lacks the menace of Polanski's game changer, it is different enough and has enough twists and turns to keep things fresh. There is none of the early ambiguity of *Rosemary's Baby* in *The Mephisto Waltz*. We are not left to ponder if it is all in Paula's mind. The occult is all too real right from the get-go and Paula's gradual realization of what's been going on and her decision to do something about it is the real plot of the movie although some will question the credibility of her desperate wish to remain with Alan Alda, regardless of who is inhabiting his body.

The movie occupies the brief period between the release of *Rosemary's Baby* and the slew of possession movies ushered in by *The Exorcist*. It is a little toothless, lacking the scares and dread-laden atmosphere of those movies and, as such, it never really rises above the TV talent behind it.

THE DEVILS (1971)

Director: Ken Russell
Writer: Ken Russell

In 1632, troubling reports emerged from the French town of Loudun where a convent of Ursuline nuns claimed to be visited by erotic visions of Urbain Grandier, a local Catholic priest who had a reputation for womanizing. Demonic possession was suspected and a series of exorcisms were conducted in public in which the nuns swore, barked, spoke in tongues and exposed themselves much to the titillation of spectators.

Grandier was a handy scapegoat. As well as insulting the Mother Superior of the convent by refusing to become its spiritual advisor, he had opposed the crown's order to demolish Loudun's walls which was part of Cardinal Richelieu's attempts to centralize control. He also had a scandalous reputation after writing a book criticizing the church's policy of celibacy for priests and was accused of fathering a child on the daughter of a local noble. By offending both church and state, Grandier's fate was sealed and the rumors mounted, claiming that he had made a pact with the devil, held a black mass and used sorcery to possess the nuns. In 1634, after horrific torture, Grandier was burned at the stake for sorcery.

These extraordinary events formed the basis of Aldous Huxley's 1952 novel *The Devils of Loudun* which was turned into a play in 1960 by John Whiting. United Artists intended to make a film adaptation of the play with Ken Russell attached to direct, hot after his 1969 Oscar winner *Women in Love*. The studio balked upon reading the screenplay and dropped the project. Warner Brothers picked it up and shooting began in 1970 on a whopping set on Pinewood's backlot designed by Derek

Jarman.

The movie shows the town of Loudun amid the wasteland of religious war and pestilence. Cardinal Richelieu (Christopher Logue) is influencing the foppish King Louis XIII (Graham Armitage) with designs on centralizing France's control over independently governed towns like Loudun by ordering their walls to be torn down. Opposing this is the philandering priest and acting governor Urbain Grandier played by Oliver Reed who had previously worked with Ken Russell in *Women in Love.*

Vanessa Redgrave plays the demented Sister Jeanne, the Mother Superior of the Ursuline convent, who is obsessed with Grandier, fantasizing about him as an eroticized Christ figure. In addition to Grandier refusing to become the convent's spiritual advisor (historically true) Sister Jeanne learns that he has secretly married a woman (historically dubious). Driven mad with jealousy, Sister Jeanne's vindictive claims that Grandier has visited the nuns of her convent in their dreams are seized upon by those who see an opportunity to rid themselves of the troublesome priest.

Enter charlatan Father Pierre Barre (Michael Gottard) who begins a series of grotesque and degrading exorcisms of the nuns as well as setting up the worst kind of kangaroo court that will find the answers it is looking for no matter what it takes. Barre's passing resemblance to a hippie complete with tinted glasses may seem anachronistic but that's kind of the movie's point. Russell is telling us that bigotry, weaponized heresy and corruption are timeless, as is the self-serving claptrap spouted by exploitative 'gurus' of the era's counterculture.

Further artistic choices that strengthen the movie's conflation of past and present are Derek Jarman's sterile sets which are nearly futuristic in their sparse whiteness and make a convent look like a subway station. They would suit some of Aldous Huxley's science fiction novels and indeed, Jarman was influenced by Fritz Lang's *Metropolis* (1927) among other gargantuan sets of the silent era.

Described by Ken Russell as his only political film, *The Devils* is a scathing critique of church hypocrisy, bigotry and the dangers of marrying church and state. Although it often feels over the top and sensationalist, the movie does a fine job of mirroring the mounting religious hysteria as more and more people are drawn into its toxic web and made complicit either by fear or their own personal ambitions. There are echoes of Arthur Miller's 1953 play *The Crucible* as the nuns, now either too terrified to admit their falsities or too wrapped up in their new-found freedom, dance naked and masturbate openly in an orgiastic mass exorcism. Incidentally, *The Exorcist* clearly took a few cues from *The Devils* including the growling throat noises and spider walking of Sister Jeanne, albeit almost drowned out by other, more shocking exhibits.

It's a stomach-churning movie but not without moments of intentional farce; in the midst of a 'bring out your dead' plague scene, Grandier hurls the ludicrous cures of the Pythonesque quack doctors out the window and then fends off an attack by the enraged father of a woman he has seduced with a stuffed crocodile.

But it's rare when Oliver Reed isn't the most shocking or mesmerizing thing about a movie. When Ken Russell goes all-out nuts (particularly if you are watching the rare director's cut), it's easy to forget that Reed is even in the movie. Until the third act, of course, when he commands every scene he is in as the screaming, frothing authorities demand a confession among some of the most eye-watering scenes of torture ever inflicted on film.

Ironically for a movie criticizing authority, *The Devils* struggled with censorship and Russell was forced to agree to cuts in order for the movie to be released in Britain with an X certificate. The most controversial scene is the notorious 'rape of Christ' in which naked nuns tear down a statue of the crucified Jesus and rub their genitals all over it. One can only imagine what UK activist Mary Whitehouse had to say about *that*. The US released an even more stripped-down cut which disjointed the narrative and robbed the movie of its ever-increasing fever pitch.

Even after a director's cut reinstated the missing scenes in 2002, Warner Brothers has remained reluctant to release it on home video in any form, a testament to the visceral power of the movie and its perceived blasphemy.

THE POSSESSION OF JOEL DELANEY (1972)

Director: Waris Hussein
Writers: Grimes Grice and Matt Robinson

Totally overshadowed by THE possession movie that came out the following year, this adaptation of Ramona Stewart's 1970 supernatural thriller has found some reappraisal in recent years. Rather than satanic possession, the movie delves into the world of Puerto Rican Santería which is perhaps the movie's most interesting aspect.

Shirley MacLaine stars as Norah Benson, an insufferably entitled Manhattan mother of two who is rude to her Puerto Rican maid Veronica (Miriam Colon), barges people aside in queues and generally looks on anything outside her privileged bubble with disdain. Her brother Joel (Perry King) has a more bohemian take on life, preferring to live in a grubby hippie pad in the East Village, much to Norah's bafflement. Ever since their mother's suicide (a topic only briefly mentioned in the movie) Norah has taken on a maternal role, smothering Joel to the point where she looks on with jealousy as he chats to his hippie girlfriend Sherry (Barbara Trentham) at a party; just one of several hints that there is something slightly incestuous about their relationship.

Things begin to go awry when Joel violently attacks the superintendent of his tenement and is carted off to Bellevue where he emerges from his episode with no memory of what he has done. Convinced he was on drugs, Norah persuades him to come and live with her for a while, clearly delighted at the prospect of mothering him at close range.

But Joel's behavior becomes even more erratic. He rapes his girlfriend and delivers an expletive-filled rant to the maid in Spanish (a language he can't speak), causing her to quit. Desperate for answers, Norah gradually comes to learn that Joel is possessed by the spirit of his dead friend, Tonio Pérez; a man the police suspect in the murder of several women. Norah is forced to leave her comfort zone far behind as she delves into the world of Puerto Rican Santería that is apparently abound on the poverty-stricken streets of the less affluent parts of New York City.

This is the New York of *The French Connection* (1971) and *Taxi Driver* (1976); a city collapsing under the weight of crime and social inequality. In some wonderful street scenes, director Waris Hussein uses contrast to further the movie's social commentary, flicking between swish Manhattan apartments where African tribal masks are relegated to objects of art and the eclectic streets of Spanish Harlem where belief in spirits and possession are alive and well.

Norah's search leads her to Don Pedro (Edmundo Rivera Álvarez), a Santería practitioner who patiently tries to broaden her horizons. "People like yourself; you try to buy God. And your mind is closed" he explains. The people of her world might go to church on Sundays but they no longer *believe*.

Shirley MacLaine is excellent throughout, playing a character who, although unlikeable, provides a POV of the sheltered and privileged, her discomfort visible in every scene. A real standout is her panicked flight through Spanish Harlem, terrified by some clearly non-existent danger born of her own prejudices and fish-out-of-water unease. During the feverish exorcism in a claustrophobic apartment complete with convulsions and chanting, Norah's mind all but breaks down and the audience is right there with her.

One of the movie's criticisms is the gut-churning climax where the possessed Joel holds Norah and her two kids hostage in their Long Island Beach house at the point of a switchblade, his terrorizing of them resulting in child nudity and forced dog food consumption. Labelled gratuitous and needlessly cruel, the scene has been a real turn-off for some and is probably why the movie isn't as fondly remembered as it should be.

Shirley MacLaine, a close friend of author William Peter Blatty, was the model for the character of Chris MacNeil in *The Exorcist* and Blatty hoped she would play the part in the movie adaptation. This was vetoed by Warner Brothers who felt it would be too similar a role to the one she had just played in *The Possession of Joel Delaney* and the part eventually went to Ellen Burstyn.

MISS LESLIE'S DOLLS (1973)

Director: Joseph G. Prieto
Writers: Joseph G. Prieto and Ralph Remy Jr.

Joseph P. Mawra directed several black and white exploitation movies in the 1960s featuring sadism, sex and drug use with titles like *White Slaves of Chinatown* (1964), *Olga's House of Shame* (1964) and *Chained Girls* (1965). One of his later movies, *Fireball Jungle* (1968) was butchered by producers who removed his name from the director's credit and replaced it with 'Jose Priete'. Often believed to be a pseudonym for Mawra, it was most likely the name of a different, Cuban director called Joseph G. Prieto who had previously helmed *Shanty Tramp* (1967) and *Savages from Hell* (1968). This has led to some confusion as to who directed *Miss Leslie's Dolls*, a low-budget piece of nonsense that blends *Psycho* (1960) with *House of Wax* (1953), with many thinking it was Mawra. He claims that the movie "doesn't ring a bell"(3). The fact that nobody really knows who directed *Miss Leslie's Dolls* only indicates how obscure this oddball horror movie is.

In a plot that absolutely would not fly with modern audiences, the titular Miss Leslie is a deranged transsexual played by Salvador Ugarte (his voice dubbed by an uncredited woman) who, through her interest in the occult, wants to transfer her spirit to the body of a female victim. This has led her to plundering a rather makeshift-looking cemetery for suitable subjects in her experiments which seem to involve hypnotism and a vat of chemicals.

During a thunderstorm, three college students called Martha (Kitty Lewis), Lily (Marcelle Bichette) and Roy (Charles Pitt from Russ Meyer's *Supervixens*) are on their way back home from a football game along with their young but prudish teacher appropriately named Miss Frost (Terri Juston). Running out of gas in the middle of the aforementioned cemetery (which they have somehow driven into), the four youngsters seek shelter in the nearby farmhouse with Roy remarking (at least three times) that he'd love a glass of bourbon.

There, they encounter the strange Miss Leslie who lives alone with her cat and keeps a macabre temple in her basement containing the lifelike mannequins of several beautiful young women. She also freaks her guests out by exclaiming that Martha is clearly a reincarnation of her childhood companion who died with her mother in a mysterious fire in a doll factory.

Miss Leslie offers the bedraggled visitors rooms for the night as well as food. Booze-hound Roy finally gets his bourbon but he clearly can't hold his liquor because, after half a snort, he makes a pass at Miss Frost who is understandably unimpressed. The movie then enters a section which feels like a sex comedy with bed-hopping shenanigans involving the two girls who are inexplicably keen for the boorish Roy who clearly thinks it's Christmas. There's also a random lesbian scene between Miss Frost (who has now thawed out and wearing a skimpy negligee) and game-for-anything Lily. This nonsensical bit of sexploitation is explained away by 'drugged coffee'. Indeed, Miss Leslie was seen toying with a bottle of pills, but what she did with them, or how our characters know about it, is unclear.

The acting and pacing are abysmal, alternating between long stretches where nobody says anything and bloated monologues from Miss Leslie where she plots her evil schemes out loud for the benefit of the audience. Conversations with the skull of her mother which she keeps in the basement provide more opportunities for infodumps and the plot device from *Psycho* is pinched by having Miss Leslie's 'mother' personality

174

occasionally take over and attempt to murder the houseguests.

There aren't a whole lot of scares or gore. Miss Leslie tries to choke Roy with an axe handle before using the axe properly on Lily's face, but, aside from a brief glimpse of the mutilated corpse, it's all pretty tame, even the sexploitation aspects falling short of anything stronger than occasional bared breasts. There is a surreal nightmare scene in which Miss Frost is assailed by the female mannequins which borders on frightening but goes on for far too long and was presumably only included because it was something else for the hired extras to do other than stand still and look pretty.

The reincarnation of Martha isn't really returned to in the movie begging the question of why it was mentioned in the first place as Miss Leslie is just as happy to possess the body of any other woman. Her occult powers aren't really gone into in any great detail either, the filmmakers apparently content to leave in some vague references and an altar with an eternal flame in Miss Leslie's shrine. They also toss in a vat of gunk and a handwave about 'science', meaning that we are dealing with a blend of the occult and some Frankenstein's lab type guff.

There are some astonishingly ridiculous things going on. Our gang never act like anybody would in such a situation. They blunder past every red flag such as the basement of eerily lifelike mannequins and the dead body under a sheet which they all walk by without comment. It's also apparently possible to hypnotize a screaming and unwilling victim by dangling a pocket watch in front of them.

Miss Leslie's Dolls is so silly it's fun and has become something of a campy cult classic, having been thought lost for years before a print was found and cleaned up for a 2018 Blu-ray release. Several of its elements are reminiscent of *The Rocky Horror Picture Show* (1975), albeit that was a comedy musical riffing on exactly the kind of low-budget drive-in schlock we have here. In fact, it's hard not to wonder if *Miss Leslie's Dolls* had been seen by Richard O'Brien, but its obscurity suggests coincidence rather than influence.

THE EXORCIST (1973)

Director: William Friedkin
Writer: William Peter Blatty

In March 1949, a Lutheran minister wrote to the Parapsychology Laboratory at Duke University, in North Carolina, describing the alarming events experienced by a family in Cottage City, Maryland. It began with scratching under the floorboards and thumping in the walls, progressing to objects being hurled across the room. The focus of the activity appeared to be the family's fourteen-year-old son, Ronnie Hunkeler, who, on several occasions, was tipped out of his chair and his mattress would shake violently when he was in bed.

Hunkeler's symptoms worsened with him speaking in a guttural voice and showing aversion to anything sacred. Several exorcisms were conducted during which the boy broke the nose of a Jesuit priest and the words 'evil' and 'hell' allegedly appeared on his body. Later, the priests claimed that the demonic spirit had left Roland's body and that the boy had gone on to live a normal life.

The Washington Post ran an article on the unsettling events in August of 1949 and one of the people who read it was William Peter Blatty, then in his final year at Georgetown University. A practicing Catholic, Blatty was fascinated by the case and began toying with the idea of writing a book about it but found that members of the clergy were less than enthusiastic to cooperate. He instead decided to pen a fictional version, swapping out the teenaged boy for a twelve-year-old girl and relocating the story to Washington D.C.

Blatty's novel, *The Exorcist*, hit the shelves in 1971. It's the story of Regan, the twelve-year-old daughter of divorced actress Chris MacNeil, who begins exhibiting strange and disturbing behavior. Starting with foul language and urinating on the carpet, Regan's symptoms worsen until it becomes clear that some demonic presence is inhabiting her body, driving her to do unspeakable things.

Blatty adapted his own novel into a screenplay which was shopped around to various directors, but Blatty wanted William Friedkin whose background in documentaries had carried over effectively in his recent hit *The French Connection* (1971). Friedkin's gritty and realistic style would give *The Exorcist* perhaps its most important edge as a serious horror movie that, much like *Rosemary's Baby* (1968) would ditch the monster movie camp of previous decades for a terrifying and uncompromising look at evil in the modern world.

Part of Friedkin's realistic approach involved using actors that weren't stars. The studio wanted Jane Fonda or Audrey Hepburn for the role of Regan's mother (originally written by Blatty for his friend Shirley MacLaine). It instead went to Ellen Burstyn who is perfect as the increasingly frantic mother; an atheist forced to question her own beliefs in her efforts to protect her daughter. She is caught between the extremes of religion and science, and we are unsure which prospect appalls her more; having her daughter exorcised or referred to a shrink.

The Exorcist presents an interesting examination of the relationship between faith and science, with the angiography scene (in which blood spurts from Regan's neck) often appalling viewers more than any of the notorious head-spinning or vomiting of the eventual exorcism. It is only after she has exhausted the routes of medicine (and a doctor recommends an exorcism, purely from a psychological perspective) that Regan's mother turns to the Catholic church.

Enter Father Damien Karras (Jason Miller), a priest who is in the midst of a crisis of faith and mired in guilt

178

for not being able to help his aging mother in the final days of her life. Karras, himself a trained psychiatrist, initially dismisses Chris's request for an exorcism, claiming that such a thing simply isn't done any more. The dual focus on an atheist mother's reversal of her beliefs and a modern priest's struggle to deal with the darkest aspects of his own faith gives the movie its real depth and makes it more about character than shock and gore.

The star of the movie is naturally Linda Blair as the possessed Regan who endured hours of make-up and torturous practical effects (resulting in back injuries during the bed-shaking scene). Blair's transformation from all-American girl into a hideous, foul-mouthed monstrosity (with a chain-smoking Mercedes McCambridge providing the voice of the demon) created one of horror cinema's most shocking and terrifying icons.

The titular exorcist is the Jesuit priest and archaeologist Father Merrin (Max von Sydow) who is introduced in the movie's opening scene as he unearths a statue of the Mesopotamian demon Pazuzu in northern Iraq. Although Von Sydow was only forty-three at the time of filming, he was used to playing older characters in Ingmar Bergman's movies and underwent extensive aging make-up for *The Exorcist*.

It's astonishing to think that *The Exorcist* was very nearly written off as a failure and shelved mere weeks before release due to it being over budget and featuring an unknown cast which failed to convince Warner Brothers that it had any hope of turning a profit. Fortunately, the movie made it into theaters and its shock value and controversy quickly made it a phenomenon. It earned Blatty an Oscar for Best Adapted Screenplay and another for its eerie sound design which, combined with Jack Nitzsche's low-key but nerve-shredding score and the occasional presence of Mike

Oldfield's 'Tubular Bells' makes the movie almost as much an audible experience as a visual one.

The Exorcist held the title of the top-grossing R-rated movie for almost half a century (eventually dethroned by *It* in 2017). Its enduring terror is no doubt due to the perversion and corruption of an innocent, not to mention the controversy of a fourteen-year-old Linda Blair playing a character required to masturbate with a crucifix and utter foul expletives making the movie notorious. Prominent evangelist Billy Graham claimed that "the devil is in every frame of that film"(4). Whether or not he was suggesting that the movie itself was possessed, that was certainly the way some people took it. Along with the unusual number of deaths related to the filming of the movie, and the subliminal images of a demonic face (Eileen Dietz in make-up), these rumors have given the movie a reputation of being 'cursed', only adding to its street cred as 'the most terrifying movie ever'.

The Exorcist leaves enough ambiguity to make us deeply uneasy. Why, of all people, did the demon possess Regan? Who desecrated the nearby church? Why does she react to tap water masquerading as holy water? Again, it is Friedkin's impartial, documentary style of filmmaking that gives the impression that he is merely recording what is happening, leaving us to try and understand what we have just seen.

The movie has lost none of its shock-value and controversy in the decades since its release. In the UK it got caught up in the 'video nasty' moral panic of the 1980s and the VHS was yanked from shelves in 1986, not being granted a certificate until 1999. This, along with remarks by the likes of Billy Graham, gave *The Exorcist* an air of sinful unattainability which has only heightened its allure.

MAGDALENA, VOM TEUFEL BESESSEN/MAGDALENA, POSSESSED BY THE DEVIL (1974)

Director: Walter Boos
Writer: August Rieger

Rapid Film, a West German production company formed in the late-fifties by Wolf C. Hartwig would achieve their biggest claim to fame in stumping up much of the budget for British-German war movie *Cross of Iron* (1977) directed by Sam Peckinpah. Before that, Hartwig was deeply entrenched in the sleazier end of the European exploitation industry, spawning the dubious 'sex report' genre with *Schulmädchen-Report* (1970); a pseudo-documentary in which schoolgirls talk about their earliest sexual experiences.

Posing as educational movies, the sex-report genre was hugely popular in 1970s Europe with over a dozen entries in the 'Schoolgirl Report' series as well as variations involving nurses and housewives. Director Walter Boos was involved in the genre right from the get-go as editor and assistant director on *Schulmädchen-Report* as well as directing several of its sequels and the 1972 *Krankenschwestern-Report* (*Nurses Report*). Such a background in Euro-sleaze made him particularly suited for this extremely sleazy possession movie.

Also released as *The Devil's Female,* and *Beyond the Darkness,* it begins with a drunken prostitute on her way home from a bar to find an old man crucified to a door. The police determine that the old man was paying for his orphaned granddaughter's tuition at a girl's boarding school but before young Magdalena (Dagmar Heidrich) can be told of her grandfather's death, she is possessed by a demon, possibly the spirit of her grandfather (the movie is rather vague on that point).

The possession gives Magdalena superhuman strength which enables her to boot open locked doors, tear bibles in half and almost twist the arm off a would-be rapist. And that brings us to what is a defining feature of the movie because the demon also makes Magdalena extremely horny. When she isn't foul mouthing the priest (interestingly played by Rudolf Schündler who played Karl in *The Exorcist*), she's on the prowl, getting a series of clueless men to engage with her before killing them.

Such low-budget fare is hardly going to come close to anything like the terrifying special effects of *The Exorcist* (although that didn't stop some of its Italian brethren from giving things a shot) but *Magdalena, Possessed by the Devil* has almost zero special effects. What it lacks in visual horror, it more than makes up for in gratuitous nudity. Dagmar Heidrich gives a decent performance, alternating between innocent schoolgirl and possessed harridan required to rip her clothes off in every other scene. There are also some icky POV rape angles as she is ravished by an invisible demon who, presumably, is simultaneously possessing her (again, the movie doesn't quite explain who or *what* is possessing her).

As with most possession movies, there is the stand-ard discourse between science and faith with Dr. Stone (Michael Hinz) performing some tests on her before it is decided that she will spend some time at a retreat in the country with him. Amid ping pong games and horse riding, there is a ham-fisted attempt at a romantic subplot, but the demon rears his ugly head whenever the two of them start to have sex. Interestingly, sex seems to initiate Magdalena's fits which could be turned into some sort of commentary on sexual liberation and coming-of-age but such things are far beyond the movie's fleapit aspirations.

The plot is repetitive in the extreme. Magdalena escapes, goes on a sex-crazed rampage, is captured and then escapes again multiple times. Story threads are started but never followed through. A pointless sequence shows some poltergeist activity in the school's attic in which furniture and paintings are hurled around but when the attic is inspected the next day, everything is back to normal. We also never find out who crucified Magdalena's grandfather or what it has to do with her possession. There is some talk of him receiving strange visitors in the night, suggesting that he was part of some sort of cult but it's never gone into. The police arrest a suspicious man breaking into his apartment and is seemingly little more than a red herring. Incidentally, the landlady is played by Ursula Reit who was Mrs. Gloop in *Willy Wonka & the Chocolate Factory* (1971).

It seems the filmmakers never really decided on where the movie was going and an abrupt and unimpressive exorcism is tacked on during one of Magdalena's many rampages, leaving us with an incredibly limp ending and the notion that the devil can be hypnotized by a regular doctor and cast out by a simple prayer from a priest. But exorcism was never really the point in a movie from the studio which pioneered the 'sex report' genre and uses demonic possession here as a plot device to show plenty of gratuitous full-frontalism.

183

Seytan (1974)

Director: Metin Erksan
Writer: Yilmaz Tümtürk

There's rip-offs of popular movies and then there's *Seytan*, a Turkish movie which slavishly copies *The Exorcist*, scene by scene, right down to the use of Mike Oldfield's *Tubular Bells*.

The Yeşilçam period (literally meaning 'green pine' and named after a street in Istanbul) of Turkish cinema was in decline by the mid-seventies. Rising production costs and competition from television had a catastrophic effect on an industry which managed to pump out three-hundred movies in 1972. Many prestigious directors of the Yeşilçam period (like Metin Erksan whose 1964 movie *Susuz Yaz/Dry Summer* had won the Golden Bear at the 14th Berlin International Film Festival) had to turn their efforts to low-budget copies of American products.

This brand of 'Turksploitation' included bizarre mashups like Captain America and Spider-man along with Mexican wrestler Santo in *Three Mighty Men* and the 'first' Star Trek movie, *Ömer the Tourist in Star Trek*. Both of these movies came out in 1973, the same year *The Exorcist* stirred up a worldwide phenomenon and Turkey's struggling movie industry wasn't about to let it slip by.

The target of this demonic possession is a twelve-year-old girl called Gül (played by Canan Perver) who lives with her single mother (Meral Taygun) and has been forgotten about by her father who doesn't even turn up for her birthday party. Gül has been fooling around with a Ouija board and talking to her imaginary friend 'Captain Lersen'. Pretty soon, there are noises in the attic, urinating on carpets and everything else from

184

the first half hour of *The Exorcist*. When Gül thumps a hypnotist in the nuts, the medical profession washes its hands of her and her mother desperately turns to more spiritual solutions.

As Turkey has a large Muslim population, it wouldn't make much sense to have a Jesuit priest as one of the main characters. Instead, we get an academic with an interest in psychiatry called Tugrul Bilge (stage actor Cihan Ünal in his second movie). He's written a book on demons and exorcisms but isn't making enough money to move his sick mother into nicer dwellings and she ends up in a mental institution before dying, giving poor Tugrul the same guilt Father Karras had.

Agah Hün plays a character known only as 'the exorcist' and was introduced in the movie's prologue as an archaeologist uncovering some sort of demon talisman in a non-descript arid country. There's very little backstory to his character in comparison with what we got with Max Von Sydow which seems to be the standard for the movie. No mention is made of Gül's mother being an actress or of any career at all in this stripped-down, essentials only take on Friedkin's movie.

Being made in an officially secular but a predominantly Muslim and conservative country, *Seytan* is also stripped of any Christian religious imagery as well as its profanity. There is no desecration of the local church and the crucifix in the most infamous scene is replaced with a sharp letter opener with a devil's head which may be somewhat nastier although less blasphemous. Even the holy water is swapped out for water from the Zamzam Well (according to Islamic narratives, a miraculously generated source of water located in Saudi Arabia). In doing so, *Seytan* nearly delivers on the fascinating premise of an Islamic possession movie but, while Agah Hün's exorcist wields a book that looks like it could be the Qur'an, the filmmakers are careful to avoid associating any overt Islamic imagery with their cheapo horror movie.

Due to its shoestring budget, the make-up and effects are naturally not a patch on the original but that doesn't stop Erksan and Co. trying to ape every aspect of it. From the bouncing bed to the levitation to the soupy vomit (that strangely comes in varying shades throughout the movie), it's all there but just not as good and without any of the shock value. The movie is particularly let down by some of the silliest medical nonsense to be had in cinema. While *The Exorcist* was praised for its (all too real for some) angiography scene, *Seytan* gives us a ludicrous 'shock therapy' scene which involves rattling poor Gül's head about with what looks like a pair of jackhammers.

There's little point in critiquing the story of *Seytan* as it all but lifts Blatty's script wholesale and changes the names. That does make it marginally better and more coherent than the average *Exorcist* copy-cat and, being around twenty minutes shorter than *The Exorcist*, it's a little tighter and faster paced. But in rushing to show us *The Exorcist*'s greatest hits, it sacrifices atmosphere and the buildup of dread which, together with the lackluster effects and makeup, make for a pretty bland imitation in every way.

L'OSSESSA/THE EERIE MIDNIGHT HORROR SHOW (1974)

Director: Mario Gariazzo
Writers: Mario Gariazzo, Ambrogio Molteni, Ted Rusoff

This Italian *Exorcist* clone has gone by a slew of titles including *Enter the Devil*, *The Devil Obsession*, and *The Tormented* as well as its UK video box title; *The Obsessed*. Its most common title came about once the 1975 musical horror comedy movie *The Rocky Horror Picture Show* started gaining a cult following. *L'Ossessa* was quickly repackaged under the title *The Eerie Midnight Horror Show* with a new poster ripping off *Rocky Horror*'s famous 'lips' poster.

But *L'Ossessa* is neither musical nor comedic. Stella Carnacina stars as art student Danila who investigates an abandoned church to see which religious sculptures should be salvaged. Apparently orgies were held here a hundred years ago resulting in the church's deconsecration which should set some alarm bells ringing.

Fascinated by one of the crucified effigies, Danila purchases it and takes it back to her studio. Closeups of the effigy's face clearly show that it is an actor in makeup so you just know the damn thing is going to come to life at some point.

At a groove-tastic party held by her parents, Danila witnesses her mother engaging in some kinky business with a tousle-headed stud (Gabriele Tinti who would go on to star in several of France's erotic *Emmanuelle* series as well as Mario Bava's *Lisa and the Devil*) who whips her savagely with a bouquet of roses.

Disgusted, Danila retreats to her studio and tries to get on with some work. As we predicted, the effigy comes to life, strips her naked and ravishes her which

187

she doesn't seem all that opposed to.

We're twenty-minutes into this breezy possession flick and we've already had two steamy sex scenes which should give you some idea of where director Mario Gariazzo's motivation lies. Allegedly one of the movie's many alternate titles was *The Sexorcist*, possibly inspired by (and often confused with) the X-rated movie of the same name which also came out in 1974.

Danila is pursued home by shadowy voices and echoing footsteps in the movie's most effective scene as she races up the stairwell to her family's apartment on the top floor. It is then that she is possessed fully which causes her to masturbate in front of her parents and even try to seduce her father (*Obscene Desire*'s Chris Avram). Needless to say, the doctor is called.

When another dream sequence (in which Danila is crucified by the demonic cackling effigy-come-to-life) results in stigmata, it is time for Italy's answer to Max von Sydow to make his entrance. Father Xeno is played by Luigi Pistilli, veteran of several *gialli* and some Spaghetti Westerns including *The Good, the Bad and the Ugly* (1966) in which he also played a priest.

The 'devil' in this movie is played by *All the Colors of the Dark*'s Ivan Rassimov, an Italian actor of Serb descent who had starred in a ton of *giallo* and *poliziottesco* flicks in the sixties as well as playing Django in a few Spaghetti Westerns. It's unclear why Satan has been hiding in the form of a crucified effigy. There is some guff about a Etruscan temple being taken over by Carthaginians in the 4th century who sacrificed newborn children to Ba'al but there is little to connect all this to Danila's possession.

The actual exorcism doesn't take up much of the movie's runtime and is a pretty bare-bones affair with none of the expensive effects of the movie it is ripping off. Stella Carnacina's performance can't be faulted however, as she really throws herself into the role of the wild-eyed raving woman possessed by the devil. Sex and flagellation aside (or 'whips and bells and other masochistic tomfoolery' as Danila's bitter father accuses his wife of), *L'Ossessa* is a fairly by-the-numbers *Exorcist* knockoff.

CHI SEI?/BEYOND THE DOOR (1974)

Director: Ovidio G. Assonitis and Roberto D'Ettorre Piazzoli
Writers: Ovidio G. Assonitis, Antonio Troiso and Roberto D'Ettorre Piazzoli

Greco-Italian movie mogul Ovidio G. Assonitis was already the head of an extensive distribution network in Southeast Asia by the late sixties before he moved into movie production, turning out a handful of gialli along with Umberto Lenzi's *Man from Deep River* (1972), the first of a wave of Italian cannibal movies. Assonitis had read William Peter Blatty's *The Exorcist* and had wanted to buy the rights but was beaten to the punch by Warner Brothers. So, he did what any other good exploitation producer would do and cobbled together his own version, using the input of around half a dozen other writers, and directed it himself.

The movie begins with the devil (English Shake-spearean actor and Italian exploitation regular Edmund Purdom, who had already played the devil in *The Devil's Lover*) having a friendly chat with us and bemoaning the fact that the current fashion demands that his is heard but rarely seen. His final line; "That stranger, sitting in the seat next to you … could be me!" must have caused some horsing around in theaters at the time.

The movie's protagonist, Jessica (Juliet Mills) flees a surreal, candlelit ceremony of some sort while the devil berates a bearded man called Dimitri (English veteran of stage and screen Richard Johnson) for letting her get away. Ten years later, when Dimitri's car is plunging off the side of a cliff, a bargain is struck meaning that Dimitri will be granted an extension of life if he can find Jessica and ensure the baby she carries is born.

We catch up with Jessica as the wife of music producer Robert (Gabriele Lavia) and mother to two of the weirdest kids you're likely to see on film. Both are foulmouthed little brats and their parents (whom they refer to by their first names) just roll their eyes at their antics. The son, Ken, drinks Campbell's green pea soup out of the can with a straw and the girl, Gail (who seems to be voiced by a 23-year-old), carries around multiple copies of Erich Segal's *Love Story* and talks in hippie slang.

Sure enough, Jessica discovers that she is pregnant but is alarmed when the doctor says that the fetus is already three months along. Soon, she is suffering more than just morning sickness but mood swings, hallucinations and levitating in the night. What's more, both she and Robert keep seeing Dimitri loitering around and reflected in windows and mirrors.

There's also something going on with the kids who are plagued by poltergeist activity. Dolls start walking about and objects are hurled around the nursery before the whole room starts tipping and shaking. Mommy is no help; when Gail tries to wake her, her head slowly rotates to reveal a demoniacal grin, her possession in full swing now.

Unlike most possession movies, there is no reassuring presence of a Max von Sydow in whom we can place our trust. Dimitri, when he does turn up and introduces himself as an ex-boyfriend Jessica has never mentioned, is presented as an ally against evil, but we know not to trust him as we are aware of his pact with the devil.

Beyond the Door is a stylish movie reminiscent of the more vibrant entries in the giallo genre. Jessica and Robert's modern house exudes seventies chic including a red-themed bathroom. The street scenes of San Francisco with it colorful stores are lovingly evoked all to Franco Micalizzi's jazzy score.

Like the best Italian horrors, there's a surreal quality to *Beyond the Door*. Much of it is overexposed resulting in a misty, dreamlike look while characters suffer delusions like eyeballs in drinks and a bathroom towel catches fire in the middle of the night, seen by nobody, and is never referenced again. Odd cutaways, freeze frames and nonsensical montages abound and the movie's final kicker, in which little Ken finally unwraps that present he received at the beginning of the movie, suggests that time isn't even linear further adding to the nightmarish atmosphere.

The movie could certainly have been cut down a little to make it tighter. Assonitis takes his time with his shots and there are many lengthy episodes of our characters simply wandering around San Francisco including one bizarre scene in which Robert is assailed by a street musician playing a nose flute for no apparent reason.

But Assonitis knew how to do horror and when Jessica falls fully under demonic control, the shots are well done, even if they were lifted straight from *The Exorcist*. They are also overused just a tad and it's nothing we haven't seen before; yellow contact lenses, head-spinning, levitation and even the pea soup vomit (leaving us to wonder if Ken's penchant for the green stuff is a deliberate in-joke).

A slightly longer version of the movie was released in the UK as *Devil Within Her* (not to be confused with the British 1975 horror movie *I Don't Want to be Born* which, confusingly, was released in the US as *The Devil Within Her*) and the movie did surprisingly well in the US. Success however, draws attention and, along with blaxploitation *Exorcist* knock-off *Abby* (1974), *Beyond the Door* was hounded by Warner Brothers for copyright infringement, a case which was eventually settled in 1979. Although the influences are obvious, *Beyond the Door* is definitely one of the better imitators.

Beyond the Door is often quoted as being part of a

trilogy but the other two entries are merely unrelated Italian movies given new titles in the US. *Beyond the Door II* (1979) is Mario Bava's 1977 movie *Shock* and *Beyond the Door III* is a 1989 movie called *Amok Train*.

L'ANTICRISTO/THE ANTICHRIST (1974)

Director: Alberto De Martino
Writers: Gianfranco Clerici, Alberto De Martino and
Vincenzo Mannino

Also released in the US as *The Tempter* (confusingly the same name as the UK release of *Il sorriso del grande tentatore,* also from 1974, which was known in the US as *The Devil is a Woman*), *The Antichrist* is a particularly vibrant entry in the opus of Italian knockoffs of *The Exorcist.* Director Alberto De Martino had a long career in Spaghetti Westerns and Eurospy movies, including *O.K. Connery* (1967) about James Bond's brother which starred Sean Connery's actual brother Neil.

We open on some extended scenes of absolute pandemonium at a sanctuary of the Virgin Mary in Rome where pilgrims writhe and scream, some seemingly possessed. One of the visitors is Ippolita Oderisi (Carla Gravina) who is wheelchair bound and keen for a divine favor. After a particularly demented pilgrim spits at the Virgin Mary and then hurls himself off a cliff, Ippolita is taken home where she lives with her father (Mel Ferrer), brother (Remo Girone) and housekeeper Irene (Italian golden age star Alida Valli who would go on to appear in *Suspiria*).

The Antichrist takes its time in getting going and we're up to the thirty-minute mark before it explained exactly what is going on. When she was twelve-years old, Ippolita was paralyzed from the waist down in a car crash which also claimed the life of her mother. Since then, she has lived a rather reclusive life with a deep emotional reliance on her aristocratic father who has recently taken up with another woman (Anita Strindberg), eliciting strong feelings of resentment from Ippolita.

Ippolita's uncle is a priest (Arthur Kennedy in a dog collar will no doubt recall the similar role he played in *The Sentinel*). He knows a parapsychologist called Dr. Sinibaldi (Umberto Orsini) who offers to try and cure Ippolita with hypnotism. He believes that Ippolita's condition is psychological, not physical and stems from the trauma of her accident.

Regression therapy results in Ippolita recalling the fate of an ancestor, also called Ippolita, who fled a convent to join a satanic sect before being burned at the stake as a witch. These regression sessions restore Ippolita's ability to walk but inadvertently allow a demonic spirit to enter her body.

Soon we're in the familiar territory of pea soup vomit and torrents of blasphemy and sexually laden obscenities. Carla Gravina writhes and snarls throughout, doing a good job of conflating demonic possession with sexual frustration. An unexplored subplot involving incest (and the resulting antichrist quickening in Ippolita's womb) suggests that the Oderisi family have more than a few skeletons in their closet, as does the ancient tome locked in a cabinet which relates the tale of their devilish ancestor. The swapping of the wealthy but regular family life of Regan and her mother from *The Exorcist* with a decaying bastion of Italy's vanishing nobility gives the movie an interesting touch of the gothic.

The movie is livened up no end by its incredible locations and sets including the actual Colosseum. The Oderisi family live in a baroque mansion with a fascinating hallway of sculpted busts set in niches in the red painted walls. For a movie that is clearly trying to ride on the coattails of *The Exorcist*, *The Antichrist* certainly doubles down on the art direction, conjuring images of *Suspiria* and even *The Devils* in the stark modernism of the historical flashbacks.

Equally impressive is the dream sequence in which Ippolita experiences her ancestor's initiation into the devil cult in a moonlit wood which is clearly a sound-stage but it's so damn beautiful that the artificiality only adds to the surreal atmosphere. Particularly shocking is the black mass in which Ippolita eats the head of a toad, licks a goat's anus and fornicates with either the devil or a high priest made up to look like him. Much of this was cut from several versions of the movie.

There isn't much in the way of special effects aside from a few dreadful bluescreen shots during the scenes where Ippolita levitates and furniture is hurled around the room. Rubber toads and snakes also fail to convince but are used sparingly. It's mostly makeup and Carla Gravina's performance that sells the possession, even if the movie pilfers wholesale from Friedkin's game changer by the final act. There are enough interesting elements to make *The Antichrist* different enough from *The Exorcist* but the general plot is the same.

The Antichrist reached the US in 1978 in a truncated version but the original, full-length version (goat included) is one of the bolder and more provocative (and therefore worthwhile) *Exorcist* rip offs. Alberto De Martino would cash in on the next great devil trend with *Holocaust 2000* which took its cue from *The Omen*.

ABBY (1974)

Director: William Girdler
Writer: G. Cornell Layne

Before *Asylum of Satan* director William Girdler made his biggest hit *Grizzly* in 1976, he dabbled in the blaxploitation genre with a couple of flicks shot in his hometown of Louisville, Kentucky. One of the was the Pam Grier-starring *Sheba, Baby* (1975) and the other was an *Exorcist* knockoff called *Abby*.

Carol Speed stars as wholesome marriage counsellor Abby, recently moved into a large house with her Baptist minister husband Emmett (Terry Carter). Emmet's father, Bishop Williams (Blacula himself, William Marshall), is a college professor who is currently on an archaeological dig in Nigeria where he finds a puzzle box carved with images of the Yoruba god Eshu, "the most powerful of all earthly deities ... a trickster, creator of whirlwinds ... chaos." Upon opening the box, a powerful wind escapes and makes its way across the Atlantic to Louisville.

Abby soon starts acting strange. She becomes foul-mouthed, violent and sexual, attacking her husband and flaunting her breasts to an aghast couple during one of their marriage counselling sessions. Whenever she turns demonic it's signaled by creepy contact lenses and renowned voice actor Bob Holt doing his best Mercedes McCambridge impression. The dubbing isn't particularly convincing however and the quick cutaways to the rubbery face of a demon have nothing on *The Exorcist*'s terrifying inserts of Pazuzu.

Emmet is desperate to help his wife and calls on his father's aid. Returning from Nigeria, Bishop Williams declares that Abby became possessed by the evil spirit Eshu when he opened that damned box. Now it's up to him, Emmet and Abby's cop brother, Cass (Austin Stoker), to rectify the situation.

While Regan was bound to her bed for much of the duration of *The Exorcist*, Abby is free to cavort around town, pick up men in bars and generally have a blast while her trio of concerned male family members look for her. But any message that Abby's possession liberates her from her role as a docile Christian house-wife is ham-fisted. One early scene has her masturbating in the shower as proof of her being inhabited by a demonic spirit and she is predictably restored to the dutiful, pious housewife before the credits roll.

There's plenty of padding in the third act in the form of shots of seedy disco bars and downtown Louisville nightlife which is entertaining enough in its own right but the climactic exorcism held in a smashed-up bar is very talky. William Marshall is convincing as an exorcist and his baritone voice resonates while Carol Speed gives it her all, foaming at the mouth and calling everybody out on their secrets. She is definitely the highlight of the movie, playing the flip sides of the coin with boundless energy. Whether she is the insufferably bubbly housewife or the foul-mouthed, wild-eyed demonic presence, she is enthralling to watch. Speed also wrote and sang the song 'My Soul is a Witness' for the movie.

The movie's focus on the Yoruba religion of West Africa is an interesting take amid the slew of competi-tors chasing some post-*Exorcist* profit. There is the concern about deities of other religions literally being demonized and used as a stand in for the Christian devil and *Abby* is certainly guilty of perpetuating the tradition begun by the 19th century Yoruba cleric and linguist Samuel Ajayi Crowther when he translated 'Eshu' as 'Satan' in his *A Vocabulary of the Yoruba Language* (1872). But non-Christian deities being translated as devils is nothing new. Even *The Exorcist*'s Pazuzu is a Mesopotamian deity, not Satan himself.

For all its faults, *Abby* is entertaining and fresh enough to stand out amid its fellow imitators but suffered from being singled out by Warner Brothers for copyright infringement. It must be admitted that they had a point, with several scenes in *Abby* seemingly lifted straight from Friedkin's movie. Warner Brothers won and *Abby* was yanked from theaters (but not before pocketing around four-million dollars for distributor, AIP).

William Gridler was the first to admit that he always aimed to cash in on popular trends with *Abby* and his *Jaws* rip-off *Grizzly* (1976) being cases in point. He would die in 1978 at the tragically young age of thirty in a helicopter accident in the Philippines while scouting out locations for his newest movie, allegedly a knock-off of *Star Wars* (1977).

LA ENDEMONIADA/DEMON WITCH CHILD (1975)

Director: Amando de Ossorio
Writer: Amando de Ossorio

Amando de Ossorio made a name for himself in the Spanish horror movie boom with his 1972 movie *Tombs of the Blind Dead*. Featuring zombified Knights Templar, the movie was influential on many Spanish horror filmmakers and Ossorio followed it up with three sequels to form the 'Blind Dead tetralogy'. He directed other horror movies of the period too, including this decent stab at the exorcism trend.

It's unfair to simply label *Demon Witch Child* as just another *Exorcist* knockoff as it does attempt to do something a little different, even if the influence of Friedkin's movie is clear. Somebody is desecrating churches and abducting babies. There's some serious racial profiling going on down at police HQ with the blame squarely placed on a local gypsy woman, Mother Gautère (Tota Alba), who has the reputation of being a witch. Unfortunately, they're right and Mother Gautère is the head of a devil cult lurking in the nearby woods who are in the habit of sacrificing unbaptized babies to Lucifer.

Dragged in for questioning, Mother Gautère prefers to hurl herself out of a top floor window than answer any questions. Her followers blame Commissioner Barnes (Ángel del Pozo) and one of them slips a demonic talisman to his daughter, Susan (Marián Salgado who was no doubt picked because she dubbed Linda Blair in the Spanish release of *The Exorcist*). That night, the spirit of the dead witch rises from her body (in a scene with the sort of special effects that belong in a silent movie) and enters the sleeping form of the teenaged Susan Barnes.

Despite the problematic approach of depicting gypsies as devil worshippers, the cult aspect is what separates *Demon Witch Child* from *The Exorcist*. Rather than a demon randomly selecting an innocent to possess, the possession is the work of a group of outsiders who have a bone to pick with the firm-handed police commissioner.

Whenever Susan is taken over by the spirit of the witch, her face actually resembles Mother Gautère's with its rotten teeth and thin, wispy hair, via the use of makeup and old-fashioned time-lapse effects. There is even an attempt to emulate the head-spinning of *The Exorcist* by rotating the whole top half of Susan's body using a primitive camera effect (it doesn't quite work).

There's not much of Regan's green vomit and blasphemy in *Demon Witch Child* but little Susan retains the foul mouth, swearing at adults and calling them out on their bullshit which adds some humor to an otherwise grim story. One neat trick is mimicking the voices of others which Susan uses to mess with the adults, calling her governess's boyfriend and getting him to meet her in the park. What she does to him then might have a few male viewers crossing their legs and is one of the nastiest bits in the movie along with the actual ritual sacrifice of a baby (so often associated with devil cults but rarely seen in movies).

There's a completely superfluous subplot in which we learn that Father Juan ditched his girlfriend to join the priesthood. She is later introduced as a prostitute, just to show how far she has fallen without him by her side. This bit of padding distracts from the plot but is brief enough not to drag the movie down.

As in most of these movies, the eventual exorcism feels way too easy and simply tacked-on as a way to bring things to a close. But *Demon Witch Child* is a fairly tight thriller that doesn't outstay its welcome, has the added creepy factor of a murderous little girl with an old woman's face and is less bizarre and slapdash than many of its ilk.

Demon Witch Child was something of a last hurrah to Ossorio's horror career. The Spanish movie industry was never able to match the success of their Italian cousins who began churning out low-budget zombie and cannibal movies in the late seventies and early eighties.

Exorcismo/Exorcism (1975)

Director: Juan Bosch
Writers: Juan Bosch, Jordi Gigó and Paul Naschy

Spanish actor and filmmaker, Paul Naschy (who had changed his name from Jacinto Molina to better appeal to non-Spanish audiences), was in the right place at the right time in 1968. Spain was in the middle of its horror boom instigated by Jesús Franco's 1962 hit *The Awful R. Orloff*. After years of playing extras, Naschy penned his own script for a werewolf movie and ended up playing the lead. *La Marca del Hombre Lobo* (known as *Frankenstein's Bloody Terror* in the US, despite having nothing to do with Frankenstein) was released in 1968 and spawned eleven sequels in which Nashy starred as the werewolf, Count Waldemar Daninsky, earning him the title of 'Spain's Lon Chaney'.

A fan of Universal's monster movies since childhood, Naschy penned many other horror scripts in the early seventies, including 1973's *Horror Rises from the Tomb* inspired by the historical Gilles de Rais, an accused satanist and child murderer. After meeting British director John Gilling who had directed several horror movies for Hammer, Naschy picked him for his unofficial entry in Amando de Ossorio's Blind Dead series, *La cruz del diablo* (*The Devil's Cross*) in which he intended to play the lead. Unfortunately, the producer sold the script which was rewritten and Gilling decided to cast a different actor (Ramiro Oliveros), effectively cutting Naschy out of the project. Understandably bitter, Naschy embarked on a new project that, unusually for him, was set in the modern day.

Directed by the reliable Juan Bosch, *Exorcism* is set in England (Bristol, to be exact, though the arid Spanish landscape suggests otherwise). It's easily forgotten until we are reminded by the occasional appearances of policemen in custodian helmets as the events largely take place on the rambling estate of the wealthy Gibson family. Its youngest member, Laila starts acting strange after a near fatal car crash. She starts swearing at her family and claims she hates everybody. Normal teenage behavior, some might say, but by the title of the movie, we know there is something more demonic afoot.

Leila has been hanging out with a free love crowd who drop acid, drink blood and hold orgies in honor of Satan down on the beach. Her home life is messy too. Her father has died in a sanitorium and her stepbrother, John (Joan Llaneras) is rather possessive of her to the point of infatuation and despises her boyfriend, hippie archeologist Richard (Roger Leveder).

The Gibson family servants are up to something too. One of the maids is having an affair with John while chauffeur Udo (Luis Induni) sneaks around and ogles naked pictures of Leila. Pretty soon, people start turning up dead with their heads twisted around 180° (which is the only head-spinning you'll see in the movie).

It's up to Father Dunning (Paul Naschy) to find out what's going on. He's been a friend of the family for years and was also Richard's tutor at college. Does that make him an archaeologist too? We never find out but Dunning certainly has enough books on his shelves about cults and Satanism to arouse the curiosity of the local police detective (Juan Velilla).

Exorcism feels more like a family drama than a horror movie and its only at the thirty-minute mark that we are treated to a mild jump scare in the form of somebody in a devil mask bolting from the scene of a crime, bowling Father Dunning over in the process.

Naschy carries the movie and is part of the action from the get-go rather than being wheeled onstage in the third act like so many other movie exorcists. It's interesting to see him as a heroic character playing detective after all his years of playing monsters and he does well with what he has here, which isn't much.

The cult angle is something of a red herring as it has little to do with Leila's possession and it seems a strange subplot to include. *The Exorcist*'s Regan never needed to be part of a cult to draw the attention of demonic forces and neither does Leila, which begs the question of why it was ever included besides the need for some obvious padding. There's nothing overtly awful about *Exorcism*. It's competently made and plods along like a murder mystery before giving us a brief exorcism as promised. The main problem is that so very little happens.

While it's true that *The Exorcist* also has a quiet buildup before Regan goes full-on demonic, Friedkin's movie also racked up the tension and filled the first two acts with mounting dread which is utterly lacking in *Exorcism*. The scary makeup, vomiting and poltergeist activity is all saved for the final twenty-minutes and even then, it's pretty tame stuff, making for a fairly low-key and mild entry in the *Exorcist* cash-in genre.

It's strange that Naschy, who was such a big voice in seventies Spanish horror, tried to ride on the coattails of one of horror's masterpieces and forgot to add anything scary. He claims he wrote the script before seeing *The Exorcist* which wasn't released in Spain until 1975 (although *Demon Witch Child* was certainly able to copy a few things despite being made several months before) and, as so few elements of what made *The Exorcist* great pop up in *Exorcism*, he might just be telling the truth.

The House of Exorcism (1975)

Directors: Lamberto Bava, Mario Bava and Alfredo Leone
Writers: Alberto Cittini, Alfredo Leone and Mario Bava

In 1972, Mario Bava, the Italian horror master behind 1960's *Black Sunday*, 1971's *A Bay of Blood* and 1972's *Baron Blood*, shot a movie in Spain called *Lisa and the Devil*. It was a surreal, gothic creeper in which tourist Lisa (Elke Sommer) gets separated from her tour group and winds up at an old mansion where she suffers hallucinations and the sinister machinations of the family butler played by Telly Savalas.

Although *Lisa and the Devil* received a limited release in Spain as *El diablo se lleva a los muertos* (*The Devil Takes the Dead*), it never received an Italian release, languishing in limbo until the worldwide phenomenon of *The Exorcist* caused international movie producers to start rummaging through their vaults to see if they had anything that might be salvageable as a quick cash-in.

And so, *The House of Exorcism* was conceived. Producer and long-time Bava associate, Alfredo Leone, along with Bava's son, Lamberto, rehashed the movie into a possession story. Elke Sommer was called back and extra scenes were shot to include the character of Father Michael (Robert Alda) who tries to exorcise the demon which is apparently at the root of all of Lisa's bizarre experiences.

German actress Elke Sommer (who was once hired as an au pair for Vicki and Anne Michelle, of *Virgin Witch*) was the leading lady in several hits of the 1960s including the Pink Panther sequel *A Shot in the Dark* (1964), *The Wrecking Crew* (1968) in which she starred alongside Dean Martin and the ill-fated Sharon Tate, and Mario Bava's previous movie, *Baron Blood* (1972).

Here, she plays Lisa, the wandering tourist who finds her way to an antique store where she encounters Telly Savalas (bearing an uncanny resemblance to the mural of the devil Lisa has just seen in the town square). Savalas is purchasing a painted dummy and both he and the storekeeper comment on how much Lisa resembles somebody called Elena and how suitable she might be for some unspoken purpose.

It is as Lisa is leaving the antique store that we are exposed to the first of the new scenes inserted by Alfredo Leone and Lamberto Bava. She collapses in an apparent fit and is examined by Father Michael before being taken away in an ambulance. While unconscious, Lisa seems to have a dream of wandering around the town and being approached by a mustachioed man (Espartaco Santoni) who looks remarkably like the dummy Savalas bought.

More dream sequences follow as Lisa finds herself arriving at a crumbling old mansion in the middle of the night in the company of two other travelers; man and wife Francis and Sophia (Eduardo Fajardo and Sylva Koscina) and their chauffeur, George (Gabriele Tinti from *The Eerie Midnight Horror Show*). The residents of the old house are Maximillian (Alessio Orano) and his blind mother known only as 'the countess' (played by Alida Valli who was in *The Antichrist* and would later appear in *Suspiria*). Lo and behold, Leandro the family butler, is played by Telly Savalas. This was just before Savalas's career-defining turn as Kojak, but not before he had traded cigarettes for lollipops to help him quit; an amusing quirk that was written into the script when he offers Lisa a Chuba Chup.

As the movie progresses, intercutting bits from Bava's nightmarish movie with scenes in which Father Michael tries to root out the demon inhabiting Lisa's body, it becomes apparent that she is experiencing flashbacks to another life in which she was called Elena. As the lover of both Maximillian and his father, Elena was at the center of a murderous family squabble, the nature of which unfolds against the gothic backdrop of the decaying mansion in a tale which drips with corruption and madness worthy of Poe.

The new scenes are drab and sterile and stick out like occasional sore thumbs amid Bava's florid visual style. The obligatory crisis of faith subplot is introduced with the devil taunting Father Michael by taking the form of his dead lover (Carmen Silva) who tries to seduce him in a full-frontal nude scene but, as with most such subplots, it has little relevance.

Feared lost forever, Bava's original version of the movie eventually emerged in the nineties but even the most ardent fan of Italian horror must admit that it is a baffling experience which no doubt was the reason it failed to fly in 1973. Bava fans will claim that *The House of Exorcism* confuses the plot further, but others may appreciate its attempt to make some sense of Bava's dream logic. By presenting the original movie as flashbacks experienced by Lisa during her possession which is taking place in another time and another place, there is the suggestion that her soul is trapped in some sort of purgatory by the devil, but it still leaves us with questions. What's with all the dummies? Is Leandro the devil? Is Lisa a reincarnation of Elena and, if so, how can she be having flashbacks of scenes she isn't in?

Now seen as Bava's crowning achievement (he would only make two more feature movies before his death in 1980, one of which was *Shock*), *Lisa and the Devil* was perhaps simply too artsy for the general public in 1973, especially ones expecting a straightforward horror movie. If rehashing it into an exorcism movie was the only way to make a buck off it, so be it. But even in this bastardized format with its ugly and generic exorcism scenes crowbarred in, Bava's delirious madness shines through and makes *The House of Exorcism* a standout and remarkably unique amid its fellow cash-ins.

I DON'T WANT TO BE BORN (1975)

Director: Peter Sasdy
Writers: Stanley Price and Nato de Angeles

Director Peter Sasdy had a prolific career in British television before he made a few horror movies for Hammer Productions at which point his movie career looked ready to take off. Unfortunately, it was derailed slightly by this unsuccessful and almost universally derided occult stinker starring Joan Collins in one of several British horror movies she made after her return to the UK in 1970. It was released under several titles including *The Monster* in the UK and *The Devil Within Her* in the US as well as *Sharon's Baby*, which is particularly inexplicable as there is nobody in the movie called Sharon.

The credits roll over a delivery room scene in which Lucy (Joan Collins) screams in labor while Donald Plesance tugs the baby out with forceps to *Doctor Who* composer Ron Grainer's prog-rock score. This clumsy and slightly tasteless opening sets the tone for the rest of the movie which concerns Lucy's unusually large (12lbs) baby and its increasingly strange abilities. Hammer veteran Ralph Bates plays Lucy's husband Gino, who is Italian, the only explanation for which is that the story was conceived by Italian producer Nato de Angeles whose company Unicapital co-produced the movie with the Rank Organisation.

Right from the get-go, Lucy knows that there is something odd about her baby. He bites and scratches and somehow gets out of his cot to trash his nursery like a drunk rockstar. The stern housekeeper (Hilary Mason) is quick to take a dislike to the baby and, at the baptism, he apparently has a fit in the arms of the priest, although it's difficult to tell what's going on as the action is so badly shot.

In fact, we never really see the baby do anything and it's debatable if the movie would have been better if we did. The idea that a newborn baby is somehow able to reach out of his pram and push nannies into lakes and drop dead mice into cups of tea is laughable, perhaps doubly so if we saw the little tot committing the acts, but even with cutaways and clumsy camera angles, it just doesn't work and certainly isn't frightening.

A feeble attempt at an explanation for the demon baby is given by Lucy in the form of a narrated flash-back. She was once part of a cabaret act with a dwarf called Hercules in a strip club. Hercules was smitten with Lucy but she was more interested in carrying on an affair with club owner Tommy (John Steiner, star of many Italian exploitation movies including *Shock*). Feeling snubbed, Hercules cast a curse on Lucy, stating that she will have a baby "as big as I am small and possessed by the devil himself!"

Lucy's situation is further confused by the fact that she was carrying on her affair with Tommy right up until her wedding night, meaning that she doesn't even know who the baby's father is. The whole business with Tommy takes up the middle act of the movie and doesn't really go anywhere; just another example of the filler needed to pad out the paper-thin plot.

That such a high-caliber cast is involved in this mess is astonishing. Donald Pleasence was no stranger to trashy drive-in fare (see *The Devil's Men*) but looks utterly bored as the sidelined family doctor here. There's some overacting from Collins, Bates and Caroline Munro who was apparently dubbed, making the movie feel even more like an Italian production despite being filmed in England with British actors. One who does manage to keep things on an even keel is Eileen Atkins who plays Gino's level-headed sister, a nun involved in some sort of scientific research (yet another side plot that is never explored). Her accent might not be any better than Bates's, but Atkins brings a sensibility to the proceedings which is laudable considering the nonsense surrounding her.

When we do catch glimpses of the baby during its murderous rampage in the final act, it takes the form of Hercules, cackling in his pram and wielding a knife as he chases Lucy about. The connection between Hercules and the baby is never gone into in any detail nor is it explained how he has the power to cast curses. A touch of actual occultism would certainly have helped the movie feel a little more thought out.

A murderous dwarf and the presence of Hilary Mason may recall *Don't Look Now* (1973), but *I Don't Want to be Born* lacks any of the atmosphere or subtlety of Roeg's masterpiece. Just as the final exorcism scene with its shaking bed and Latin prayers is lifted from *The Exorcist* and the overall concept of a devil baby is from *Rosemary's Baby* (1968), *I Don't Want to be Born* happily plunders ideas from far better movies and mixes them together in an ineffectual hodgepodge. Like *To the Devil a Daughter*, *I Don't Want to be Born* was a sign of the dying British movie industry which, by 1975, was helplessly grasping at straws and trying to jump on the devil bandwagon as American investors headed to more profitable pastures.

LA SEXORCISTA/SATÁNICO PANDEMONI-
UM/SATANIC PANDEMONIUM (1975)

Director: Gilberto Martínez Solares
Writers: Jorge Barragán, Adolfo Martínez Solares and
Gilberto Martínez Solares

The witch-hunt genre of exploitation movies hit its stride in the 1970s in the wake of *Witchfinder General* (1968) with *Cry of the Banshee* and *Blood on Satan's Claw* being rare examples where the occult was depicted as a real source of power. Most lacked any supernatural elements, content to simply offer up a platter of nudity and sadism in an early form of the 'torture porn' genre of the 2000s. A cousin genre also emerged in the 1970s after Ken Russellhad outraged the Catholic Church with his controversial movie *The Devils* about the supposedly possessed nuns of Loudon which bore some hallmarks of the witch-hunt genre, mixed in with the notions of repressed sexuality bursting forth in the unlikeliest of places.

Inspired by the titillating prospect of showing habits being cast aside for carnal pleasures, the 'nunsploitation' genre saw many a low-budget pusher of grindhouse fare churn out movies concerning masturbating nuns, sadistic torture and possession (which usually manifested itself as lesbianism or at the very least, sexual awakening). And all this before *The Exorcist* made demonic possession a near requisite in religious horror movies.

Prompted by both *The Devils* and Matthew Lewis's 1796 novel *The Monk*, producer Jorge Barragán came up with the idea for *Satanic Pandemonium*, handing it over to his friend Adolfo Martínez Solares to pen the script on the condition that Solares's father, the prolific

Mexican director Gilberto Martínez Solares would direct.

There's nothing like a naked man to spoil a pleasant walk. That's what Sister Maria (Cecilia Pezet) discovers while out picking flowers not far from her convent. The naked man in question is the devil himself, played by Enrique Rocha, whose state of undress sends Sister Maria fleeing in fright. But the devil has somehow got into her head and appears at the window of the convent, seen only by Maria, offering her an apple in a not-so-subtle bit of symbolism.

Terrified, Maria indulges in a bit of self-flagellation, which she seems to enjoy by the sound of her orgasmic moaning. As with most nunsploitation movies, sexual repression is the word of the day and Maria also seems to have lesbian cravings as well as masochistic tendencies. A fantasy about being made love to by one of her fellow sisters goes downhill when it is revealed that she is being ravished by Lucifer.

She tries to fulfil her sexual desires for real by sexually assaulting another nun, sister Clemencia (Clemencia Colin) who, at first seems receptive, only to squirm away. Sister Mary doesn't take rejection well and plunges a knife into Sister Clemencia's back. She also tries to seduce a local shepherd boy, even visiting him in the night and clambering stark naked into his bed in perhaps the movie's most shocking and uncomfortable scene. That also results in murder when the boy wakes up and starts resisting.

Lucifer has infected Maria's every waking moment, making her see snakes in her water cup and transforming a portrait of the pope into the grinning visage of the devil. Is Maria going mad or has she truly been possessed? That question lies at the heart of the movie which toys with madness and sexual repression as much as it does with the supernatural.

It's more tactful than the average nunsploitation flick, despite having all the necessary ingredients (lesbianism, torture, nudity and repressed sexuality) and is sparing in their use, saving most of it for the shocking finale. An unfortunate result is that it's incredibly slow-paced. We watch nuns eat, pray, and walk down corridors in something of an historical drama reminiscent of *Black Narcissus* (1947) rather than *The Devils*. It's a pretty-looking movie however, with the dusty Mexican convent against the arid landscape complimenting the baby blue of the nuns' habits and the red of the blood that will eventually be spilled.

Its original title of *La Sexorcista* never quite fit, having nothing to do with exorcism but, considering it came out in the wake of *The Exorcist*, it must be lauded for not aping that movie's plot as so many others did. It's a possession movie of a sort, but of a more existential type. One doesn't get the impression that the devil is making Maria do all the terrible things she does, but rather the evil is within her already and he merely removes the barrier of self-control and morality. The restrictive monotony of the convent and the tyranny of the mother superior is dwelt on at length, including the bullying of two black nuns (convent life being no escape from colonial-era racism), that it's almost easy to side with Sister Maria or at least understand where her rage comes from. *Almost.* She is, however, a murderer and potentially a pedophile, so the movie's message is a little muddled, as is its style and tone. Nicely shot with admirable cinematography, the movie seems at odds with its grindhouse subject matter which is generally seen in less competent affairs.

The movie's revised name of *Satanico Pandemonium* is a better fit than any attempts to cash in on *The Exorcist*, and, in a bit of Hollywood trivia, was used as the name of Salma Hayek's character in Quentin

Tarantino and Robert Rodriguez's ode to grindhouse, *From Dusk till Dawn* (1996).

UN URLO DALLE TENEBRE/THE RETURN OF THE EXORCIST (1975)

Directors: Angelo Pannacciò and Luca Damiano
Writers: Giulio Albonico, Aldo Crudo and Franco Brocani

Released as *The Possessor* and *Naked Exorcism* in the US, *Un urlo dalle tenebre* was also cheekily given the title *The Return of the Exorcist* to fool people into thinking it was a sequel to Friedkin's movie. The UK video release took this one step further after the official *Exorcist II* had come out, by calling it *The Exorcist III: Cries and Shadows*.

While most attempts to copy *The Exorcist* lack the intense buildup of dread Freidkin achieved, *The Return of the Exorcist* drops the buildup entirely and introduces us to Piero (Jean-Claude Vernè); a teenage boy who is already possessed and tied to his bed. It's up to his sister Elena (Patrizia Gori), a nun just returned from missionary work in Africa, to fight the powers of evil and explain to us exactly what has been going on.

Elena's exposition dump to her priest (and us) shows Piero out wandering with his friends in the mountainsides surrounding his village. He spots a naked woman (Mimma Biscardi) standing outside a cave and snaps a photo of her before she promptly vanishes. His companions aren't impressed, especially his girlfriend, Sherry (Sonia Viviani) which is somewhat understandable. Back home, Piero develops the pictures he took and sees no sign of the naked woman.

Going back to the spot the next day, Piero finds an amulet inscribed with an inverted cross and the word 'Tahal'. Deciding to wear this, strange things start to happen to him. He experiences chest pains and hallucinations of the mysterious woman as well as a black mass in which she was the centerpiece of a satanic orgy (presumably in the cave where he saw her). When she appears to him in his bedroom and tries to seduce him, he slits her throat with a knife. This has the undesired effect of killing Sherri who collapses on the dancefloor of a local club with blood gushing from her throat.

This interesting telekinetic killing suggests that we might be in for something a little more original than a run of the mill exorcism movie. Unfortunately, it's never really expanded on, and the movie quickly hits its intended gear; namely titillating sleaze. The naked devil woman keeps popping up and trying to seduce everybody, man or woman. Sister Elena is ravaged in the middle of the night and even Piero's mother (Françoise Prévost) isn't safe from having her clothes torn off her by the succubus before tumbling down the stairs to her death in one of the movie's more tasteless scenes.

There's some convoluted backstory given to us via another flashback to the 18th century in which a heretic priest and his demonic companion (the succubus we keep seeing) together seduced a nobleman's daughter called Anna. The resulting 'spawn of sin' was named 'Tahal, Son of Satan'. His mother met her fate at the hands of the Inquisition, but the fate of the baby is left unexplained.

Return of the Exorcist is short on character work. Scenes with actual people in them feel rushed but there's plenty of padding in the form of lengthy shots of the mountainous Italian village, the orgy in the cave, a papal address confirming the existence of the devil over shots of the Vatican and Sister Elena's flashbacks to her own time in a mental institution which were cribbed from another movie, *La casa delle mele mature* (1971).

Richard Conte (known to American audiences as Don Barzini in *The Godfather*) shows up towards the end as this movie's exorcist. This was Conte's final movie and it's a shame he didn't get much to do in it. He's there to play word battles with the demon in a very lackluster exorcism which seems to go on forever and doesn't involve much but a little vomiting (blood and not pea soup for once) and a floating bed.

That both directors, Angelo Pannacciò and the un-credited Franco Lo Cascio would go on to have lengthy careers in the porn industry (Cascio under his famous pseudonym Luca Damiano) is an indication of where the *The Return of the Exorcist*'s goals lie. There's nothing particularly scary going on and the whole exorcism angle seems like a way to cash in on a popular trend while dishing up plenty of skin and lesbian undertones in an otherwise dull and convoluted movie.

EL JUEGO DEL DIABLO/DEVIL'S EXORCIST (1975)

Director: Jorge Darnell
Writer: Jorge Darnell

As well as distributing the deluge of mostly foreign attempts to cash in on *The Exorcist*'s success, US distributors also unscrupulously retitled foreign horror movies which had nothing to do with the devil or exorcism, hoping to hoodwink audiences looking for the next pea soup-spewer. For example, the 1971 Spanish *Las melancólicas*, which was about a woman in a mental asylum, hit US theaters in 1974 under the nonsensical title *Exorcism's Daughter* starring Spanish child actor Inma de Santis.

As well as bit parts in other Spanish horrors like *Murders in the Rue Morgue* (1971) and *The Killer of Dolls* (1975), de Santis played the main part in this little-known *Exorcist* cash-in which also fails to deliver on the exorcist/exorcism front but at least hints at demonic possession as well as containing some deeper interpretations.

De Santis plays Catholic schoolgirl, Sheila, the only offspring of wealthy but distant parents. She's having a weird time of it, experiencing hallucinations and night terrors of being pursued by a tall, creepy man (José Lifante) who is somewhat reminiscent of Angus Scrimm's Tall Man in the *Phantasm* movies. With her behavior rapidly turning for the worse, it's off to the hospital for psychiatric evaluation.

While there, Sheila turns off the oxygen to a boy in intensive care, killing him. And this is just for starters. In fairly quick succession, Sheila shoves her mother over a balcony *Omen* style and hangs the dog of the family's elderly gardener (José Orjas), causing the poor old man to die of a heart attack. With three murders on her hands (four if you count the dog), Sheila clearly needs help and Dr. Liza Greene (Maria del Puy), whose work strangely has more to do with animals than children, takes the child on and tries to get to the heart of her troubling behavior.

Although Catholicism is present in *Devil's Exorcist*, there is little discussion of faith versus science as in other examples of the genre and no priests turns up in the final act to combat the forces of darkness. In fact, without giving away the ending (which borrows from *The Exorcist* as well as deviating sharply from it), the movie is incredibly bleak without the triumphant power of God which render many possession movies as so much Christian propaganda.

There are some creepy and well-shot set pieces to show Sheila's visions, like a snake uncurling from the hair of an effigy of Christ and, in particular, a wall of groping hands in the movie's final moments which recalls Roman Polansky's *Repulsion* (1965). But these moments are all too seldom with most of the movie wallowing in tedious conversations between Dr. Greene and her colleagues and her pointless relationship with her lover, (Jack Taylor, who we've seen in *Exorcism*, not to mention the Blind Dead series). The movie lacks the building atmosphere of better entries in this particular cannon with far too much time spent showing us things that have no real relevance such as the elderly gardener visiting the grave of his wife or the other patients of the hospital where Sheila is being evaluated.

But perhaps Jorge Darnell (whose brief directorial career never really descended into exploitation fare) meant for *Devil's Exorcism* to be a more cerebral take. As Sheila writhes around in the throes of demonic possession, it's hard not to interpret her cries as the moans of orgasm. She is the product of a strict upbringing and Catholic education and, as already discussed, this is not a movie that goes out of its way to extoll the virtues of Catholicism.

Sexual repression has often been linked to anti-social behavior and is often utilized by horror movies, but there is also a fear in Sheila, particularly of the mysterious man who appears in her visions (and is never explained). The previously mentioned allusion to Polanski's *Repulsion* hints at a fear of men, exemplified by the groping hands emerging from the wall and in the water of her swimming pool. In the beginning of the movie, Sheila's class visit a creepy waxwork museum and she seems both enchanted and frightened by the men on display which perhaps signals Darnell's intention right from the start; this is a story about a girl's fears and desires on the cusp of puberty and sexual awakening.

Ordinarily, such psychoanalyzing is overthinking it when it comes to low budget horror movies but, as *Devil's Exorcism* contains no gore, grisly special effects, gratuitous nudity or any other hallmarks of exploitation cinema, perhaps there is some messaging in there somewhere, however slowly and drily it is presented.

J.D.'s Revenge (1976)

Director: Arthur Marks
Writer: Jaison Starkes

Arthur Marks had a long run at directing episodes of *Perry Mason* before moving into feature films, directing several blaxploitation classics like *Detroit 9000* (1973), *Friday Foster* (1975) and this blaxploitation possession movie which, while not big on horror, pulls no punches in other regards.

In 1942 New Orleans, hustler J. D. Walker (David McKnight) stumbles across the corpse of his sister in a meatpacking plant, her throat slashed by persons unknown. Fellow gangsters, the Bliss brothers, burst in on him and, thinking he is the murderer (Elija Bliss was his sister's lover), gun him down before he can get a word in edgewise.

Thirty-odd years later, law student and cab driver Isaac Hendricks (Glynn Turman) is out on the town with his girlfriend, Christella (Joan Pringle) and some friends. They go in for a hypnotism act and Isaac is brought on stage as a volunteer. A fun time is had by all but something else happened to him on stage it seems, as Isaac begins acting mighty strange afterwards.

He becomes abusive, sexually violent and starts dressing and talking like a zoot-suited gangster of the 1940s. That's because Isaac has been possessed by the spirit of J. D. Walker and is out for revenge on the brothers who murdered him, but not without having a good time while he's at it. That spells bad news for Christella whom he slaps around and rapes before going on the rampage, murdering an old lady in his taxicab just for kicks and picking up women in bars who marvel at his old dress style and manners. And when J. D. turns nasty, he *really* turns nasty, wielding his straight razor

223

to deadly effect.

As with *Cathy's Curse*, *J. D.'s Revenge* is a possession movie that refreshingly doesn't draw heavily on *The Exorcist*. As with most hauntings, the spirit cannot be laid to rest until some terrible wrong is righted, and this is what lies at the core of *J. D.'s Revenge*. J. D. seeks out his murderer, Elija Bliss, who is now a celebrity preacher, and even gets frisky with his daughter, Roberta (Alice Jubert who also played J. D.'s sister in the flashbacks). When we stop to consider that this is his own niece, we get a real idea of just how unhinged J. D. is.

It's interesting to see the fish-out-of-water scenario of an old school gangster dropped into 1976 and highlights just how much had changed in America in thirty short years. Isaac ditching the Afro for straightened hair draws some derision from his friends and family, the celebration of natural hair being very much a part of the Civil Rights Movement which J. D. never lived to see.

Speaking of the 1970s, *J. D.'s Revenge* has some great scenes of the discos and topless bars of 1970s Bourbon Street. As with its fellow blaxploitation possession movie *Abby*, we get a real sense of downtown nightlife but *J. D.'s Revenge* feels a lot more open with scenes in taxi ranks, hospital cafeterias and police stations evoking the era nicely.

Aside from the rape and knife violence, the horror is kept to a minimum and the movie feels more like a crime thriller, although there is some effective juxtaposing of the flashbacks to the murder of J. D.'s sister with shots of cattle being slaughtered, the lidless eyes of carcasses and blood flowing down the grate which is quite unnerving. The movie is also light on the occult and the supernatural, using no special effects other than glimpses of J.D. in mirrors. The burden of conveying possession is squarely on the shoulders of Turman, and he does a magnificent job, playing two characters; the wholesome and loving Isaac and the snarling, abusive J. D.

Jekyll and Hyde is what comes to mind when seeing Turman's performance rather than *The Exorcist* and the fact that the possession is the result of a bungled hypnotism act leads us into some interesting territory. As the story develops, there is no doubt that the spirit of J. D. is real but there is the insinuation that hypnosis is an occult practice which has the potential to open doorways to the spiritual realm through which anything might come.

Being a blaxploitation movie, there's plenty of violence, naked breasts and jive talking, but at its heart, *J. D.'s Revenge* is a character driven piece which relies on acting a lot more than it does on action and effects. Turman is superb and, as we watch a thoroughly unlikable and nasty man go about getting his revenge, it's impossible to really root for him, but the tension is kept high as we have no idea of who will still be standing when the credits roll.

CRASH! (1976)

Director: Charles Band
Writer: Marc Marais

Not to be confused with David Cronenberg's 1996 adaptation of J. G. Ballard's novel of the same name, or the all-star 2004 drama about racial tensions in L.A., *Crash!* is a product of prolific director and producer of largely direct-to-video horror, Charles Band who founded the production companies Empire Pictures and Full Moon Productions, mostly famous for cult classics like *Re-Animator* (1985) and *Puppet Master* (1989). Written by Marc Marais (who's only other writing credit was for Ray Austin's 1974 *House of the Living Dead*), *Crash!* is another mashup of occult horror and car chase thrills somewhat in the spirit of *Race with the Devil*, further highlighting how the occult craze was starting to peter out in the late seventies and required a fuel injection from other genres. It also beat similar possessed car movie *The Car* to theatres by mere months which, despite hiring Anton LaVey as a 'technical advisor', really doesn't provide any explanation for its possession, occult or otherwise.

José Ferrer and Sue Lyon play unhappily married couple Marc and Kim. Marc is wheelchair bound and terminally bitter due to a car accident while Kim seems to be little more than a trophy wife. While perusing a flea market, Kim buys a strange one-eyed talisman (from character actor Reggie Nalder who starred in 1977's *Dracula's Dog* with José Ferrer which was directed by Charles Band's father, Albert), intending it as a gift for her occult-interested husband. The couple argue upon her return and Kim keeps the talisman, attaching it to her keychain and heading back out.

While driving along a country road, a Doberman

(another cast member from *Dracula's Dog*?) leaps into the car and attacks her, causing her to crash. She is able to crawl away from the wreckage (clutching her keyring) where Charles Band in a cameo, picks her up and takes her to hospital.

Kim's in a bad way, having lost her memory and is almost mummified in bandages, muttering only "Akasa" to the confusion of Dr. Martin (John Ericson) and nurse Logan (Kathy Parrish). Meanwhile, Kim's husband (who dispatched the dog to murder her) learns of her survival and makes his way to the hospital to finish the job by disconnecting her drip, which results in blood running down onto the talisman in her grip. Fortunately, nurse Logan notices in time while Dr. Martin decides to do some digging about the strange talisman that is forever in Kim's grasp. He is led to John Carradine's professor who identifies it as a representation of the Hittite goddess Akasa.

Peppered throughout this threadbare narrative, are scenes of Kim's driverless 1967 Chevrolet Camaro causing no end of destruction across the state. It is later revealed that it became possessed when Kim's blood touched the talisman. The trouble is, the car starts its rampage before this happens. This can only be explained by Charles Band using footage intended for the climactic action-filled finale to liven up the rest of the movie, thus giving us something in the way of flashforwards. It has to be admitted that he was on to something – the movie would be incredibly dull without the occasional car going up in a blazing fireball – but it confuses the narrative no end and the audience may be forgiven if they think they're watching scenes from two different movies spliced together.

The spirit of Akasa has possessed Kim who can apparently control the car from a distance as well as Marc's wheelchair which she uses to flatten the dog which nearly killed her. While Marc continues to plot the death of his wife (who, handily for him, no longer recognizes him), Kim's powers grow, leading to the movie's insane car-versus-wheelchair climax.

The car crashes are spectacular and are the movie's real draw. The rest of the movie falls flat as it makes little sense and is padded to the extreme. From the pointless bickering of an old couple before they are flattened by an out-of-control police car to a highlight reel of reused footage in the movie's climax showing us the car stunts one more time, Band spreads his butter incredibly thin. There's some real silliness too, from a dog being trained to run for miles to be at the exact place it needs to be to attack Kim, to a sauna with a lock on the outside, the movie is full of contrived nonsense. However, familiar faces, red-eyed possession, and some great car carnage rescue *Crash!* from being a complete wreck.

JADU TONA (1977)

Director: Ravikant Nagaich
Writer: Aziz Quaisi

Ravikant Nagaich directed several Hindi crime and spy thrillers but briefly turned to horror with this bizarre possession movie starring Reena Roy, who was just reaching the apex of her career in 1977. The previous year, she had starred in the hugely successful horror movie *Nagin* about mythical shapeshifting cobras which also featured Feroz Khan, one of Bollywood's top actors. The two reunited for *Jadu Tona* (also known as *Black Magic*) along with an impressive supporting cast of well-known faces of Hindi cinema.

The argument between faith and science is almost always a part of possession movies but it really takes center stage in *Jadu Tona* in the manner of juxtaposing a modern, city-dwelling family with their more rustic relatives in the countryside. Amirchand (Prem Chopra) and his daughters are westernized sceptics, constantly dropping English phrases and scoffing at the superstitions of the locals as they make their way out into the countryside to visit Amirchand's parents. Amirchand waves away a local's suggestion that they should pay their respects to the nearby sacred tree and teenage daughter Varsha (Reena Roy) refuses to touch the feet of her grandparents in the old way of respect, highlighting the generation gap between modern India and its traditional past.

The bored Varsha and her bubbly younger sister, Harsha (Baby Pinky) explore the local area resulting in the first song and dance number (oh yes, this is a *musical* possession movie). Harsha wanders into a ruined house and encounters a mysterious man who asks her to open a bottle of medicine. She does so and releases a vengeful spirit which possesses her, causing her to have a violent fit and even spew the trusty old green vomit.

Back in the city, Harsha is taken in for psychiatric evaluation by the hunky Dr. Kailash (Feroz Khan) who has no time for talk of possession. He seeks only rational answers and puts it all down to mental illness. All this is intercut with ridiculous scenes with the other patients, clearly played for laughs as they mug for the camera and talk gibberish. In fact, the movie is big on humor with all sorts of slapstick silliness going on. There are several scenes with Indian comic actor, Jagdeep including one where a roast chicken cooked by his wife comes to life on his plate. Why he is suffering from hallucinations connected to Harsha's possession is left unexplained.

Varsha's engagement is broken off by her fiancé's father who doesn't want his son getting involved with all this evil spirit stuff (and Varsha has a few choice words for him too). Fortunately the handsome doctor is dropping by several times a day to check on Harsha which gives ample opportunity for a blossoming romance (and more Bollywood musical numbers) with her big sister.

There's a lot of romance in *Jadu Tona*, as much as there is any horror. When the scary stuff does kick off, it manages to elicit a mixture of hilarity and unease at just how *out there* it all is. Harsha's fits are triggered whenever a doctor pricks her finger or if she skins her knees, resulting in her eyes rolling about like gumballs and exaggerated zoom shots before she goes off on a superhuman rampage. She also pulls the same trick Susan Barnes does in *Demon Witch Child*, namely changing her voice to impersonate others and getting them to meet her places so she can murder them.

That's because the spirit possessing Haarsha is that of Pannalal, a criminal who was betrayed and murdered by his associates, and he wants revenge. When a man's body is found in the hanging gardens with his head almost twisted off and one of Harsha's hairpins nearby, it's up to veteran of Indian cinema, Ashok Kumar as the comedic police inspector, Jolly Goodman, to find out what's going on.

With a runtime of over two hours, there's a bit of everything in *Jadu Tona*. Horror, comedy, romance, police procedural, and songs. If you don't mind choppy editing, hopeless special effects (like plastic scorpions and double exposures that barely line up) then there's some fun to be had with it. All this aside, there is perhaps a deeper significance to the movie in the context of the period in which it was made. Dr. Meraj Ahmed Mubaraki emphasizes *Jadu Tona*'s role in the cultural backlash against the secularism and modernism of 1970s India and the part it played in championing Hindu orthodoxy against scientific rationalism(5). Like *The Exorcist*, *Jadu Tona* decidedly sides with the believers in the spiritual world and, while the movie might be seen as a foreign attempt at an American trend, it utilizes the folklore and political context of its country to its benefit.

Nurse Sherri (1977)

Director: Al Adamson
Writers: Michael Bockman, Greg Tittinger and Al Adamson

Al Adamson knocked out a slew of low-rent exploitation movies in the sixties and seventies with a Corman-esque commitment to quantity over quality. Fast and cheap shockers like *Blood of Dracula's Castle* (1969) and *Horror of the Blood Monsters* (1970) showcased his desire to repackage the gothic and sci-fi cliches of the forties and fifties for new audiences, injecting them with sleaze in a more permissive era. He also jumped on contemporary trends like the biker movie in *Satan's Sadists* (1969) and *Hell's Bloody Devils* (1970). With the possession craze hitting its peak in the mid-seventies, Adamson did his own take on it, set in a hospital, resulting in something like the Corman-produced *Candy Stripe Nurses* (1974) mixed with *The Exorcist*.

It starts out like a cult movie with suited leader 'Reanhauer' (Bill Roy, who had played the villain in Adamson's 1974 blaxploitation karate movie, *Black Samurai*) and his mismatched collection of followers hanging out in the Californian desert. One of their number has recently died as Reanhauer persuaded him to stop taking his insulin shots. Ranhauer is of the evangelical preacher type cult leader rather than the Charles Manson hippie guru which is an interesting switch for Adamson who had made several biker and hippie movies, a couple of which were shot at Spahn Ranch while the Manson family were still living there.

Reanhauer attempts to demonstrate his supernatural powers by reviving the deceased cult member, but the effort nearly kills him and he ends up in a woefully understaffed hospital that seems to have only three nurses and two patients. The doctors are unable to save the preacher and his vengeful spirit possesses nurse Sherri (Jill Jacobson) as a green animated blob that looks like something from *Ghostbusters*, and I mean the cartoon, not the movies. Sherri is soon acting weird, missing lunch dates and losing track of time because she's out murdering people while her doctor boyfriend, Peter (Geoffrey Land), tries to figure out what's wrong with her.

Not that you'd understand all of this first time watching the movie because Adamson manages to create a narrative jumble by pointlessly delivering the story in flashbacks that come along too late while the first act mostly focuses on the sexual escapades of the hospital staff. It's not until much later that we find out that Sherri and Reanhauer even had a conversation during which he suggested that she was 'the one' and that he refused medical care which is why he's so pissed at the hospital staff. Some of that information might have been useful upfront. There's also the abandoned character of Stevens (J. C. Wells), a cult member who expressed second thoughts during the movie's opening and is never referred to again.

Some of the confusion is explained by the fact that there were two radically different cuts of the movie. The original, titled *Nurse Sherri,* was more of a sexploitation movie and hit drive-in theatres in 1977 while a second version called *The Possession of Nurse Sherri*, removed several of the sex scenes and replaced them with a subplot involving Stevens trying to destroy the corporeal remains of Reanhauer. But the clumsy first act is present in both movies, confounded in the *Nurse Sherri* version by a couple of titillating scenes where Peter and Sherri exchange flashbacks of their weirdest sexual encounters; hers a poolside lesbian fling with a friend and his getting sucked off while delivering a lecture by

233

somebody we hope isn't one of his students.

A subplot that is present in both versions of the movie is the relationship between black nurse Tara (Marilyn Joi, another alumnus of *Black Samurai*) and her patient, Marcus (Prentiss Moulden), an NFL champ who was blinded during a car crash. Marcus's grandmother was a Voodoo priestess so he recognizes what's up with Sherri and has just the answer; the body of Reanhauer must be exhumed and burned, leading to a spooky trip to the cemetery in the dead of night for nurses Tara and Beth.

The special effects aren't much to write home about, being almost nonexistent aside from the aforementioned green sparkly blob and some low-key gore including a decent pitchforking. *Nurse Sherri* is more of a softcore porn flick than a horror with Adamson's attentions focused far more on the naked breasts of his female cast, even moving into Carry On-style comedy in one scene in which nurse Beth gives some 'special treatment' to a patient who goes cross-eyed with pleasure.

There's quite a well-done ending in which Tara and Beth try to burn the body of Reanhauer before Sherri kills Peter in a tense race against time, but ultimately, *Nurse Sherri* can't seem to decide what sort of movie it wants to be. There are remnants of Adamson's experimentations in blaxploitation but then the movie focuses mostly on the sexual escapades of a white doctor and nurse while trying to cash in on *The Exorcist* and simultaneously present a story of a cult. The result is a silly, meandering mess. There was even a ludicrous attempt to put the movie in the blaxploitation genre when it came out on video by retitling it *Black Voodoo* and slapping an afro on Jill Jacobson on the poster.

THE CAR (1977)

Director: Elliot Silverstein
Writers: Dennis Shryack, Michael Butler and Lane Slate

Jaws on land. That was the requirement for director Elliot Silverstein who, after a prolific TV career, switched to feature films with 1965's *Cat Ballou* shortly followed by *The Happening* (1967) and *A Man Called Horse* (1970). Never mind that Steven Spielberg himself had begun his career with a Jaws-on-land movie with his 1971 TV movie *Duel* about a hapless man pursued by a homicidal truck driver.

And then there was *Crash!* which hit screens mere months before. While that movie struggled to give its possessed vehicle some backstory by way of a Hittite goddess called Akasa and a mysterious talisman, *The Car* gleefully refuses to offer any such explanation. It's an evil car much in the way that the 1983 adaptation of Stephen King's novel *Christine* portrayed its car as being inherently 'bad' with no real motive behind its actions.

James Brolin plays Deputy Wade Parent who finds himself promoted after Sheriff Peck (John Marley) gets run over by the mysterious car which thunders out of nowhere apparently set on mass murder. As well as struggling with his family life which consists of his daughters (real-life sisters Kim and Kyle Richards) and girlfriend, Lauren (Kathleen Humphries), Deputy Parent has to stop this seemingly invulnerable machine of death.

The *Jaws* influences are clear. The lawman of a small town desperately tries to protect his flock, ordering public functions to be cancelled. That doesn't stop the car from charging a band rehearsal involving Deputy Parent's daughters and girlfriend in a too-close-to-home moment reminiscent of the shark attack in

Amity's lagoon in *Jaws*. And, just like in *Jaws*, Parent heads out to hunt down and destroy the car with some explosives and the help of a drunken and unlikable old grouch (played by *Race With the Devil*'s R. G. Armstrong).

Of course, the real star is the chopped 1971 Lincoln Continental Mark III made by Hollywood custom car legend, George Barris. With no license plates, no door handles and conveniently tinted glass to hide the stunt driver, the titular car seems otherworldly in its design, as if it wasn't made by human hands. Its appearance is heralded by a gust of desert wind and, if *Jaws* relied on its iconic score, the car announces itself with a roar of its engine and celebrates each kill with a triumphant horn blast (which allegedly spells 'X' in morse code).

The kills are inventive but surprisingly bloodless, making this a PG outing but fun nevertheless. The car has a particularly sadistic sense of humor, toying with its victims, in one instance, trapping a cop in his car and slowly edging him off a cliff. It can also open its doors, whapping its victims viciously if they get too close.

Silverstein uses Utah's desert location to great effect, panoramic shots of the dusty terrain making *The Car* almost feel like a Western. With no cover to hide behind, the open landscape adds to the horror as the plume of dust streaks towards its prey like a shark's fin. It's a creepy touch accompanied by Leonard Rosenman's eerie score, which, like that of *The Shining* (1980) was based on the hymn *Dies Irae*.

The movie did itself a PR favor by hiring Church of Satan founder Anton LaVey as a 'technical advisor' (whatever that entailed). LaVey had been involved in movies before, providing a similar service on *Rosemary's Baby* and *Lucifer's Women* and even starring in *The Devil's Rain*. It's likely that having him onboard was little more than a publicity stunt for the movies he allegedly advised on and, in the case of *The Car*, it's hard to see what he could have contributed other than the quote at the beginning of the movie, somewhat altered from the "Invocation Employed Towards the Conjuration of Destruction" found in *The Satanic Bible*.

LaVey's involvement and the opening quote, along with an image of a demonic serpent as the car is finally destroyed in a fireball, are the movie's only satanic references. The car is unable to enter hallowed ground for some reason, but it's never revealed what is possessing the car or why.

As such, *The Car* is little more than dumb B movie fun, never deep enough to really earn its stripes as an occult movie, but fun enough to tag along with the satanic crowd and become a cult classic.

EXORCIST II: THE HERETIC (1977)

Director: John Boorman
Writer: William Goodheart

Rip offs of *The Exorcist* were coming out left, right and center in the latter half of the decade and, with Warner Brothers hurling lawsuits at imitators like *Abby*, it was only a matter of time before they hopped on the cash-in bandwagon and made a sequel.

A script by Broadway playwright, William Goodhart drew heavily on the philosophies of Pierre Teilhard De Chardin (the Jesuit priest William Peter Blatty modelled Father Merrin on in his original novel) who got in hot water with the Catholic Church for claiming that evolution was part of God's plan. With Oscar-nominated director John Boorman and a cast including Richard Burton and Louise Fletcher, hot after her Oscar win for *One Flew Over the Cuckoo's Nest* (1975), it's baffling how a movie with such talent behind it became such an incomprehensible mess notoriously labeled the worst sequel ever.

The heretic of the title is presumably Father Merrin, the titular exorcist from the first movie played by Max Von Sydow, whose controversial writings on the devil don't gel with the church's efforts to modernize and distance themselves from things like exorcisms. Concerned that Merrin lost his faith and may even have thrown in his lot with the devil, the Vatican charges Father Lamont (Richard Burton) to investigate his death and find out exactly what went on in that bedroom in Georgetown, Washington.

Lamont's first port of call is Regan MacNeil (Linda Blair), the subject of the first movie's exorcism. Now sixteen, Regan is living in a fancy New York penthouse with her guardian, Sharon, played by Kitty Winn who, besides Blair and a cameo from Von Sydow, is the only returning cast member from the original. Like Friedkin and Blatty, Ellen Burstyn (who played Regan's mother) wanted nothing to do with the sequel and her character is mentioned as being away on a film shoot for the duration of the movie.

Regan is dealing with the trauma of her past, suffering from nightmares and pretending to her therapist, Dr. Gene Luskin (Louise Fletcher), that she doesn't remember anything about her ordeal. Dr. Luskin uses a device that really belongs in a science fiction movie to 'synchronize brainwaves' in order for both her and Regan to delve into Regan's memories. Father Lamont has a go and suspects that the demon Pazuzu still has a hold on Regan's soul (negating Father Karras's sacrifice in the previous movie). He also learns of a young boy in Africa called Kokumo whom Father Merrin had performed an exorcism on many years ago. This necessitates a trip to Africa in search of the grown-up Kokumo (James Earl Jones) who is now a scientist working on preventing locust swarms.

In fact, locusts play a big part in the movie and we certainly see a lot of them. Kokumo explains that destructive swarms occur due to overpopulation and the brushing of one locust's wings against another which drives them into a frenzy. He is trying to breed a type of locust which can resist the brushing of wings and thereby break the chain reaction.

Locusts are also the embodiment of the demon Pazuzu who apparently is attracted to people with psychic abilities. And it is here that *Exorcist II* attempts to explain why Regan was possessed in the first place. She is a psychic healer and one of a select few who are spiritually advanced. Father Merrin believed that these individuals are the next stage in evolution and the hope for humanity which has become locust-like in its greed and ravaging of the planet.

The story is utterly confusing and annoyingly repetitive with Father Lamont going back and forth in search of something we're not too sure of. The usual culprits behind terrible movies were present in its making such as the script being rewritten while shooting and no real ending decided upon before cameras started rolling. There are some interesting ideas like the aforementioned locust analogy but they are unfortunately bungled. The juxtaposition of science and faith from the first movie is still present in the conflicting interpretations of Regan's trauma by Dr. Luskin and Father Lamont. Luskin is a rational psychologist, but her logical approach is undermined by the silliness of the brain-wave device.

Despite the nonsensical plot, Boorman does give us some interesting visuals. There's a great use of reflections to isolate characters and superimpose the past on the present but, in contrast to the almost documentary style of Friedkin, *Exorcist II* feels incredibly studio bound with an overreliance on miniatures and constructed sets, beautiful they may be. Even the house and its iconic adjacent steps from the first movie were recreated on a sound stage as permission to film at the original location was denied.

There are also some terrible flashback sequences which attempt to recreate scenes from the previous movie with Von Sydow putting in a cameo and a double as the possessed Regan (Linda Blair firmly stated that she did not want to go through the torturous make-up process a second time around). But what is most notably absent are the husky tones of Mercedes McCambridge as the voice of the demon. In all, the flashbacks to the possessed Regan feel like one of the many parodies of *The Exorcist* which was no doubt partly responsible for the reported laughter from audiences upon the sequel's release.

Linda Blair seems out of her depth this time around with the role of Regan demanding her to play an innocent teenager, a survivor of serious trauma and a seductive succubus in the movie's dumbfounding climax. Her father/daughter relationship with Father Lamont is fairly touching but Burton does seem distracted throughout, most likely due to being in the middle of his second divorce from Elizabeth Taylor and a losing battle with alcohol.

Exorcist II: The Heretic utterly lacks focus and has none of the mounting terror of the original. There are no real scares and it's arguable that it isn't even a horror movie. John Boorman, a director interested in meta-physical concepts as well as ecology crafted a strange, dream quest of a movie that focuses on the nature of the battle between good and evil when audiences really just wanted another *Exorcist*. The worst thing about this misguided sequel is that it's just so dull.

Fortunately, William Peter Blatty wrote a sequel to *The Exorcist* in 1983 called *Legion*. He directed this himself in 1990 as *The Exorcist III*, a movie not without its own troubles, but decent enough to wash out the bad taste left by *Exorcist II*, the events of which it totally ignores.

CATHY'S CURSE (1977)

Director: Eddy Matalo
Writers: Myra Clément, Eddy Matalon and Alain Sens-Cazenave

This Canadian possession chiller eschews the tropes of its brethren which had become very tired by 1977 and feels more like a haunted house flick with a touch of *The Omen* and *Audrey Rose* (which came out mere months before). There isn't a Catholic priest in sight, nor any mention of the devil meaning that *Cathy's Curse* isn't so much a *demonic* possession movie but a haunting, only in this case, the haunted is a little girl and the ghost is the spirit of her dead aunt.

We open in 1940s Montreal and a young girl called Laura has been left all alone in the house clutching her doll by her mother who has done a runner, along with little brother George, for reasons unknown. Laura's father turns up in a hell of a mood ("Your mother's a bitch!" goes the movie's favorite line). Dragging Laura with him, he tears off in his vintage car in search of his missing wife and son but there is a terrible accident and both Laura and daddy perish in a fiery inferno.

Some thirty years later, brother George (Alan Scarfe) has grown up to inherit the old house and is moving in with his wife, Vivian (Beverley Murray) and young daughter Cathy (Randi Allen). Vivian is highly strung and there is talk of the death of a newborn and a nervous breakdown, setting things up for the old 'hysterical woman nobody believes' schtick.

Little Cathy is left to her own devices and, while rummaging around in the attic, finds a creepy portrait of her dead aunt Laura and an old doll with its eyes sewn shut. What would be a major 'nope' for us adults has no effect on Cathy who takes the doll as her own and becomes very attached to it.

As expected, Cathy starts acting weird. She has telekinetic powers and is able to shatter ornaments and slam windows and doors at will. A series of unfortunate adults (all elderly for some reason) start being bumped off *Omen* style. Vivian begins to suspect that not all is well with her daughter but, as previously mentioned, a depressive housewife recovering from a nervous breakdown is believed by nobody.

There's some pretty terrible acting (apart from Randi Allen who is on point as the sweet girl-turned nasty) and a script that seems to have been written by somebody who doesn't understand how human beings interact. The dialogue is stilted and characters don't seem too phased by some extraordinary events (like Cathy vanishing into thin air right in front of her mother). Ideas are hinted at but never developed like a tray of food turning moldy and then appearing fine in the next scene, and a police detective who clearly has suspicions about the death of the housekeeper and then never turns up in the movie again.

What's most frustrating about *Cathy's Curse* is that there's so much we don't find out. Why is the spirit of Laura so keen on killing everybody? What has the doll got to do with it and why were its eyes sewn shut? Perhaps there was always something strange about Laura which caused her mother to flee with George in the first place. The most baffling thing is that nobody in the neighborhood seems to remember Laura and her death. Not once does George mention that he ever had a little sister. Perhaps he was too young to remember but, with an attic full of knickknacks including her portrait, some sort of revelation is expected at some point to give us some exposition but it never happens.

Cathy's Curse was mauled by the critics on release and vanished into obscurity for many years. It was rather unfairly regarded as an *Exorcist* knock-off but, bad acting, nonsensical plotting and shoddy editing aside, *Cathy's Curse* is an intriguing movie which could have been fairly solid if we were just told a little more about what the hell is going on.

SCHOCK/SHOCK (1977)

Director: Mario Bava
Writers: Lamberto Bava, Gianfranco Barberi and
Alessandro Parenzo

Shock was Mario Bava's last movie before his death in 1980 of a heart attack. It was made during a difficult period for Italy's horror pioneer after he had been burned by the butchering of his most personal movie, *Lisa and the Devil*. Written (and partly directed) by his son Lamberto, *Shock* stars Daria Nicolodi who, at the time, was in a relationship with Dario Argento and getting him interested in the occult while helping him conceive his masterpiece, *Suspiria*. As with *Cathy's Curse* (which also came out in 1977), *Shock* mixes the 'evil kid' genre no doubt inspired in part by *The Omen*, with the possession craze while also feeling like a haunted house movie which also enjoyed much popularity in the 1970s.

Dora (Nicolodi), her son, Marco (David Colin Jr. who had been through the whole possession thing before in *Beyond the Door*) and Dora's new husband, Bruno (*I Don't Want to be Born*'s John Steiner) move into an old house. It's rather a strange setup as Dora lived in that very house seven years ago with her previous husband, Carlo (Marco's father). She seems to have inherited it as her ex-husband has only just been declared dead, having gone missing at sea seven years previously.

There are the usual haunted house tropes; a swing moving despite there being no breeze, a piano playing itself, doors creaking open etc. More effective are the occasional instances of a moldering hand groping for Dora in what may be hallucinations. But it's the increasingly strange behavior of Marco that really gets under Dora's skin. He becomes very possessive of her, to the point of jealousy, and seems to develop sexual feelings for her, pinning her on the grass in the garden, ogling her in the shower and stealing her underwear. It's clear that he's not quite himself but who then, is influencing him?

With her pilot husband away for much of the time, Dora is left to fend for herself against supernatural forces and the murderous actions of her son. He seems to possess psychic powers, making blinds crash down and even disrupting one of his stepfather's flights by some sort of Voodoo involving the aforementioned swing. When we find out that Dora's ex-husband was an abusive drug addict, we start to wonder exactly what really happened to him and if his malevolent spirit may have possessed Marco.

There's some silliness which may draw laughs from the viewer rather than screams. A floating box cutter terrorizes Dora at once point and a piano seems to laugh as its lid opens and closes like a guffawing mouth. This is somewhat made up for by an exceedingly good jump scare in the movie's frantic climax that wouldn't be out of place in the modern *Conjuring* universe.

Shock was released as *Beyond the Door II* in the US, despite having nothing to do with *Beyond the Door* other than David Colin Jr. being in it. The plan was to scoop some of the success of *Exorcist II: The Heretic* (released that same summer) but when word of mouth and critical derision sent that movie into a nosedive at the box office, plans to release *Beyond the Door II* were shelved. It eventually limped out in the US in 1979. There was also a *Beyond the Door III* released in 1989, again, totally unconnected to the other two movies, being a retitled Italian movie originally called *Amok Train* or *Death Train*.

It's unclear how much of *Shock* was shot by Bava's

son, Lamberto, but there is a definite inconsistency to the directorial style. Bava's movies tend to work more on the psychological level and there seems to be some attempt to make *Shock* play on the old archetype of the delusional housewife. Is it all in her mind? Apparently not, as other, more visceral shots which aren't from Dora's POV, leave us with no doubt that there really is something supernatural going on. This conflict of styles along with the mishmash of genres puts *Shock* in danger of trying to be too many things but it never gets dull and Nicolodi's acting in particular, carries the movie through to its pulse-pounding finale.

The impact of Dario Argento cannot be understated (particularly in the use of Goblin-esque prog rock band, Libra which feels out of place at times). Italian horror was in a period of transition in the late seventies. The giallo movement, of which Bava was a founding father, had been changed irrevocably by Argento, but the era of the gory cannibal and zombie movies of the 1980s had not yet begun. As such, *Shock* is a solid chiller that relies on acting rather than gore but is a perfectly fine swansong for Mario Bava his body of more subtle gialli.

ALUCARDA, LA HIJA DE LAS TINEBLAS/ALUCARDA (1977)

Director: Juan López Moctezuma
Writers: Alexis Arroyo and Tita Arroyo

Mexican director Juan López Moctezuma only made six movies in a sporadic career that started in 1973 and ended in 1994. Always insistent on making movies on his own terms, he was too much of an auteur to capitalize on the success of his 1973 debut, *The Mansion of Madness*, by following it up with any attempt at a commercial career. Moctezuma only directed two more movies in the 1970s, both horror; *Mary, Mary, Bloody Mary* (1975) and the cult classic *Alucarda, la hija de las tinieblas* (1977).

Often lumped in with all the *Exorcist* rip-offs of the late seventies, *Alucarda* is an intriguing and unique little movie that caused a degree of controversy for its religious imagery and apparent criticism of the church. Although possession is at the center of its story, it's framed in a way that sets it wholly apart from *The Exorcist* and its imitators.

A brief prologue shows a woman (Tina Romero) give birth to a baby in some cobweb-shrouded crypt with a witchy-looking woman playing midwife. How she got here or what her story is isn't explained but she dies shortly after birthing 'Alucarda' (a variant of the oft-used palindrome for 'Dracula') leaving instructions for her to be delivered to the nearby convent.

Years later, teenage Justine (Susana Kamini) arrives at the convent after the recent death of her parents. She is quickly befriended by Alucarda (Tina Romero again) who has been living at the convent all her life. The relationship between the girls becomes close and

248

borders on sexual. They frolic in the woods, visit the local gypsies and investigate the ruined mausoleum where Alucarda was born. Here, they swear a pact that when they leave the mortal realm, they will do it together. Alucarda then opens the coffin belonging to her mother and *something* is released which possesses the girls.

Soon the girls are acting up, fainting during prayers and showing aversion to crucifixes. In what looks and feels like a dream sequence, the girls take part in a satanic ritual overseen by a gypsy dwarf (Claudio Brook). The devil himself shows up and there is an orgy, witnessed by the Mother Superior who seems to be seeing the whole thing in her dreams. The flailing arms of the satanic priestess matches the nun's desperate prayers in one of several scenes in the movie which deliberately draws comparisons between Christian and satanic rituals. After the girls break out into profanity and blasphemy during bible study, the priest is summoned. Deeming them possessed by Satan, an exorcism is prepared with disastrous consequences.

There is something of the vampire movie about *Alucarda*, especially when the local doctor (Claudio Brook in his second role) goes all Van Helsing and seeks out the cursed girls in the mausoleum armed with crucifix and holy water. The basic plot is reminiscent of the classic vampire story Carmilla by Sheridan Le Fanu published in 1872 (predating *Dracula* by a quarter of a century) and some of the dialogue is lifted wholesale. Known for its queer undertones, Carmilla involves the seduction of a young nobleman's daughter by the vampire Carmilla.

The church's conflation of lesbianism with satanic possession in the movie makes some pretty strong comments on the repression of sexuality by religion. It is suggested that by allying themselves with Satan, the

249

girls are liberating themselves from the shackles of the church. Alucarda even flaunts her satanic freedom to Father Lázaro (David Silva), claiming that she worships life while he worships death.

The girls might be possessed but audiences are far more likely to side with them than the religious authorities and as such, the movie evokes secular horror movies like *Witchfinder General* (1968). There are no kindly Max Von Sydows here, only fire and brimstone priests and nuns who are more interested in searching for the devil's mark on the girls' bodies and pricking them with needles than they are in saving their souls. As the nuns descend into hysteria with the fear that they too might become possessed and, in so doing, *act* as if they are, we are also reminded of Ken Russel's *The Devils*.

The problem is that Satan *is* real and a force to be reckoned with in *Alucarda*. This leads to some rather mixed messaging; on the one hand the movie seems thoroughly critical of organized and fanatical religion but on the other it totally legitimizes it by presenting the devil and all his evils as a real threat.

It's not just the message that is confused. *Alucarda*'s narrative is disjointed enough to give it a surreal flavor laced with dream logic. Alucarda's mother seemed to fear for her daughter's soul but it was the opening of her coffin that caused Alucarda's possession. Are we then to assume that she was possessed by the spirit of her mother? Also, what part do the gypsies play in it all? We see them preside over a satanic orgy in which Satan himself shows up to encourage Alucarda and Justine to drink each other's blood, but did this really happen or is it the fevered nightmare of a prejudiced nun? And what was the reason for Claudio Brook playing both gypsy hunchback and doctor?

With this kind of dream logic, Moctezuma manages

to create an atmosphere that feels nightmarish but also disconnected from time. The movie is set sometime in the 19th century but, as we spend most of the time in the catacomb-like convent, it might as well be at some point in the Middle Ages. Rather than black and white habits, the nuns are dressed in what looks like bloodied bandages and, as they are revealed to be flagellants, that may very well be the case.

As the movie reaches its climax, the shock factor is dialed right up, including a coffin full of blood, decapitations and nuns being set alight. There is a definite spectacle factor in *Alucarda* but amid all the blood and boobs, there are some interesting themes that raise the movie above the level of mere grindhouse sleaze.

DEATH BED: THE BED THAT EATS (1977)

Director: George Barry
Writer: George Barry

What was once a piece of cult folklore on the bootleg VHS circuits of the eighties and nineties became official in 2003 when George Barry's $30,000 unreleased independent movie got its first theatrical showing followed by an official home media release on DVD.

Death Bed: The Bed That Eats was shot in Detroit in 1972 with a largely Canadian cast (to dodge paying union fees) after which, writer, director and producer George Barry spent four years editing the movie and trying to get it distributed. He came close with an offer to put it out on VHS in the UK if he stumped up the cost of the credits, but he couldn't and so the movie fell into limbo.

Portland Films, a British company who put out bootleg videos (proudly claiming that they were 'So cheap they could have almost fallen off the back of a lorry!') included *Death Bed* as part of their 1983 Christmas video offer and the movie entered the realm of secondhand tapes, becoming an underground cult classic. It wasn't until 2001 that Barry (wholly unaware that his one and only movie had developed a cult following) spotted a review of it online and the wheels were set in motion to give it a belated official release.

The titular death bed is a gargantuan fourposter in a derelict mansion which it shares with a painting by 19th century Decadent artist, Aubrey Beardsley, in which the spirit of the artist is trapped (portrayed by music critic Dave Marsh and voiced by Patrick Spence-Thomas). The artist is something of a narrator, frequently scolding the bed as it devours a series of unsuspecting victims, none of whom seem to find it icky in the slightest to jump into an old bed without changing the sheets.

How exactly does a bed eat people? A yellow foam rises from the mattress and sucks down whatever it wants to be dissolved in a sickly yellow liquid below (stomach acid?). But the bed seems to have control over the whole house and can cause doors to lock and curtains to close as well as give hallucinations to anybody near it. It also destroys the house in a fit of hungry despair, causing cracks to appear and statues to cry blood, after which, it languishes in the cellar, awaiting new victims.

The bulk of the plot focuses on three hippie(ish) teens – Diane (Demene Hall), Sharon (Rosa Luxemburg) and Suzan (Julie Ritter) – who stop over at the ruined house. Suzan has recently run away from home and her brother (William Russ) is out looking for her. The bed greedily guzzles her up (snatching her PJs off first, naturally) but there's something about her friend Sharon which puts the bed off its appetite.

The artist spends the middle chunk of the movie giving us flashbacks to the bed's origins (it was created by a demon who fell in love with a mortal woman who then died) and pondering why the bed is so frightened of Sharon. There's something special about Sharon and we don't find out what until the end of the movie which, suffice to say, involves an occult ritual and unearthing the grave of the woman the demon loved, now referred to as the bed's 'mother'.

Considering its pocket change budget, *Death Bed* is an impressive feat. It doesn't get overambitious, keeping its effects simple and yet surprisingly nasty. A chain necklace sawing through a girl's neck will make many viewers squirm and the visceral munching and slurping sounds are quite off putting. It occasionally lets itself down with silliness, however. In one flashback, a gangster fires his gun into the mattress, accompanied by pathetic gunshot sound effects (the gun clearly not even loaded with blanks), and one sequence in which a victim almost escapes the bed and crawls across the floor seems to take forever.

When Suan's brother turns up and thrusts his hands into the bed only to pull them out as skeletonized digits, the flesh dissolved by the bed's stomach acid, he's more irritated than in agonizing pain ("Great. Cartilage decay" he grumbles). This must be intentional humor and indeed, the movie does occasionally make light of itself. After devouring Suzan, the bed then gobbles up her suitcase in order to get at a bottle of Pepto Bismol.

Such a ludicrous contraption as a bed that eats people could never really be taken seriously and the movie has often been ridiculed and made fun of as a 'so bad, it's good' movie. It's not brilliant of course, but there does seem to be a layer of intentional camp running through it and, considering its budget and the fact that it was a first (and only) outing in the careers of many involved, one can't help but be at least a little impressed with such an audacious effort.

SEASON OF THE WITCH: BLACK MAGIC

"Look what we have today. Young minds looking to the unknown for answers, some seeking God with great sincerity, others seeking thrills any way they can get them." – Dr. Helsford, *Blood Orgy of the She-Devils*

In the first century A.D., there lived a man in Samaria called Simon Magus who was a reported sorcerer with a large following. He was baptized by Philip the Evangelist but caused an uproar by offering two of Jesus's disciples money in exchange for the power to confer the Holy Spirit (thus originating the term 'simony'; the charge of buying or selling positions or sacred objects within the church).

This curious but brief episode found in the *Acts of the Apostles* is the earliest allusion to the mysterious figure of Simon Magus but he was influential enough to inspire a body of legends and myths over the following centuries in which he founded a Gnostic sect called the Simonians, fell in love with a prostitute from Tyre whom he held up as the reincarnation of God's 'Ennoia' (his first thought), set himself up as an alternate to Christ and, ultimately, engaged Peter the Apostle in a contest of powers before Emperor Nero during which he levitated and was brought crashing down to his death by the prayers of Peter.

Simon Magus, whoever he was, serves as an early example of the friction between religion and the occult, the contest between divine miracle and self-serving magic. Simon's influence on the Faust legend aided the development of a category of occult fiction that works on the fear not of a satanic or pagan cult, nor demonic possession, but of the lone sorcerer, the magician, the practitioner of *black magic*.

255

Simon, King of the Witches, a 1971 movie about a young hippie sorcerer who sells occult trinkets and tries to work his way up the social ladder with his end goal being godhood is a clear nod to the legend of Simon Magus. In a similar vein, AIP's *The Dunwich Horror* (1970) updated H. P. Lovecraft's short story for the counterculture and featured Dean Stockton as the offspring of a demon who seeks an occult grimoire to call back 'the old ones' while a similar demonic tome appears in the stop-motion filled student movie *Equinox* from the same year.

Sometimes the practitioner of the occult ropes in several acolytes to help carry out their dark incantations. While not exactly cults, these groups are often just kids out for kicks who inadvertently fall under the sway of somebody with much darker intentions. *Children Shouldn't Play with Dead Things* (1972) is about an amateur film group hoping to shoot a horror movie on an abandoned island but, due to the occult antics of their leader, accidentally summon a zombie uprising. *The Demon Lover* (1976) features a similar group of teenagers who tire of their leader's bombastic pretentions and are picked off one by one by a demon summoned by the vengeful sorcerer. *Psychomania* (1973) is essentially a biker zombie movie concerning a bored biker who learns the secret of immortality and encourages his minions to follow him beyond the veil of death.

Then there are the groups of youngsters who wind up on the wrong end of the occult in cursed European castles peopled by creepy inhabitants in plots reminiscent of *Scooby-Doo*. Often emerging from Italy and Spain, these movies tap into the gothic tradition of family curses, madness and sadism. *The Devil's Nightmare* (1971) plays with the motif of the seven deadly sins, dispatching its seven mismatched guests in various gruesome ways while Rosalba Neri gets more than she bargained for in *The Devil's Lover* (1972) when she and her friends spend the night at a castle purported to belong to the devil. Both *Baron Blood* (1972) and *Horror Rises from the Tomb* (1973) deal with the resurrection of evil noblemen with occult powers who then stalk the corridors of their modernized estates while *Curse of the Devil* (1973) has a 19th century nobleman cursed by a witch his ancestor executed.

The concept of the witch gained a fresh wind in the sixties and seventies courtesy of the rise of Wicca; an occult branch of the feminist movement that attempted to rehabilitate the image of the witch, dispelling negative stereotypes in favor of an empowering figure of feminine magic. With talk of 'witches covens' popping up in suburban environments, the witch, like the satanist, became a hot topic for horror movies, many of which took little notice of what the Wicca movement was trying to do and instead focused on the medieval image of the witch as a practitioner of evil.

Sensuous Sorceress (1970), *Lorna the Exorcist* (1974) and *Sex, Demons and Death* (1975) all placed the figure of the witch in starkly modern environments but retained the negative connotations while *Touch of Satan* (1971) and *Hex* (1973) conversely presented the witch as a sympathetic figure yet one to be crossed at one's peril. George A. Romero's *Season of the Witch* (1973) explored the feminist aspect of witchcraft as a tool for empowering bored and mistreated housewives.

Vampires, with their association with the devil, have always had a touch of the occult about them, even if they are rarely cast as practitioners in the same way witches are. *Disciple of Death* (1972) attempted to show a vampire as a leader of a coven of like-minded blood-suckers and Hammer desperately tried to keep its flagship series afloat by using black magic to conjure the undead count in *Dracula A.D. 1972* and insert him into a contemporary setting. AIP did something similar with *Blacula* (1972) and its sequel, *Scream Blacula Scream*, mixed things up the following year with a touch of Voodoo. The emergence of the blaxploitation genre in the 1970s saw several horror movies use Voodoo as a source of occult power. Baron Samedi had become a household name after appearing as a villain in the 1973 James Bond movie *Live and Let Die* with a similar incarnation in *Sugar Hill* the following year which was one of several zombie movies of the decade which returned to its pre-Romero occult roots. More zombies appeared in *Vengeance of the Zombies* (1973) and *Devil's Kiss* (1976), ditching the Voodoo for a more generic brand of witchcraft.

Another kind of zombie-in-all-but-name continued to lurch its way across screens despite appearing increasingly crusty amid the wave of new horror. Mummy movies started under the stewardship of Universal Pictures with Hammer Productions carrying the torch into the era of color. Always involving ancient curses, forbidden texts and occult dabbling, the mummy movie rarely offered much variation on the theme, with each installment almost feeling like a remake of the last. The final Hammer mummy movie, *Blood from the Mummy's Tomb*, crept onto screens in 1971 and ad-dressed concerns of mummy fatigue by not actually having a mummy in it. Paul Naschy, ever one to lovingly pay homage to the years of gothic cinema, made *The Mummy's Revenge* in 1973 which did have a mummy and every other trope besides.

Stock horror figures like vampires and zombies might be far-fetched concepts, but their increased association with black magic in the 1970s was a symp-tom of an era in which very real concerns surrounded the occult. Werewolves and mummies might not be real, but witches apparently were, and, in an era that

258

saw a boom in occult bookshops that sold crystal balls and tarot cards alongside academic books on every subject of esoteric knowledge, when Time Magazine pondered the occult revival as a response to the failures of science and reason, the young generation's interest in black magic was, for many, both perplexing and frightening. From Simon Magus to teenagers drawing pentagrams and idolizing Aleister Crowley, the long history of people striving for occult knowledge has been seen as disturbing, rebellious and, potentially, liberating. And for movie producers, the thought of youngsters dabbling in the occult was a positive grimoire of horror movie potential.

THE DUNWICH HORROR (1970)

Director: Daniel Haller
Writers: Curtis Hanson, Henry Rosenbaum, Ronald Silkosky

By 1960, Roger Corman had made a name for himself directing cheap black and white movies for American International Pictures (AIP) which were distributed as double features. With each movie shot over ten days for less than $100,000, this low budget formula was profitable but had begun to wear thin. Corman, a life-long fan of Edgar Allan Poe, approached AIP's executives James H. Nicholson and Samuel Z. Arkoff with the idea of spending his next budget on one movie, shot in widescreen and in color over fifteen days instead of ten. A more lavish production like this might be able to compete with the popular foreign movies of the time like Britain's Hammer productions and Italy's *giallo* films. The subject? Poe's classic short story, *The Fall of the House of Usher*.

House of Usher (1960) starring Vincent Price was a huge success and more Poe adaptations followed with the ever-economical Corman recycling sets and footage to bring these public domain stories to life. But even the most generous Poe fan would struggle to recognize much of the master of the macabre's work in some of them which gleefully used the titles of Poe's stories but not much of their plots. A case in point is *The Haunted Palace* (1963) which takes its name from one of Poe's poems but was actually an adaptation of H. P. Lovecraft's story *The Case of Charles Dexter Ward*.

After five Poe adaptations, Corman had wanted to branch out into Lovecraft but AIP, keen to continue the Poe cycle, had changed the movie's title without Corman's agreement (just one example of studio meddling that drove Corman away from AIP to form his own production-distribution company, New World Pictures, in 1970). Nevertheless, there were a couple of other AIP efforts to bring Lovecraft to the screen. 1965's *Die, Monster, Die!* is a loose adaptation of *The Color Out of Space* and in 1970 they distributed Tigon's British Film Productions *Curse of the Crimson Altar* (1968) as *The Crimson Cult* which claimed to be inspired by Lovecraft's *Dreams in the Witch House*.

An adaptation of Lovecraft's classic *The Dunwich Horror* had been in the works since 1963. Daniel Haller, production designer on several of Corman's Poe movies, had gone on to direct AIP's previous Lovecraft adaptation, *Die, Monster, Die!*. After helming a couple of biker pictures to ride on the coattails of Corman's successful *The Wild Angels* (1966), he returned to Lovecraft country to direct *The Dunwich Horror* with Corman as a producer. The updating of this tale of witchcraft and demonic pregnancies to a modern setting was no doubt encouraged by the success of *Rosemary's Baby* (1968), along with the decidedly un-Lovecraftian addition of a female protagonist.

Sandra Dee's days as the wholesome star of *Gidget* (1959) were well behind her and she had finally got out of her suffocating contract with Universal leaving her free to pick her own roles. Here she plays Nancy, a student at the Miskatonic University in Arkham. Her professor is Dr. Henry Armitage (Ed Begley) who entrusts her with returning the dreaded *Necronomicon* to the library; a grimoire so rare and dangerous that it is kept in a glass case.

It is then that Wilbur Whateley enters, described by Lovecraft as 'exceedingly ugly' and 'goatish'. Here he is a handsome but odd Manson-esque occultist played by Dean Stockwell, a former child star who had ditched acting for the love-ins of the Topanga Canyon hippie set, rubbing shoulders with Neil Young and Dennis Hopper before playing a bit part in AIP's hippiesploitation flick *Psych-Out* (1968).

Wilbur is after the *Necronomicon* and Nancy, seemingly falling for his hypnotic eyes, agrees to let him look at it, much to the disapproval of her librarian friend Elizbeth (Donna Baccala). Dr. Armitage arrives to intervene and apparently knows the Whateley family of Dunwich and the rumors that surround them.

When Wilbur 'misses' his bus home, Nancy agrees to drive him back to Dunwich. He invites her in for tea (which he drugs) and then sabotages her car, effectively stranding her with him in his family's creepy old mansion. Nancy suffers vivid nightmares of pagan rituals in the old AIP tradition of filters, dry ice and Vaseline-smeared lenses.

Concerned that Nancy never returned home, Dr. Armitage and Elizabeth travel to Dunwich to find out what's going on. They meet Nancy and Wilbur and are alarmed to learn that she has agreed to spend the weekend with Wilbur. After doing some asking around in the town, they discover how much the locals hate the Whateleys and with good reason too. Wilbur needs Nancy and the *Necronomicon* for an occult ritual that will bring back 'the Old Ones'; monstrous gods from another dimension.

Sadly, Sandra Dee has little to do here other than be a catatonic victim for most of the movie in which she is drugged, raped and abused in hideous occult rites. Considering the oppressive contract Universal had her locked into for the early part of her career (studio execs wouldn't allow her to smoke or drink in public in case it ruined her wholesome image), it doesn't feel like she found the freedom she desired in *The Dunwich Horror*.

The movie really belongs to Dean Stockton doing his Charlie Manson bit and it's not a great stretch to wonder if he ever crossed Manson's path during his Topanga Canyon days (Neil Young certainly did).

The movie is a little slow and the script leaves a lot to be desired, but it scores high on the visuals even if Lovecraft's New England looks decidedly Californian due to the movie being shot in Little River, Mendocino County. Haller's days of creating the gothic, gloomy sets for Corman's Poe outings serve him well here as the Whateley mansion is cluttered with oddities. The surreal dream sequences and psychedelic colors of the monster's final rampage and the animated title credits are particularly impressive.

Skräcken har 1000 ögon/Sensuous Sorceress (1970)

Director: Torgny Wickman
Writers: Inge Ivarson and Torgny Wickman

Sweden's reputation as a sexually liberated society dates back to the 1950s with *One Summer of Happiness* (1951) and *Summer with Monika* (1953) courting controversy with their scandalous scenes of nudity. Although serious drama movies, they were distributed in the US to grindhouses and drive-ins as well as arthouses, with lurid promotion focusing on their titillating aspects. An appetite for 'Swedish sin' developed in the 1960s with *I, a Woman* (1965) and *I Am Curious (Yellow)* from 1967 pushing boundaries and inciting protests and heated debates over obscenity (as well as making buckets of cash).

Often posing as educational films, these quasi-documentaries fed sensational appetites as the sexual revolution hit its stride in the US. Torgny Wickman's *Language of Love* (1969) is notable for being the first mainstream movie to depict a real act of sex. Wickman followed this up with *Eva: Diary of a Half Virgin* (1969) starring Solveig Andersson who would make a name for herself in similar movies including *Swedish Wildcats* (1972) and *Wide Open* (1974). Before that, she worked with Wickman on a couple of other movies, one of which was *The Lustful Vicar* (1970); a sex comedy about a witch who curses a vicar with a permanent erection and *Skräcken har 1000 ögon*; an attempt to blend Swedish sexploitation with occult horror.

Skräcken har 1000 ögon literally means 'Fear has a 1000 eyes' but was released in the US with the more fitting title of *Sensuous Sorceress*. It's the story of

Swedish couple Sven (Hans Wahlgren and Anna (Anita Sanders, who had starred in several Italian movies including Frederico Fellini's *Juliet of the Spirits* in 1965) returning to their home in northern Sweden. Anna is pregnant and, utilizing an all-too familiar trope, is mentally fragile and seems to have spent some time in an institution, so we can just tell that whatever happens to her isn't going to be believed by a soul. Anna's friend, Hedvig (Solveig Andersson), comes to stay to help Anna out during her pregnancy.

Pretty soon, strange things start to happen. A glowing hand creeps about at night, scaring both Anna and the neighbors. It's clear from the get-go that Hedvig is the cause of it, having dipped her gloved hand in phosphorous. For reasons as yet unclear, Hedvig is using Anna's vulnerability to manipulate her into thinking she is going insane. In one scene, she swaps a pair of baby leggings Anna is knitting with a three-legged set, causing Anna to scream and faint. There is also black magic afoot with Hedvig jabbing pins into dolls she is making and, in one case, a knife into a loaf of bread that resembles a local man's face, killing him.

She also starts to play sexual games, donning a blonde wig and making love to Sven in the middle of the night as he sleeps in the guest room, thinking that she is Anna. Hedvig is also clearly attracted to Anna, evidenced by some soft-core lesbian action in the movie's climax in which both Sven and Anna are under Hedvig's control. The eroticism is kept pretty low with shots of breasts and buttocks but nothing that would place *Sensuous Sorceress* in the highest tier of Swedish sin.

It's a slow-moving domestic drama for the most part, spiced up with a few sex scenes and a bit of horror towards the end involving a decapitated body and inverted crosses carved into flesh during the climactic orgy. There's some interesting discourse on the similarities between Christian rituals and occultism but little else to add any depth to the proceedings.

For the most part, the story meanders along, failing to follow up on anything interesting such as the doctor noticing that Hedvig is wearing an inverted crucifix in her x-rays, or Sven finding a box containing human finger bones (presumably belonging to Hedvig). Equally vague is Hedvig's motivations. She murders her way through the movie without any apparent goal in mind other than sexually enjoying both Anna and Sven. Copying *Rosemary's Baby* would have been an obvious choice, but Anna's pregnancy is left unaddressed and is included in the plot purely to cover for her fragile state and delusions.

As an erotic horror movie, *Sensuous Sorceress* fails on both fronts being neither scary nor particularly erotic. It makes up for this somewhat with the cold, bleak Swedish atmosphere and its 1970s trappings which will no doubt appeal to connoisseurs of the sleazier, low budget side of the era.

EQUINOX (1970)

Directors: Jack Woods, Dennis Muren and Mark Thomas McGee
Writers: Mark Thomas McGee and Jack Woods

In 1967, future visual effects wizard Dennis Muren, winner of several Oscars for his work with ILM on *The Empire Strikes Back* (1980) and *Jurrassic Park* (1993) among others, was fresh out of high school and eager to make a start in the business. He managed to raise $6,500 and, with stop-motion animators Dave Allen and Jim Danforth, made a 71-minute, 16mm occult monster movie. It was called *The Equinox: Journey into the Supernatural* and attracted the attention of producer Jack H. Harris (responsible for 1958 cult classic *The Blob*). Harris hired editor Jack Woods to shoot ten more minutes of footage to make it feature length, rearranged it a little, and released it in 1970 as *Equinox*.

A man called David (Edward Connell) winds up in a psychiatric hospital after being hit by a car and the movie unfolds via his flashbacks. David and his friend Jim (Frank Bonner), along with Jim's girlfriend Vicki (Robin Christopher) and a blind date for David called Susan (Barbara Hewitt) head up into the mountains to visit David's professor, Dr. Arthur Waterman (played by legendary sword and sorcery writer Friz Leiber).

They find the professor's cabin destroyed and can see no trace of him. After hearing evil cackling from a nearby cave, the gang unfathomably decide to investigate. Within the cave, they come across a crazy old man who gives them a book filled with occult symbols. There's a lot of sitting about having a picnic and examining the book in the first half of the movie. Gargantuan exposition dumps reveal that Dr. Waterman was using the book to bridge the gap between worlds and there are descriptions of various demons which dwell beyond the barrier, one of which was a giant cephalopod which destroyed his house.

Things pick up in the second half as the gang are accosted by a series of demons from the book. This is the good stuff. The monsters are animated with stop-motion and have the look and feel of Ray Harryhausen's creations (apart from a green giant which is disappointingly not stop-motion but an actor in a costume). The monsters want the book back, as does the local park ranger (played by the director, Jack Woods) who calls himself Asmodeus (subtle!).

Equinox certainly feels like a Harryhausen creature feature but, while the master of stop-motion's monsters tended to be of the sword and sandal variety, *Equinox* has an occult vibe to it that perfectly suits the period in which it was made. Considering most of it was shot in 1967, before *Rosemary's Baby*, it preceded the occult mania, and even features a couple of demonic possessions. The gang learn that they have to protect themselves with occult signs and fashion some from willow twigs (all except Susan who has a cross which is apparently just as good). The book itself is a dead ringer for Lovecraft's *Necronomicon* and the movie bridges the gap between the monster movies of the fifties and sixties and the occult-themed horror of the post-counterculture revolution such as *Phantasm* (1979) and *The Evil Dead* (1981), both of which bear some resemblance to *Equinox*.

But in all honesty, the only reason to watch *Equinox* is to enjoy the early stop-motion efforts of several men who would go on to become titans in the visual effects field. Everything else about the movie is sub-par. From the one-note characters played by actors who were all but amateurs to the lackluster direction and cinematography, without the charm of its monsters, *Equinox*

would be even more obscure and forgotten that it
already is.

SIMON, KING OF THE WITCHES (1971)

Director: Bruce Kessler
Writer: Robert Phippeny

Black masses! Incantations! Ceremonial sex! The psychedelic posters for this obscure entry that came out at the tail end of the hippie period make it out to be a lot saucier (and more exciting) than it actually is. It's a difficult movie to place in any genre. It's not scary or gruesome enough to be horror, nor is it funny enough to be comedy. It is perhaps a satire of the occult movement or maybe a parody of the movies it inspired. It's quite possible that *Simon, King of the Witches* attempts to be all of these things.

Simon Sinestrari (Andrew Pine) is a low-grade ceremonial magician living in the storm drains of Los Angeles. He earns a crust by fashioning occult trinkets and selling them to wealthy socialites at parties. After being arrested for vagrancy, Simon befriends male prostitute Turk (George Paulsin) and, upon their release, takes him under his wing as a combination of servant, chauffeur and companion.

While seen as a joke by some and a con artist by others, Simon is deadly serious and seeks to increase his powers to godhood by working his way up the social ladder. He sparks up a relationship with trendy stoner Linda (Brenda Scott) who turns out to be the daughter of the District Attorney which inevitably doesn't go down so well with daddy.

When Simon is given a bum check after performing a tarot reading, he 'curses' the man who then dies after a falling plant pot lands on his head. The low-key nature of Simon's powers (indicated only by the presence of a glowing red light) is what makes the movie's 'magic' seem a little more grounded in the real world as opposed to other movies, leaving the possibility that it could all be smoke and mirrors. It's unclear for a good portion of the movie whether or not Simon is a phony (and that might have been an interesting movie in itself) but by the halfway mark, it becomes clear that Simon is the real deal and that's when the movie shifts gear.

Simon gatecrashes a witches' coven and ridicules their leader (played by Andy Warhol superstar, Ultra Violet) and then tricks a partygoing gentleman into taking part in his rituals. Simon's stoner buddies urge him to bump off a troublesome narc while Linda's father tries to frame Simon as a drug pusher. There's also a plotline involving police corruption. With all this going on, Simon is constantly distracted in his ploy to depart this dimension and take his place in the cosmos which makes for quite a meandering plot. With this in mind, it's almost possible to see the movie as a parable for the counterculture in general in which the lofty pretensions of the hippies became mired in sex, drugs and ultimately, murder.

That said, there's a fair bit of humor. When Simon chalks a pentagram on the wall of his new apartment, his landlord says; "Please don't think I'm prejudiced, Rabbi." Later, Simon uses his magic to give Turk an erection which he can't get rid of until Simon threatens to lop it off with his knife (his erection quickly disappears 'just like magic').

It's easy to criticize the movie for the banality of its protagonist and early Doctor Who era special effects but Andrew Pine's performance is almost convincing enough to make it work. Simon is a ceremonial magician rather than a man with superhuman powers and he employs psychology and psychodrama to cast his 'spells' just as occult practitioners do in real life. The movie simply hints at what might happen if such people really did have command over supernatural forces.

But this doesn't help the movie's unfocused script and long scenes of dialogue which sadly feel like filler. Despite a lengthy career in TV directing episodes for *Mission: Impossible*, *The Monkees* and *CHiPs* among others, director Bruce Kessler's only other feature films were *Angels from Hell* and *Killers Three* (both 1968). *Simon, King of the Witches* certainly feels like it belongs on the small screen, never providing much to look at other than colorful clothes and primitive light effects amid the humdrum knife twirling and occult mumbo jumbo.

Simon, King of the Witches was double billed with the fantastically titled *Werewolves on Wheels* but even that couldn't save it at the box office. It bombed and vanished into obscurity for several decades. It has received minor cult status in recent years but not enough to become a full-blown cult movie.

THE TOUCH OF SATAN (1971)

Director: Don Henderson
Writer: James E. McLarty

Director Don Henderson's only other movies were a couple of exploitation flicks for Crown International Pictures produced by (and starring) George E. Carey; *The Babysitter* (1969) and *Weekend with the Babysitter* (1970), both of which were written by James E. Mc Larty. A third entry in the trio of Carey/Henderson/McLarty productions was this regional folk horror rereleased under a slew of alternate titles such as *Curse of Melissa*, *Touch of Melissa* and *Night of the Demon* (not to be confused with the 1957 *Night of the Demon*; a British adaptation of M. R. James's *Casting the Runes* which was released as *Curse of the Demon* in the US).

College boy Jodie Lee Thompson (Michael Berry) is taking some time out before joining his father's law firm and is driving around the US in his Ford Maverick. He stops by an idyllic pond to eat his lunch and is approached by the young and pretty Melissa (Emby Mellay). Romantic tension builds and Jodie is invited back to the family walnut farm (which city slicker Jodie amusingly refers to as a 'walnut ranch').

But Melissa and her parents harbor a dark secret. Melissa's great grandmother, Lucinda (Jeanne Gerson), horribly disfigured from a fire in her childhood, lives with them and has a tendency to sneak out at night and murder people with farm implements. Melissa's parents, Luther (Lee Amber) and Molly (Yvonne Winslow) are at first hesitant to welcome Jodie, but Melissa gradually wins them around with talk about Jodie being 'the one'.

Jodie ends up staying for what feels like a few days. He learns that the local townsfolk think Melissa is a witch. They're not wrong as we find out that Melissa is

127-years old and Lucinda is actually her sister. Back in the 1850s, the townsfolk tried to burn Lucinda as a witch (a little improbable by the 19th century). Melissa made a pact with the devil to save her sister and extinguished the fire with her powers but was cursed with immortality which can only be undone if she has sex with a man who loves her. Apparently, it took her over a century to find the right man for the job.

The plot raises more questions than it answers such as why Lucinda aged into a decrepit old lady while Melissa stayed young and why Lucinda feels the need to randomly kill people. Another thing that is never explained is who the hell Luther and Molly are, as they sure aren't Melissa's parents. Some well-meaning couple roped into protecting a witch's pact with the devil? Perhaps they are Melissa's own children who now appear older than her? What could have been another interesting aspect to the plot is unfortunately left unmined.

It's a nicely shot movie (which shouldn't be surprising considering that its cinematographer, Jordan Cronenweth, went on to lens *Blade Runner*). The sun-dappled pastoral scenes belie the darkness underneath which only adds to the folk horror feel of the movie. The most shocking scene, in which Lucinda butchers a cop with a hay hook, happens in broad daylight and is followed by a great 360-degree shot that circles Melissa as she sinks to her knees in appalled desperation.

Perhaps the most interesting aspect of *Touch of Satan* is its sympathy for its witch which is at odds with most occult horror movies. Far from being an evil satanist who uses black magic for material gain, Melissa is forced into making a pact with the devil to save her sister who is a victim of small-minded prejudice. When faced with the angry mob who want to destroy everything they don't understand, it's hard not to side with

274

the witch.

Touch of Satan has an interesting story at the heart of it and some memorable scenes with a chilling ending but is too lumbering in getting to the good stuff. Horror fans will find their patience tested by what feels like a TV episode stretched into a feature presentation with plenty of long pauses and walks in meadows amid some truly awful dialogue such as Melissa pointing to a pond and saying, "This is where the fish lives". It's worth sticking around for the ending, though.

BLOOD FROM THE MUMMY'S TOMB (1971)

Director: Seth Holt
Writer: Christopher Wicking

Blood from the Mummy's Tomb was Hammer Film Productions' fourth and final mummy movie in a run they started with 1959's *The Mummy* (itself a remake of Universal's 1940 movie *The Mummy's Hand*). Loosely based on Bram Stoker's 1903 novel *The Jewel of Seven Stars*, *Blood from the Mummy's Tomb* doesn't really feature a mummy, despite its title, and is more concerned with ancient Egyptian sorcery, possession and reincarnation.

Veteran of many a Carry On movie and star of Hai Karate aftershave commercials, Valerie Leon, plays Margaret Fuchs, the daughter of a famed Egyptologist who is suffering nightmares of an ancient sorceress who was buried alive in a tomb by Egyptian priests (who cut off her hand and throw it to the jackals). These symptoms are worsened when her father, Julian Fuchs (Andrew Keir), gives her an enormous ruby ring from one of his expeditions.

When Julian Fuchs is attacked by an unknown force in his study leaving him comatose, his old expedition partner-turned-rival, Corbeck (a dastardly James Villiers) turns up to fill us in on what all this is about. Years ago, Fuchs, Corbeck and three others discovered the tomb of Tera, a wicked Egyptian sorceress and previous owner of the ruby ring (which they find on a severed hand near the sarcophagus). When Fuchs read the name 'Tera' on the ring, his wife back in England died giving birth to their daughter, Margaret.

Tera is gradually exerting her influence over Margaret and, while it's not fully a possession (Margaret is still in control of her senses), she is using her as a tool to collect the necessary items for her resurrection. These are sacred relics from her tomb in the form of a snake, a cat and a jackal's skull, each owned by the other members of the expedition. Also necessary is the Scroll of Life which Corbeck has found along with Tera's missing hand. Corbeck is in league with Tera and wants to bring her back but, by doing so, Margaret will die.

There are altogether too many MacGuffins in *Blood from the Mummy's Tomb* and a general confusion about what they all mean. Fuchs doesn't seem to understand the ring's power as he gives it to Margaret as a protective talisman when all it seems to do is strengthen her connection to Tera. Tera needs the sacred relics from her tomb to resurrect fully but the relics come to life and kill their owners before making their way to the Fuchs household of their own volition so why does she need to seek them out in person?

There is also some ambiguity as to the link between Margaret and Tera. Both are played by Valerie Leon suggesting reincarnation (as is so often the plot of mummy movies) but Margaret is also possessed by Tera, begging the question why Leon had to play both. Adding to the confusion is the perfectly preserved body of Tera (minus a hand) which Julian Fuchs has brought home from Egypt and kept in a shrine in his house. With a perfectly good body available, why does Margaret need to be possessed at all?

Part of the reason for the movie's incoherence may be down to its difficult production. Peter Cushing was initially cast in the role of Julian Fuchs but, after a single day of shooting, learned that his wife had been diagnosed with emphysema and left the movie with Keir taking over his role. Producer Howard Brandy and writer Christopher Wicking had a falling out resulting in Wicking being barred from the set and director Seth Holt died of a heart attack on set with one week of shooting left. It was left to Hammer executive Michael Carreras to finish the movie, cobbling together what Holt had shot with new scenes into some sort of narrative.

The contemporary setting and low-level nudity show this as part of Hammer's attempts to modernize in the early seventies, ditching the period dress of their earlier success to better compete with horror coming out of America. But the movie hardly capitalizes on the modern setting (unlike they would do in the following year's *Dracula A.D. 1972*), with most scenes taking place in dim basements, cluttered studies and a grim asylum where one of the expedition's survivors (George Coulouris) is locked up with only occasional glimpses of the foggy English suburbia of the 1970s.

There's some good visceral horror which is fairly strong for 1971. Fresh blood oozing from the stump of Tera's wrist is well done and there are several nasty throat gashes. The animal kills wisely avoid the use of rubber snakes and puppet cats, instead relying on shadows and suggestion amid wind machines and lightning effects. The movie does, however, include one of the most unconvincing car crashes in cinema history involving a car which is clearly standing completely still moments before ploughing into a tree.

Blood from the Mummy's Tomb, although mis-named, is a stylish, atmospheric movie with good performances let down by a muddled narrative and confusing character motivations. A little slow in parts, it at least offers an original take on the mummy genre which had become formulaic even in Universal's days.

LA PLUS LONGUE NUIT DU DIABLE/THE DEVIL'S NIGHTMARE (1971)

Director: Jean Brismée
Writers: Pierre-Claude Garnier, Patrice Rhomm and Jean Brismée

Not too many horror movies have come out of Belgium, *Daughters of Darkness* (1971) and *Rabid Grannies* (1988) being notable examples. Even *La plus longue nuit du diable*, given the generic and slightly nonsensical title of *The Devil's Nightmare* in the US, was a co-production with Italy and it certainly looks and feels like something Mario Bava would have made.

Berlin, 1945. As the allies bomb the city, Baron von Rhoneberg (Jean Servais) hides in a bunker (Hitler is presumably in a similar predicament nearby). Also present is his wife who is in labor. She dies giving birth to a girl which the baron then murders by sticking his knife into it in a contender for most shocking movie opening ever.

Is this part of the Nazi mass suicide in the face of defeat? Nope, it's to do with a curse on the Von Rhoneberg family after an ancestor in the Middle Ages made a pact with the devil resulting in the first-born girl of every generation turning into a succubus. Decades later, a tourist bus filled with colorful characters turns up at the baron's castle (Antoing Castle in Belgium) seeking shelter from a storm.

As the guests are shown to their rooms by the scarred-faced butler (Maurice de Groote), who fills them in on the various grisly deaths that have plagued members of the Von Rhoneburg family, we spend an awful lot of time getting to know the odd collection of not-so-happy campers. There's the gluttonous bus driver Ducha (Christian Maillet), bickering married couple Howard and Nancy (Lorenzo Terzon and Colette Emmanuelle), the perpetually grumpy old man Mason (Lucien Raimbourg), mild-mannered priest in training Alvin (Jacques Monseau) and gorgeous young ladies Corrine and Regine (Ivanna Novak and Shirley Corrigan) who immediately engage in lesbian sex as soon as their door is closed in a lengthy scene which seems to be entirely inconsequential to the plot, dragging the movie into the realm of Euro-sleaze.

It's surprising that Brismée resorted to such a cheap money shot in a movie that otherwise relies on atmosphere and slow burn chills. Once the guests have departed the dining room for coffee, port and chess in the parlor, the movie begins to drag with occasional stock horror movie tropes such as the storm knocking out the electricity and blood dripping from the ceiling (which turns out to be from a dead cat in the torture chamber in the attic). Things are livened up somewhat by the arrival of an eighth guest, the stunning redhead Lisa (Erika Blanc, star of many Italian horrors including Mario Bava's *Kill, Baby, Kill*).

It becomes clear that Lisa is the succubus of the curse that has plagued the Von Rhonebergs (although how she is connected to the family is saved for the movie's end). We then enter slasher territory as the guests are pursued by Lisa through the castle and offed in various interesting ways including being guillotined, shoved in an iron maiden and even drowned in gold dust (the baron is an alchemist and has a cellar full of hokey-looking apparatus for the turning of lead into gold).

Although it sags in the middle as we are forced to watch unlikable characters play chess and discover that all the doors to the castle are locked, *The Devil's Nightmare* is heavy on the atmosphere with its gothic location put to good use. The colors are vibrant and, although the death scenes are quick and fairly bloodless, they are pulled off without looking too hokey. Erika Blanc is fantastic as the haunting succubus Lisa, switching between seductive beauty and pallid, dark-eyed ghoul when she is required to murder. She even looks genuinely concerned as she dispatches the guests in gruesome ways, suggesting that she is a reluctant tool trapped in her role.

Many of the movies in this book seem to side with Christianity and have been accused as bordering on religious propaganda in which the devil is a real force of evil and can be combatted by priests armed with bibles and crucifixes. *The Devil's Nightmare* definitely fits into that category with seminarian Alvin standing in for the warrior in a dog collar fighting against the forces of evil. As for his fellow guests, they are such an unlikable bunch that we can't help feeling that they get their just desserts. There's even an ironic line from doomed grouch Mason who declares at the dinner table; "I'm an atheist, thank God!" It's no accident that the number of guests is seven either, with each of them representing one of the seven deadly sins and their deaths have a certain correspondence to them decades before David Fincher gave us *Seven* (1995).

The Devil's Nightmare was released under several titles on video in the 1980s like *Succubus, The Devil Walks at Midnight, Nightmare of Terror, Castle of Death and The Devil's Longest Night* with most releases cutting the lesbian scene between Novak and Corrigan.

DISCIPLE OF DEATH (1972)

Director: Tom Parkinson
Writers: Tom Parkinson and Mike Raven

Jack-of-all-trades Austin Churton Fairman rose to fame during that strange British phenomenon of the 1960s when pirate radio stations broadcasted popular music (which wasn't catered for by the BBC) from offshore ships and disused sea forts. Using the pseudonym Mike Raven, Fairman eventually became a Radio 1 DJ with a penchant for rhythm and blues and was influential in the promotion of African American music in the UK. In 1971, his interest in the occult led him into the horror movie business where he starred in *I, Monster* for Amicus Productions and was cast as Count Karnstein in Hammer's *Lust for a Vampire*.

That he was inexplicably dubbed in Hammer's follow up to *The Vampire Lovers* (1970) must have stung for Raven had the deep baritone that, along with his tall, dark suaveness, almost gave Christopher Lee a run for his money. It was an image he cultivated, often dressing in black complete with cape and allowing his curious interests to be used for the purposes of promoting the movies he starred in. He even stumped up part of the cash for a low-budget shocker for Glendale Film Productions; *Crucible of Terror* (1971), a whodunnit proto-slasher in which Raven plays a curmudgeonly artist who hosts various hip types in his windswept Cornish cottage only for them be picked off one by one by persons unknown.

Crucible of Terror wasn't a financial success but that didn't stop Raven from taking another stab at horror stardom, this time taking on joint writing and production duties while *Crucible*'s producer, Tom Parkinson, directed. The result was *Disciple of Death*, a movie very much in the vein of *Witchfinder General* (1968) and *Blood on Satan's Claw*. Set in the 18th century, *Disciple of Death* keeps the Cornwall setting of *Crucible of Terror* (Mike Raven fell in love with the coastal area and moved his family there). Star crossed lovers, Julia (Marguerite Hardiman) and Ralph (Stephen Bradley) meet in secret as Julia's family don't approve of Ralph and his meager means. The lovers decide to cut their thumbs and make a blood tryst but unfortunately a drop lands upon the stone they are sitting on, and they inadvertently resurrect a dark man known only as 'The Stranger' (Mike Raven).

The Stranger poses as a man from foreign parts who has returned to claim his inheritance, namely the nearby abandoned manor. Taking quite a fancy to Julia, the Stranger strikes up a friendship with her. This is concerning as young women have started going missing in the immediate area, including Ralph's twin sister, Ruth.

The Stranger is up to shady occult business. With the help of some pasty-faced young virgins in night-dresses, he sacrifices Ruth before the Sigil of Baphomet, cutting out her heart in a surprisingly grisly scene which didn't make it into the UK theatrical release.

While many movies of this ilk leave us wondering exactly what the bad guy's endgame is other than general skullduggery, the Stranger helpfully outlines his plans for us; "My task on Earth is to supply my master Satan with an endless line of virgin sacrifices, unless I find a maiden willing to accept death and spend eternity with me in my dark place in the depths of Hell!" Naturally, he has his eye on Julia for this role and, as Julia gradually falls under his seduction, the possibility of her agreeing to this shady deal increases.

The local parson (Ronald Lacey who had starred in *Crucible of Terror* and would become most famous for his turn as the Nazi, Arnold Toht, in *Raiders of the Lost Ark*) is having none of this and teams up with Ralph to foil the Stranger's dastardly plans. They recruit the aid of the Jewish sorcerer Melchisidech (Nicholas Amer) who comes across as more of a children's entertainer than anything from an actual horror movie. The parson reluctantly accepts the need to use the occult to defeat the occult. "Trinity Shminity. This is none of your Christian schmattas. This is your kosher yiddische magic!" says Melchisidech before giving them some magical talismans (a flask of holy water, a bag of sand and a gold talisman). The movie then enters family friendly sword and sorcery territory as the Stranger summons a spell-casting dwarf (Rusty Goffe) to thwart our brave heroes as they traipse across the Cornish landscape on their quest to defeat him.

Mike Raven is a hammy theatre villain but is more than adequate in the role, clearly trying to out-Dracula Christopher Lee, alternating between dark, seductive aristocrat by day and powder-haired (and slightly blue) vampire by night. The occasional use of sudden closeups of his bloodshot eyes border on fairly effective jump scares and one scene, in which the undead Ruth appears at Ralph's window to warn him of the Stanger's inten-tions, is particularly creepy. Sadly, the Cornish landscape, which might have been put to use in creating atmosphere, is almost unseen due to pitch black night scenes and poor cinematography and the plot, which starts out intriguing, descends into farce in the third act. It's not as laughably bad as the similarly budgeted American effort *Invasion of the Blood Farmers* that came out the same year, but not by much.

While *Crucible of Terror* was unprofitable, it en-joyed a long syndication on late-night British TV but *Disciple of Death* simply vanished into obscurity after its limp release to critical derision. It was the last straw for

Mike Raven's acting career and he became a sheep farmer and a sculptor until his death in 1997. Eccentric in life, he was no less so in death and was buried on the Cornish moors in a grave he had dug for himself.

L'AMANTE DEL DEMONIO/THE DEVIL'S LOVER (1972)

Director: Paolo Lombardo
Writer: Paolo Lombardo

This obscure entry was helmed by Paolo Lombardo, primarily a writer, who turned in scripts for low budget Italian swashbucklers including *The Defeat of the Barbarians* (1962) which he co-directed. It would be ten years before he stepped behind a camera again and one gets the impression (certainly from this entry) that directing wasn't really his forte. He would only direct one more movie, the following year's poliziottesco, *Dagli archivi della polizia criminale*.

The Devil's Lover stars Italian cult actress Rosalba Neri, a veteran of many sword and sandal, spy and Spaghetti Western movies before she became a stalwart in the horror genre, particularly in those with an erotic slant. It's a folksy demonic horror plot mostly set in the past which seems to have suited Lombardo.

Neri and two friends (none of whom are given names) visit an old castle (Italy's Castello Ruspoli) because they heard that it belonged to the devil and they want to see if that's true. They find the castle's servant (John Benedy) more than helpful. He gives these strangers a tour and, incredibly, sets out a candlelit dinner for them before allowing them to stay the night.

After this flimsiest of setups, Neri gets up in the middle of the night and goes exploring in her nightie with a candelabra. She comes across a portrait of a burning woman who looks just like her. Assailed by some unseen force, she passes out and awakes in the sunshine of the 16th century. This is some sort of flashback as Neri is now playing a girl called Helga who

286

seems to have no memory of her modern-day counter-part.

Some historical soap opera guff unfolds involving Helga's engagement to Hans (Ferdinando Poggi) and the jealousy of another woman, Magda (Maria Teresa Pingitore), who is also in love with Hans. Then there's Helmut (Robert Woods) who is in love with Magda and will do nearly anything for her, except murder Helga. That leaves Magda with no choice but to go to the local witch and secure a cursed necklace which will kill Helga on her wedding day.

But Helga has other problems. Satan himself has popped up in the village, dressed not very conspicuously in a black cloak and red Klan hood. He's played by Edward Purdom (who would play the devil again, at least his voice, in *Beyond the Door*) and has unfortunately seen Helga's wedding dress. This not only spells bad luck but in fact *taints* the dress, meaning Helga also has to visit the witch to find out how to un-taint it. But the devil wants Helga for himself and demands that she sacrifice her husband and become his lover, the title of an Italian gothic horror movie being accurate for once.

There's an utterly superfluous section in which two of Helga's friends are waylaid by a couple of men in cheap-looking Halloween masks. They are led into a cave where some neanderthal rapists live and engage in an orgy before a beautiful vampire woman appears (who is never seen nor mentioned again) and turns them both into vampires. They approach Helga the following night and bite her, but this too is never referenced again, the whole subplot feeling like it came from another movie.

The meat and potatoes of *The Devil's Lover* concerns folkloric superstitions surrounding the covenant of marriage and the puritanical fears of witchcraft and sleeping with the devil. The village seems to be set in Germany, judging by the characters' names and the references to ballads of Lorelei and Valkyries. Indeed, the castle from the beginning of the movie plays no part, suggesting that this is all taking place somewhere else. There's a fairytale aspect to it all and one of the waylaid girls even wears a red riding hood.

For the most part, *The Devil's Lover* is the usual Italian skin flick with the barest pretense of an occult storyline as an excuse to have women strip off and make love with the devil. But even by Italian skin flick standards, *The Devil's Lover* is amateurish, bargain basement stuff. There are several references to it being nighttime, but not even day-for-night shooting was attempted rendering lines such as "It's so dark out!" unintentionally hilarious.

The only real reason to watch *The Devil's Lover* is the striking and statuesque Neri who carries the movie. Lombardo's direction leaves a lot to be desired but he occasionally conjures allusions to Dutch paintings in his compositions of period life which is a nice touch. There's a couple of swordfights involving people who at least look like they've held a sword before and Lombardo appears to be in familiar swashbuckling territory, but the movie is such a meandering and tedious mess with far too many subplots not followed through on, that it's really not worth anybody's time other than die-hard Neri fans.

GLI ORRORI DEL CASTELLO DI NORIMBER-GA/BARON BLOOD (1972)

Director: Mario Bava
Writers: Willibald Eser, Mario Bava and Vincent Fotre

As the son of Eugenio Bava, a cinematographer and special effects pioneer of Italy's silent movie period, Mario Bava was born to the craft. He followed in his father's footsteps in the 1940s, becoming a cinematographer and eventually an uncredited co-director called in to complete the movies of others before his directorial debut with 1960's *Black Sunday*, a classic of Italian horror about witchcraft and possession.

Bava was also one of the founding fathers of the giallo movement with his movies *The Girl Who Knew Too Much* (1963), *Blood and Black Lace* (1964) and *A Bay of Blood* (1971) considered touchstone examples. But, like Spain's Paul Naschy, Bava had a taste for the old-fashioned gothic and returned to it again and again throughout his career. He followed up *Black Sunday* with the unrelated *Black Sabbath* (1963), an anthology of horror tales presented by Boris Karloff, and then *Kill, Baby... Kill!* (1966), an eerie tale of a ghostly girl haunting a Carpathian village.

It would be six years before Bava would return to gothic horror. Producer Alfredo Leone (who would frequently collaborate with Bava) enticed him with a script for a gothic chiller set in an old castle which had a lot in common with Naschy's *Horror Rises from the Tomb* in that it dealt with a bloodthirsty nobleman of the past along the lines of Vlad the Impaler and Gilles de Rais. Such vintage fare was in danger of looking old hat in 1972 but somehow, Bava made it work through his impeccable directing and use of color and atmosphere

289

that drips from every corner of Burg Kreusenstein (a 19th century Austrian construction cobbled together from bits of medieval castles from all over Europe).

Baron Blood is the story of American Peter Kleist (Antonio Cantafora) who travels to his ancestral country of Austria to reacquaint himself with his family roots, namely Baron von Kleist, a sadistic 16th century noble-man who tortured and murdered his way through a hundred or so local villagers. One of his victims was a witch called Elizabeth Hölle who placed a curse on the baron.

Peter meets his uncle, Karl (Massimo Girotti), who takes him up to his ancestor's old castle which is now being remodeled as a hotel. Here he is introduced to Eva (Elke Sommer wearing some *very* short skirts through-out), a historian who is helping restore the building. Peter and Eva hit it off and Peter interests her with a document he found in his grandfather's belongings which relates to the infamous 'Baron Blood'. It seems to be an incantation to bring the baron back to life when read aloud in the castle bell tower at midnight.

Just for a jape, Peter and Eva sneak up to top of the tower that night and read the incantation resulting in the baron's moldering (and for some reason, bloody) corpse rising from its grave and going on a murderous rampage. With the bodies piling up (including the prospective hotelier's), the castle goes up for auction and is bought by the mysterious Alfred Becker (one of Hollywood's golden age leading men, Joseph Cotton). With the parchment required to send Baron Blood back to his grave destroyed by fire, Peter and Eva resort to a local medium who is a descendant of the witch, for some occult help.

It's a hokey script that feels like it should have been made by AIP with Vincent Price a decade earlier but perhaps Bava was paying homage to the horror of yesteryear as *Baron Blood* drips with gothic tropes. There are echoes of *Son of Frankenstein* (1939) in the American returning to his ancestral castle while the disfigured murderer in a cape and hat recalls *House of Wax* (1953) and *The Phantom of the Opera*. The portrait of the baron with its face slashed to prevent anybody knowing what he actually looked like feels like a plot device pinched from Arthur Conan Doyle's *The Hound of the Baskervilles* and even Bava's own early movies are referenced as somebody gets tossed into an iron maiden in the style of *Black Sunday*'s spiked masks.

The cobwebby castle, mysterious curse and people being grabbed by a shadowy figure (the identity of whom isn't revealed until the end), also makes *Baron Blood* feel a little like an episode of *Scooby-Doo*. It's tame for a horror movie with little in the way of gore aside from a few drops here and there and the afore-mentioned iron maiden scene. It certainly strikes a different tone from Bava's other movies which are more psychological, dreamlike and erotic but Bava seems to be having a bit of fun with this one as if he knows *Baron Blood* is B-grade schlock and still goes out of his way to make it beautiful and stylish.

A real highlight is the eerie chase through the foggy streets of the town in which Eva is pursued by the dastardly Baron Blood and the stunning location of an actual castle does the movie some great favors too. Bava uses every angle to his advantage, letting us peep at the actors through tangled torture devices and panning the camera across both interiors and exteriors to take in every gothic feature.

Baron Blood might not be one of Bava's best nor have much weight to it but it's a fine-looking movie all the same. It did very well in the US which encouraged Leone to give Bava *carte blanche* for his next project; a much more personal piece shot as *Lisa and the Devil* which was unfortunately shelved and then mutilated into an *Exorcist* cash-in called *House of Exorcism*.

CHILDREN SHOULDN'T PLAY WITH DEAD THINGS (1972)

Director: Bob Clark (as Benjamin Clark)
Writer: Bob Clark (As Benjamin Clark) and Alan Ormsby

In the late 1960s, Florida was the home of a booming industry in low-budget exploitation flicks. One filmmaker to emerge from this was Bob Clark who would later hit the big time as the director of the nostalgic favorite *A Christmas Story* (1983). It was a very different story in 1970 however, as Clark (who, at that point, had only directed the 1967 sexploitation movie *She-Man: A Story of Fixation*) teamed up with fellow University of Miami alumnus Alan Ormsby on a Z-grade zombie movie. The result was this horror comedy about a theatre group of young hopefuls who get more than they bargain for when they attempt to raise the dead on a remote island.

The script attracted the attention of the legendary low-budget movie mogul Ted V. Mikels who served uncredited as executive producer. He visited the cast and crew in Miami and, disappointed with what they had done so far, told them to trash what they had shot and start over, after giving them a few pointers on how to actually make a movie(6).

Featuring a bunch of colorfully dressed kids who get into a jam in a spooky setting, *Children Shouldn't Play with Dead Things* sits alongside *The Texas Chainsaw Massacre* (1974) in the 'Scooby-Doo for adults' genre of horror movie. Bizarrely, most of the main characters are named after the cast, something which recalls a couple of much later movies about projects in the woods gone wrong; *The Blair Witch Project* (1999) and *Book of Shadows: Blair Witch 2* (2000). But while

The Blair Witch Project pretended to be real footage and its nearly forgotten sequel pretended to be a dramatization of events in which names were changed to protect the identities of those involved, there is no such reason here other than a slapdash 'make it up as you go along' approach which permeates the whole movie.

The troupe's director, Alan (Alan Ormsby) takes his budding young stars on a boat to an island off the coast of Miami which has been reserved for the burial of the criminally insane. Besides Alan, the gang consists of the handsome leading man Paul (Paul Cronin), the loopy hippie Anya (Alan's real-life wife Anya Ormsby), the tubby and jovial Jeff (Jeff Gillen), the sardonic Val (Valerie Mamches) and attractive newcomer Terry (Jane Daly) who, for some reason, was the only one who got to change her name in the script.

The gang don't like Alan very much and we can't blame them. Alan is a letch, attempting to invoke the right of 'primal juncture' (first dibs) with Terry as some sort of initiation into the company. She wants none of this bargain basement Harvey Weinstein, in fact, none of them do but are prepared to put up with his nonsense as they are desperate for their paychecks (exactly what Alan is paying them or where he gets *his* money is left unexplained).

Alan's nonsense extends to performing a satanic ritual intended to bring a rotting corpse back to life, seemingly just for kicks. The others aren't entirely down with this and suffer a prank at the hands of Alan who has dressed up two of his buddies (unfortunate gay stereotypes played for laughs) as corpses.

Once he's had his chuckles, Alan gets serious and attempts to resurrect a corpse for real, complete with silly robe and moldy grimoire. When it doesn't seem to work, a triumphant Val offers to take over, giving the impression that she's far more knowledgeable about the

294

satanic stuff than the disgruntled Alan.

It's interesting to see a zombie movie return to the black magic side of things in the wake of George A. Romero's genre-defining *Night of the Living Dead* (1968) which swapped Voodoo for science fiction. That said, the undead on show here are very much the rotting corpses crawling from their graves with a hunger for human flesh popularized by Romero rather than the mind-controlled puppets of yore, no matter what the cause of their reanimation is.

Giving the resurrection angle up as a lost cause, the gang head to the old caretaker's cabin where they intend to spend the night. Alan brings the corpse with them and much horsing around ensues despite none of the others really wanting to be there. But it appears that either Alan's or Val's ritual worked for the dead eventually begin rising from their graves and converge on the unfortunate group.

There's some serious overacting in the movie but none of the cast come across as genuinely terrible. Some performances are downright enthralling, especially Valerie Mamches in her satanic ritual and Anya Ormsby who gives it her all in a full-on mental breakdown as the horror of what they are doing finally becomes too much for her.

The movie is mostly a corny (if dark) comedy about some kids fooling around with a corpse for an hour until the final act kicks in, but when the dead rise en masse in the final twenty minutes, *Children Shouldn't Play with Dead Things* really earns its stripes as a horror movie. With such a tiny budget, the zombies are surprisingly good (with primitive but effective makeup courtesy of Alan Ormsby) and eerie enough when they are hit with a spotlight while guzzling down somebody's guts in the darkness. The house under siege by the living dead is, of course, something we've seen before, but for such a low-budget effort, Bob Clark and all others concerned manage to ramp up the tension to a respectable degree.

The Canadian distributors were so impressed that they funded Bob Clark's and Alan Ormsby's 1974 zombie venture; *Dead of Night* (aka *Deathdream*), about a returning Vietnam war vet loosely inspired by W. W. Jacobs short story *The Monkey's Paw*. This marked the beginning of Clark's foray into Canadian cinema (provided by Canada's generous tax shelter of the 1970s) which included the proto-slasher *Black Christmas* (1974) and the sex comedy *Porkies* (1981).

DRACULA A.D. 1972 (1972)

Director: Alan Gibson
Writer: Don Houghton

British studio Hammer Film Productions was inadvertently quick off the mark with the whole devil trend, their lauded 1968 adaptation of Dennis Wheatley's 1934 novel *The Devil Rides Out* hitting cinemas the same summer Roman Polanski was redefining American horror with *Rosemary's Baby*.

Hammer being Hammer, *The Devil Rides Out* was a sumptuous period piece starring Christopher Lee as the Duke de Richeleau who combats black magic in the lordly manors of the English countryside. Good as it was, Hammer's old England routine was starting look a little old hat in the wake of *Rosemary's Baby* and *Night of the Living Dead*. Horror set in the modern world was the flavor du jour rather than the gothic past and the success of the modern-day vamp movie *Count Yorga, Vampire* (1970) across the pond showed that Americans were able to beat Hammer at its own game. If Hammer wanted to stay relevant, they had to get with the times.

Enter *Dracula A.D. 1972*, part one of two movies commissioned (the other being the following year's *The Satanic Rites of Dracula*) that would drag Hammer's best export out of his coffin and into the modern world. It was to be the seventh Hammer Dracula film, the sixth starring Christopher Lee, and the first to pair Lee and Peter Cushing since the original *Dracula* in 1958.

Filmed under the title *Dracula Today*, the movie drew heavily on the occult atmosphere of the era, in particular the media sensation surrounding a series of disturbing events occurring at Highgate Cemetery in London where several witnesses claimed to have seen supernatural figures late at night. Self-proclaimed

297

exorcist, Sean Manchester declared that a satanic cult had resurrected a 'king vampire' which now haunted the cemetery and that he would hold an exorcism on the 13th of March, 1970 to expel the evil spirit. The media circus surrounding this exorcism turned into a mob of vampire hunters which stormed the cemetery. The most disturbing aspect of the whole thing was that several months later, three schoolgirls discovered the charred, headless remains of a disinterred corpse outside of a broken vault. Evidence of a satanic ritual? Or the work of volunteer vampire hunters?

Right from the get-go it's clear that Hammer wanted to wipe the slate clean with *Dracula A.D. 1972*. A prologue set in 1872 (contradicting the events of the first Hammer Dracula which takes place in 1885), Dracula (Christopher Lee) is vanquished by Lawrence Van Helsing (Peter Cushing) who stakes him with a broken cartwheel before dying of his efforts. A mysterious stranger (Christopher Neame) turns up and collects Dracula's ashes in a vial and buries them in a churchyard near the freshly dug grave of Van Helsing.

Cut to a jet flying overhead accompanied by a seventies funk soundtrack. It's a hundred years later and we are introduced to a group of hip young things who have crashed a fancy party and are outraging the establishment stiffs by dancing on the grand piano and making out under the tables. That these so-called 'kids' are a hilarious caricature of post-Summer of Love youth (either by accident or design) is what makes *Dracula A.D. 1972* so notorious. In trying to bring Dracula up to date, Hammer created the most dated Dracula movie ever.

Chief among the group is Jessica (Stephanie Beacham) while a familiar shifty-eyed fellow played by Christopher Neame has weaseled his way into a position of influence over the young bohemians. He calls himself

Johnny Alucard ('Alucard' is, of course, 'Dracula' backwards; a now tired tradition which originated in Universal's 1943 movie *Son of Dracula*). Alucard persuades his groovy friends to take part in a black mass, just for kicks. One of them points out that they need unhallowed ground and Alucard knows just the spot; a deconsecrated church nearby is slated for demolition.

Jessica isn't so keen on the whole thing. Her grandfather, played by Peter Cushing (hullo?) is an authority on the occult and has written a treatise on the black mass. We can see where this is going. Jessica is the great-granddaughter of Lawrence Van Helsing and her grandfather, *Lorrimer* Van Helsing has inherited his ancestor's desire to vanquish evil along with some rather strong genetics.

In the churchyard that night, Alucard demands a volunteer for his black mass and gets it in the form of Laura played by Caroline Munro in one of her first screen roles before her starring turns in *The Golden Voyage of Sinbad* (1973) and *The Spy Who Loved Me* (1977). Alucard mixes his blood with Dracula's ashes and empties the lot over Laura, causing the rest of the group to flee in disgust.

The ritual results in Dracula rising from the grave and feeding off poor Laura whose body is later found by the police. Inspector Murray (Michael Coles) suspects an occult angle and calls on the help of Lorrimer Van Helsing in getting to the root of it. The body count rises and Van Helsing realizes that his family's nemesis has returned and is closing in on his granddaughter with the help of his sinister acolyte, Alucard, who has traded his life and soul for immortality.

The plot is thin and unfortunately, Jessica Van Helsing, who would have made an interesting and fresh protagonist, is largely sidelined once Peter Cushing starts doing his thing and is little more than a hypnotized victim by the movie's final act. That said, it's a thrill to see Cushing pitted against Lee's Dracula after so long, even if Dracula never leaves his crumbling abode to mix with the hot-blooded denizens of the modern world as the title suggests.

Dracula A.D. 1972 didn't receive much love on its release. It was too much of a departure to satisfy Hammer purists while not being frightening or serious enough to compete with other horror movies of the period. Hopeless attempts to appeal to contemporary youth results in cringe-inducing dialogue ("Dig the music, kids!") which made the movie look out of touch even by the time it hit theaters. But that's what made the movie a cult favorite. It's campy, ridiculous nonsense but breezy and colorful enough to never get boring.

BLOOD ORGY OF THE SHE-DEVILS (1973)

Director: Ted V. Mikels
Writer: Ted V. Mikels

By 1972, Ted V. Mikels, the musketeer-mustachioed mogul of low-budget exploitation, was living in a faux-gothic castle in Glendale, California which he had purchased with the profits of his latest movie, *The Corpse Grinders* (1971). Filled with antique weapons, suits of armor and plenty of arches and passageways, the castle was the perfect setting for a new horror movie.

Always a showman, Mikels started out as a magician, ventriloquist and accordion player before heading into the movie business in which he was a stuntman and archery instructor on Westerns like *The Indian Fighter* (1955). But it was behind the camera that his heart truly lay. He started making his own 35mm movies by buying the end pieces of unfinished rolls of film from the studios on the cheap and directed short educational movies as well as exploitation flicks. In the late sixties he was most notable for his movies *The Black Klansman* (1966), *Girl in Gold Boots* (1968) and *The Astro Zombies* (1969).

It was his 1971 movie *The Corpse Grinders* which resulted in the horror label being irrevocably attached to Mikels. Ostensibly a comedy about a cat food company which turns to human flesh as a cheap source of meat, *The Corpse Grinders* was marketed as a horror movie and did big business, enabling Mikels to buy his castle in Glendale (in which some scenes in *The Corpse Grinders* had been shot) and invest in *Children Shouldn't Play with Dead Things*. But Mikels had his heart set on shooting his next movie within the walls of his new home.

Mikels started studying the occult and attending

301

seances in preparation for *Blood Orgy of the She-Devils*; a movie intended to make every use of Mikels's castle and a cast which he peopled with friends and alumni from his previous movies.

The movie is centered on the modern-day witch Mara (played by New York theatre actress Lila Zaborin in her only screen role), who holds seances in her mansion and hires out her black magic services to unscrupulous types. One such type is Rodannus (Ray Myles) and his associate Barth (Paul Wilmoth) who hire Mara to assassinate the United Nations Ambassador of Rhodesia. She does this by way of submerging a picture of him in a vase of water, effectively drowning him from a distance.

Instead of paying Mara, Rodannus pulls a sneaky one and dispatches Barth to murder her. Mara then reincarnates herself as a cat and gets her revenge on Barth by dropping a Voodoo doll into a jar of ants (causing him to leap out of a top floor window) while Rodannus is dispatched in the more traditional way of sticking pins into a doll.

The plot is a disjointed series of anecdotes. Random scenes open to deliver the bare necessities by way of exposition with zero character work and it's a while before the viewer even realizes who the main characters are supposed to be. The eventual main players who do emerge are Mark and Lorraine (Tom Pace and Leslie McRae who had both starred in *Girl in Gold Boots*).

Mark and Lorraine are lovers who spend most of the movie on the sidelines not really getting involved in anything until the final act. Lorraine is another of Mara's paying customers and regularly attends seances. She drags the skeptical Tom along and we are subjected to an embarrassingly offensive invocation of an 'Indian spirit guide'.

Lorraine and Mark also spend a lot of time with

their college professor Dr. Helsford (played by Victor Izay, another veteran of *Girl in Gold Boots*) who warns them about dabbling in the occult. He's something of an authority on the subject and his monologue segues into a couple of flashbacks to the persecution of witches (one of whom is played by Mikel's then girlfriend, Sherri Vernon) that are as necessary to the plot as they are convincing. Dr. Helsford does make an interesting comment on the occult craze of the 1970s; "Look what we have today. Young minds looking to the unknown for answers, some seeking God with great sincerity, others seeking thrills any way they can get them." It's unusual for a movie of this ilk to confront the contemporary trend it is very much a part of head on.

When Lorraine drags Mark back to Mara's mansion for an age regression séance under hypnosis, Dr. Helsford decides that enough is enough and calls on the help of his fellow occult experts to break up Mara's coven. Assembling in the grounds of the house, Helsford and his chums unleash their own brand of magic to exorcise the house, causing chaos inside.

The minimalist approach to plotting makes the movie mercifully short and, once it hits its stride, surprisingly straight forward. Lila Zaborin is enthusiastic and convincing as Mara, but her magic is an ethnic hodge-podge of the occult that blends spiritualism, Satanism, African drums and Voodoo dolls which, like the movie, has no real direction other than getting onto the next scene.

But the biggest crime of *Blood Orgy of the She-Devils* is that it's so tame. It joins the ranks of *Werewolves on Wheels* as a movie that utterly fails to live up to its title. There's very little blood, no orgy and, as for the 'she-devils', one can only assume the interpretive dancers in leather bikinis are meant. Ted V. Mikkels, for all his outlandish titles promising grindhouse sleaze, managed to turn in some surprisingly dull and PG-rated movies and *Blood Orgy of the She-Devils* is no different.

LES DÉMONS/THE DEMONS (1973)

Director: Jesús Franco
Writer: Jesús Franco

Spanish director Jesús Franco (known to many as 'Jess' Franco) got off to a promising start in 1962 with *The Awful Dr. Orloff* kickstarting a boom in Spanish horror. His obsession with the writings of the Marquis de Sade saw him adapt several of de Sade's works as well as a couple of Fu Manchu movies starring Christopher Lee whom Franco worked with again on a remarkably faithful adaptation of Stoker's novel, *Count Dracula* (1970), and an early witch-hunt movie *The Bloody Judge* (1970).

Erotic movies were a tough sell in Francoist Spain, so Jess Franco (no relation the general) moved to the slightly more liberated France where he was able to indulge more freely in his interests i.e. sexual sadism, lesbian vampires and women in prison. Clearly inspired by Ken Russell's *The Devils*, Franco embarked on his own version. But, while Russell's movie was a harrowing criticism of the marriage of church and state based on real events, Franco's decidedly less subtle effort is an orgy of Renaissance sex scenes featuring nuns with bikini tan lines to the wacka-wacka of an electric guitar.

At some point in the 17th century, a trio of dastardly aristocrats – the icy Lady De Winter (Karin Field), Lord Justice Jeffries (Cihangir Gaffari) and Thomas Renfield (Alberto Dalbés) – torture a confession out of an old woman and then burn her at the stake as a witch. Before the flames consume her, the old woman curses the trio, claiming that her daughters will exact her revenge on them, hinting that this movie falls into the 'witchcraft is real' category.

Naturally hoping to avoid this fate, the three villains start looking for the offspring of the deceased witch. At a local convent, two sisters have earned the ire of the sadistic mother superior (Doris Thomas) and seem to fit the bill when Lade De Winter and Renfield come knocking. Kathleen (Anne Libert) and Margaret (Carmen Yazalde) were left at the convent as orphans and their upkeep is paid for by a mysterious stranger. After examining the girls, Lady De Winter declares that Kathleen is no virgin and is therefore a ripe subject to be investigated for witchcraft (i.e., tortured until she confesses).

Renfield, who has taken a shine to Kathleen, helps her escape and is then dispatched to recapture her. He does so and declares his love to her, asking her to flee to Holland with him. She agrees, no doubt spotting a chance of freedom even if it means marrying a tubby man twice her age, but the two lovers are captured by Justice Jeffries's men and tortured.

Meanwhile, Margaret has fled the nunnery after being visited by the devil himself who naturally has his way with her and causes her to seduce the mother superior, leading to the sadistic nun's suicide. Margaret falls in with a witch who helps her bring her latent powers to fruition which manifest in an ability to turn anyone she has intercourse with into a skeleton.

This bare-bones plot manages to clock in just short of two hours due to the movie being bloated with sex scenes. Every time a couple meet, they are almost guaranteed to start romping about in the bedroom. This is something of a common feature in Franco's movies but, unlike so many of them, *The Demons* has a solid attempt at a coherent plot which can only count in the movie's favor. As well as all the backstabbing and shifting loyalties, there are references to Charles II and a plot involving William of Orange's invasion of England which give some semblance of a historical backdrop

306

other than a vague Renaissance setting.

Franco makes good use of his locations and the castles and convents surrounded by Mediterranean countryside (despite the story apparently taking place in England) are an impressive backdrop to the sordidness going on. The movie is well shot with Franco's trademark zooms kept to a tolerable minimum and the whole thing certainly looks a cut above what you'd expect in a softcore venture from Spain's exploitation king, despite Jean-Bernard Raiteux's funky but out of place soundtrack.

PSYCHOMANIA/THE DEATH WHEELERS (1973)

Director: Don Sharp
Writer: Arnaud d'Usseau and Julian Zimet

Directed by Don Sharp who helmed several Hammer horrors, this bizarre but colorful supernatural British biker movie was made by Benmar Productions who were behind a trio of historical adventure movies shot in Spain. In 1972 they moved into sci-fi and horror, putting out *Horror Express*, starring Christopher Lee and Peter Cushing and written by Arnaud d'Usseau and Julian Zimet. The two writers would work together on *Psychomania* which was released as *The Death Wheelers* in the US on a double bill with *Horror Express*.

A biker gang appropriately calling themselves 'The Living Dead' enjoy tearing around the English country-side, terrorizing pensioners, plowing through shopping centers and generally causing havoc. Their leader, Tom (Nicky Henson, who played a soldier in *Witchfinder General*) is bored and looking for the ultimate thrill; life beyond death. This is no doubt encouraged by his bizarre home life. He lives with his mother (British veteran of stage and screen Beryl Reid) and the family's faithful retainer, Shadwell (played by a deteriorating George Sanders mere months before his suicide) in a massive house with an unbelievably retro 1970s interior that wouldn't look out of place in *A Clockwork Orange* (1971).

Tom's mother is some sort of clairvoyant who not only gives séances but knows plenty about how to come back from the other side (something involving the worship of a toad god and a deal with the devil). Shadwell is also deeply involved in the occult and it's possible that he is the one influencing the old matriarch. He certainly has an aversion to crosses *ala* Dracula and is privy to the toad cult's secrets. One such secret is how to come back from the grave. The details aren't gone into in any great depth, but Nicky decides to give it a try and the next day he rides off the edge of a bridge to a watery death.

His gang bury him (seated upright on his motorcycle) in the local stone circle and the next day he roars out of the grave on his hog, good as new and ready to terrorize rural England once more. His gang are initially miffed by his ability to cheat death but, one by one, are convinced to follow suit and start offing themselves in increasingly elaborate ways, leaving much confusion in the wake of bodies vanishing from morgues and coffins at funerals.

It's up to Inspector Hesseltine (Robert Hardy) to find out what the hell is going on and he finds a reluctant ally in Tom's girlfriend Abby (Mary Larkin) who isn't quite down with the whole group suicide thing and deliberately botches her own. But Nicky and his gang aren't too keen to have one of the living in their number which puts Abby in a tricky spot.

Surprisingly, there is no zombie makeup for what is essentially a zombie biker movie. The gang look entirely normal upon resurrection (the movie never explains how somebody can appear unscathed after leaping out of an airplane with no parachute). Also unexplained is why they still feel the need to wear their helmets if they are now immortal.

Psychomania is also surprisingly tame in the gore department for a horror movie. These zombies don't feast on human brains and in fact, seem content to carry on doing what they had done in their previous lives; namely roaring around and smashing things up. It does beg the question as to what the whole point is.

But it's a fun ride nevertheless. There are some excellent shots of biker mayhem and some impressive stunts. The movie also has a surreal acid trip feel to it in parts. The misty circle of standing stones gets plenty of screen time as well as dream sequences, magic mirrors and the aforementioned emphasis on toads. All this thrums along to a prog-rock soundtrack courtesy of John Cameron.

It's an impressive cast too with Reid and Sanders hamming it up in something that is far beneath them and a young Robert Hardy playing a copper. Nicky Henson gives a good turn as an unpleasant but damaged youth on a path of self-destruction. There are also a few minor faces to spot in the crowd; biker chick Jane is played by Ann Michelle, star of the previous year's *Virgin Witch* and ginger mop-top Hatchet is played by Denis Gilmore, who had been starring in British movies and TV since the age of four and was one of Angel's cultists in *Blood on Satan's Claw*.

HUNGRY WIVES/SEASON OF THE WITCH (1973)

Director: George A. Romero
Writer: George A. Romero

After he helped redefine horror in 1968 with *Night of the Living Dead*, George A. Romero deliberately stepped away from the genre. He made two left-field misfires before apparently tossing in the towel and returning to more familiar territory with 1973's *The Crazies*. First up was a romantic comedy called *There's Always Vanilla* (1971) followed by this strange suburban commentary on feminism and the empowerment of witchcraft which, although having something of the horror movie about it, is far more subtle than his other movies, even with their critiques of racism and capitalism.

It opens with a surreal, symbol-laden sequence in which frustrated housewife, Joan (Jan White) follows in the wake of her cold, domineering and abusive husband, Jack (Bill Thunhurst) as he walks through a forest, letting branches snap back into her face, while engrossed in a newspaper, entirely oblivious to her pain. He eats an egg. There is a baby. He attaches a red dog collar to Joan and makes her sit in a cage.

Thankfully this is just a dream, but Joan's waking life isn't much better. With her husband gone on long business trips, she is left with the isolation of keeping house for people who aren't there. Her teenage daughter, Nikki (Joedda McClain), is out having a much better sex life than Joan who has to content herself with domestic chores and bridge games with other housewives while occasionally catching glimpses of herself in mirrors as a white-haired old hag. It's basically everything the counterculture of the time was so terrified of, and this is where the movie's strong points lie. *Season of the Witch* is an interesting oddity that couldn't have

311

been made at any other time. Informed by the feminist movement, Romero uses the occult of the counterculture as a tool for women's liberation as housewife Joan gazes with jealous eyes at the freedom of youth.

There are a few knowing winks at the audience such as Jack lurching up from the bedroom floor to give Joan a fright as if he were a zombie from Romero's big hit only to reveal that he's just doing his morning stomach crunches. There's even a reference to that other hit from 1968 when Joan's friend Shirley jokingly warns her about not eating the chocolate mousse if it tastes 'chalky', before name-dropping *Rosemary's Baby*.

That's because Joan and Shirley are on their way to visit a local witch, just for kicks, but Joan develops a cautious interest in the occult and is soon shopping for witchy equipment and ingredients to the tune of, what else but Donovan's 'Season of the Witch'. Armed with new powers, Joan works a charm on sleazy college professor Gregg (who has already had his way with her daughter), and they end up doing the dirty on the kitchen floor. She even tells Gregg that she was responsible for bringing him to her, at which he scoffs, and we might be inclined to scoff with him, knowing that it would hardly require witchcraft to lure the horny professor who has already expressed an interest in her. But ambiguity is the key word in *Season of the Witch*. Joan seems to cause a coffeepot to shake and rattle just by looking at it but, other than that, we don't really see any other concrete evidence of her powers. They may not amount to anything other than a newfound confidence and agency; the true purpose of most ceremonial magic which relies on the psychological powers of suggestion and imagination rather than actual supernatural abilities.

The horror of the movie is all in the mind too, with little to satisfy those seeking Romero-esque visceral blood and guts. There are some well-shot nightmares of Joan in which a masked man breaks into her house and attacks her in frantic sequence of close-ups and tilted angles which is very reminiscent of the house under siege in *Night of the Living Dead* (and the masked man is even played by S. William Hinzman, the 'graveyard zombie' from Romero's classic), but it is Joan's predicament and the predicament of many other housewives which seems to be the real threat Romero is trying to convey.

And, for all its talk of women's lib through witchcraft, the movie's finale in which Joan finally joins the coven of witches, is a bleak one. A red rope is tied around her neck in a kinky initiation ritual that recalls the red dog collar from the prologue, suggesting that she has traded one form of bondage for another making the ending nearly as nihilistic as *Night of the Living Dead*'s.

Originally filmed as *Jack's Wife* in 1972, distributor Jack H. Harris chopped out over half an hour and released it under the title *Hungry Wives* with the baffling tagline 'Caviar in the kitchen, nothing in the bedroom' and a poster that suggested it was a softcore skin flick. Audiences (no doubt disappointed) disregarded the movie and it vanished from screens only to reappear in 1974 with the new title *Season of the Witch* and a more appropriate poster marketing it as a horror movie.

But even that isn't quite right and Romero himself has claimed that *Season of the Witch* isn't really a horror movie. It's more of a feminist drama that relies on metaphor. Unfortunately, the negative for Romero's original 120-minute cut has been lost, leaving us with this truncated and badly edited version of what might have been a very good movie. As it is, in a 104-minute cut, *Season of the Witch* is an intriguing, if incomplete entry from a director showing a more intimate and sensitive side in a career that was mostly fixated on flesh eating zombies.

SCREAM BLACULA SCREAM (1973)

Director: Bob Kelljan
Writers: Joan Torres, Raymond Koenig and Maurice Jules

The 1972 horror comedy *Blacula* managed to do what Hammer failed to, namely, put a centuries-old vampire into a hip, modern environment and make it work. By mixing up gothic horror with blaxploitation, director William Crane created a funny parody which also carried some social weight. It's the story of African prince Mamuwalde, whose efforts to stop the slave trade end up with him being turned into a vampire by Count Dracula. As a sympathetic protagonist cursed for centuries by European racism, *Blacula* was deeper than any horror comedy needed to be.

It was the first blaxploitation horror movie and inspired a small subgenre that included similar takeoffs of horror staples *Blackenstein* (1973) and *Dr. Black, Mr. Hyde* (1976), the possession movies *Abby* and *J. D.'s Revenge* as well as the zombie movie *Sugar Hill. Blacula* was a huge hit and one of the top-grossing movies of 1973. Bob Kelljan, director of the Count Yorga movies (similarly about an ancient vampire brought into the 1970s), was called in to direct the sequel with Joan Torres and Raymond Koenig returning for writing duties.

A ten-minute opening segment introduces us to Lisa Fortier (Pam Grier) and Willis Daniels (Richard Lawson), members of a Voodoo cult who are in the running to replace its high priestess, Mama Loa, who has just died. As her son, Willis thinks he should be the one to take over but the rest of the congregation plump for Lisa which enrages Willis and he storms off. In an act of vengeance, he purchases the bones of the deceased Prince Mamuwalde/Blacula and performs a ritual to bring the vampire back to life. Things don't quite go to plan as Willis becomes Blacula's first victim and finds himself little more than a pawn of the newly arisen vampire.

Blacula wants to get himself exorcised of vampirism and is drawn to Lisa as the only one who can help him. He still needs to feed, however, and an army of vampires spring up in his wake while Lisa's boyfriend, ex-cop Justin (Don Mitchell) is on the case, desperately trying to convince his racist old boss, Sherrif Dunlop (Michael Conrad) that there might be a vampire on the loose.

While the first movie was more of an outright comedy, the sequel wisely realizes that it can't get by on the same laughs and opts for a more serious tone. Unfortunately, this reveals that there isn't much plot beneath the concept and *Scream Blacula Scream* feels like a bit of a bloodless retread of its predecessor, albeit with a new motivation for its undead star. There are elements of humor, such as a newly-vampirized hip cat dismayed at not being able to see himself in a mirror. The racial issues are also given some lip service in Blacula's admonishing two pimps who have 'made a slave' of a black woman (unfortunately this is undermined by Blacula's own enslavement of his vampire minions).

The blend of Voodoo and vampirism had been done before, notably in the 1945 horror movie, *The Vampire's Ghost* and, while black magic rituals were often employed in the raising of vampires from the dead, particularly in *Dracula A.D. 1972* and *The Satanic Rites of Dracula, Scream Blacula Scream* is one of the first movies to use Voodoo as a source for resurrecting vampires (usually it concerns itself with zombies, at least in Hollywood movies). It also takes the interesting step of painting vampirism as something that can be exorcised. *The Exorcist* hadn't come out yet, but Blatty's book was already kicking up a storm and 'exorcism' was something of a hot topic the writers were no doubt aware of. The climactic exorcism in which Lisa tries to cure Blacula via the use of a Voodoo doll while cops storm the house and battle Blacula's army of servants is exciting enough to make up for a rather plodding narrative.

There's little in the way of special effects other than Blacula turning into a bat which is an almost identical effect Universal used in their old Dracula movies. A lot of the action takes place in Willis's mansion which is impressive enough to give the movie a touch of the gothic to go with its shots of contemporary Los Angeles.

William Marshall still gives it his all, oozing suave charm and generally rising far above the silliness around him. It was to be his last outing as Blacula but he would play the exorcist role in the following year's *Abby*. Pam Grier is also excellent as the tough but ultimately kind-hearted Voodoo practitioner who will even try to save the life of a racist cop. Her breakout hit *Coffy* had only hit screens a month previously and she was on the cusp of moving on from the sleazy women-in-prison fare of her early career to the tough-as-nails characters she would be known for in *Foxy Brown* (1974), *Sheba, Baby* and *Friday Foster* (both 1975).

EL ESPANTO SURGE DE LA TUMBA/HORROR RISES FROM THE TOMB (1973)

Director: Carlos Aured
Writer: Paul Naschy

Argentinian director Leon Klimovsky had already directed a couple of Paul Naschy's *Hombre Lobo* movies by the time Naschy started penning other non-werewolf horror movies and was Naschy's first choice to direct *Horror Rises from the Tomb,* a gothic chiller that clearly takes its cue from *The Thing that Couldn't Die* (1958). Klimovski was still busy working on another project so his assistant director, Carlos Aured, directed in his stead, making this his directorial debut and the first of four collaborations with Naschy in the 1970s.

Filmed at Naschy's parents' sprawling country estate in Spain doubling for France, *Horror Rises from the Tomb* starts with the prologue of the evil Alaric de Marnac, a 15th century nobleman beheaded for a number of atrocities involving Satanism, human sacrifice, cannibalism as well as being both a vampire *and* a werewolf. Also accused is his mistress, Mabille de Lancre (Helga Line), who is stripped naked and strung upside down before being executed (the stripping naked of women before killing them is a common motif in this movie).

In modern-day Paris, a group of friends led by Hugo (Paul Naschy) attend a séance in an attempt to contact the spirit of Hugo's villainous ancestor. Hugo doesn't put much stock in it all and invites his friends to his family estate where the headless body of Alaric de Marnac resides in the crypt (his severed head was buried elsewhere).

Hugo and his girlfriend Sylvia (Betsabé Ruiz) and

their friends, Maurice (Víctor Barrera) and Paula (Cristina Suriani) set out in a car but are accosted on a lonely mountain road by a pair of thieves. Fortunately, a local militia turn up and, after shooting one of the thieves, string the other one up from a tree. While this is one of the movie's several superfluous subplots, the sequence does let us know that we are far from the bounds of civilization where the law seemingly has no presence, increasing the sense of nightmarish isolation.

Upon arrival at the house, Hugo instructs some local workmen to start digging in the villa's grounds looking for Alaric's lost fortune (which apparently, he's never considered looking for previously). They find a chest which they are unable to open. During the night, the workmen break into the chest and find the head of Alaric who promptly possesses one of them who goes on a murderous rampage.

In addition to this, both Maurice and Paula are also possessed and reunite Alaric's head with his body, resurrecting him. They also resurrect Mabille by sacrificing Sylvia. Hugo is too busy to notice as he's getting fresh with Elvire, the caretaker's daughter (Emma Cohen).

The movie then becomes something of a vampire flick with Alaric and Mabille heading out to seduce and murder young men and women in the town while Hugo and Elvire look for a talisman that can destroy them (for some reason this talisman depicts 'the hammers of Thor'). There's also a completely left-field zombie siege which is slow moving and a little on the dull side as Alaric's victims converge on the house and are easily driven off.

The plot is a jumbled mess and hurls in the kitchen sink, seemingly unable to decide whether it's a vampire movie, a zombie movie or a possession movie. While it's certainly entertaining enough, it's difficult to get a handle on exactly what Alaric de Marnac's powers are or the fine details of the lore surrounding him. He sleeps in a coffin and seduces young women but is only interested in eating their hearts, not drinking their blood. The pagan symbol of Thor's hammers acts like a crucifix on a vampire but why would a pagan symbol have any effect on a satanist? Also, it's seemingly random who becomes a possessed servant and who is killed to be brought back as a zombie (zombies that can't be stopped by a shotgun blast to the chest, but shriek when set on fire).

Plot questions aside, *Horror Rises from the Tomb* is a fine-looking horror movie with some decent gore effects considering its low budget. The blood is a refreshingly more realistic hue than the red paint we usually get in movies of this period and there is a surprisingly good sequence in which a heart is ripped out of somebody's chest that really feels like it belongs in a better movie. Also of note are the clever shots of Naschy's head being removed from its box which manage to avoid the usual obvious dummy head (although it does turn up in a very badly done decapitation at the end of the movie).

That said, the old horror movie trope of no electricity, necessitating the need for candles dials up the atmosphere a bit but isn't exactly made the most of as the house seems to be brightly lit throughout. Put to better use is the damp, misty Spanish countryside which sells the idea that our characters are truly isolated in a bleak part of the country.

In all, it's a messy, nonsensical movie that gets far too distracted from its central plot and relies on more than one deus ex machina to move things along. Paul Naschy turned to directing in 1976 with a Spanish take on Ken Russell's *The Devils* (1971) called *Inquisición/Inquisition*. He carried on starring in his own movies and even played Alaric de Marnac (along with a different descendant) in a 1983 sequel to *Horror Rises from the Tomb* called *Latidos de Pánico* (*Panic Beats*).

La Rebelión de las Muertas/Vengeance of the Zombies (1973)

Director: León Klimovsky
Writer: Paul Naschy

After sitting out the previous entry in the Naschy canon – *Horror Rises from the Tomb* – Paul Naschy's favorite director, León Klimovsky, returned to helm this British-set zombie movie, his third collaboration with Naschy.

A masked killer is popping up around London murdering people and, in a rather convoluted way, using their blood to resurrect a member of the opposite sex by dripping it over a wax figure of them and setting it alight, thus creating an army of ghoulish slaves. The cousin of one such victim is Elvire (a name Naschy was clearly taken with as he had a different Elvire in *Horror Rises from the Tomb*) played by a redheaded Spanish actress known as Romy. Elvire is a regular client of the guru Krisna (Paul Naschy in brownface, unfortunately) who asks her to spend some time with him at his mansion near the Welsh-sounding village of Llangwell (although the architecture and suspiciously arid landscape betray the Spanish shooting location).

Elvire's boyfriend Lawrence (Víctor Barrera who played Maurice in *Horror Rises from the Tomb*) is skeptical but she goes anyway and is soon trapped in a nightmarish scenario not knowing whom to trust. Back in London, the murders continue in a gialloesqe way leading us to wonder how it is all connected to Krishna's mysterious guru retreat.

As with most of Naschy's scripts, there is a large cast of characters and multiple subplots which do add some depth to the straightforward story but also risk distracting the movie from its main task. While the mystery unfolds at Krishna's mansion, Elvire finds that she has a rival for Krishna's affections in the form of his assistant, Kala (Mirta Miller), which certainly spells trouble down the line. Meanwhile, Scotland Yard is on the case of the murders and recruits the help of Elvire's boyfriend, Lawrence who, it turns out, is an expert on the occult. Lawrence sets out for Llangwell but gets distracted from his task (and the fact that he has a girlfriend) by the lovely Elsie (María Kosty from a slew of Amando de Ossorio movies) and ends up making out by the lake instead of rescuing Elvire, suggesting that Elsie may have ulterior motives of her own.

Vengeance of the Zombies joins the ranks of *Psychomania* and *Scream Blacula Scream* in that it eschews the sci-fi origins of most post-*Night of the Living Dead* zombie movies for the more traditional occultism, albeit a mishmash of Satanism, Indian mysticism and Voodoo that references Baron Samedi in almost the same breath as the Thuggee cult. The exoticization of foreign religious beliefs as things to be feared is part and parcel of this brand of zombie movie and the importation of dark, foreign magic to the British countryside is reminiscent of Hammer's *Plague of the Zombies* (1966).

The discovery that the victims are from prominent families who lived in India gives an interesting political subtext to an otherwise run of the mill shocker. The idea that the western world's colonialism might come back to bite them in the form of foreign curses and black magic is a common feature in occult fiction. This gives some extra meaning to the title of *Vengeance of the Zombies* and is probably the reason it was set in Britain which, by the 1970s, had encouraged massive postwar immigration from India, Pakistan and the West Indies to fill the gaps in its workforce.

Another plot thread left unaddressed is the references to Krishna's mansion being previously owned by a family who made a pact with the devil. This is never touched on again other than Dr. Lawrence's comment that occultists tend to choose haunted spots for their rituals to ensure a stronger connection with the spiritual world. Elvire also suffers a nightmare at the mansion in one of the movie's most memorable scenes which involves Paul Naschy as a rather good devil.

There's far too much slow motion in *Vengeance of the Zombies*, especially whenever the zombies attack. One gets the feeling that Klimovski was going for a dreamlike feel as his horrors float towards their victims, but it ends up being more tedious than thrilling. That said, the movie scores high on the gore for its period, with plenty of throat cutting, beheadings and a particularly nasty 'death by beer can' scene.

One thing which is really out of place is the music. Juan Carlos Calderon's upbeat fusion jazz score plays incessantly regardless of the tone of the scene it is accompanying, be it a zombie attack, a funeral or stock footage of Piccadilly Circus, sapping the movie of any creepy atmosphere it might generate.

While not as muddled and contrived as some of Naschy's movies (like *Horror Rises from the Tomb*), *Vengeance of the Zombies* is a solid B-grade entry that doesn't go to great lengths to do anything original. The melting pot of occultism is silly but there's a good twist finale coming and enough blood and pasty-faced ghouls to keep us entertained along the way.

EL RETORNO DE WALPURGIS/CURSE OF THE DEVIL (1973)

Director: Carlos Aured
Writers: Paul Naschy

The seventh entry in Paul Naschy's twelve movie *Hombre Lobo* series, gives the werewolf count Waldemar Daninsky a new origin story. A previous entry explained his lycanthropy by having him being bitten by a yeti for some reason, but this time it's a curse placed on his ancestor by a satanic coven. Its title (which literally means 'Return of Walpurgis') was clearly intended to cash in on Naschy's biggest hit, 1970s *La Noche de Walpurgis* ('Walpurgis Night', released in the US as *The Werewolf vs. The Vampire Woman*) which was the fifth entry in the *Hombre Lobo* series.

Paul Naschy seemed to have been greatly interested in Renaissance serial killers. His 1974 movie *The Devil's Possessed* was a heavily fictionalized take on the life of Gilles de Rais, the 15th century child killer, who also inspired the character Alaric de Marnac, who appears in both *Horror Rises from the Tomb* and its sequel *Panic Beats* (1983). This time it's Elizabeth Bathory, the 16th century Hungarian countess accused of torturing and murdering hundreds of young women and girls, who gets the Naschy treatment.

The credits roll over footage of two knights hacking and slashing at each other. One is local lord Irineus Daninsky (Paul Naschy) and the other, Barna Bathory (Jorge Matamoros), whose wife Elizabeth (María Silva) heads a coven of devil worshipers. When Daninsky kills Barna and then rumbles his wife's black mass, Elizabeth is burned at the stake while her disciples are hanged from the castle drawbridge (the real Elizabeth Bathory was walled up inside her own castle).

Before she dies, Elizabeth lays down a strangely specific curse on the Daninsky bloodline which states that one day, one of his descendants will kill one of hers by accident, thus cursing his bloodline for ever.

Centuries later, the current Count Daninsky (Naschy again) accidentally shoots a gypsy while out hunting wolves. The man's clan are enraged and enact a dark ritual to bring the curse to fruition. Satan himself appears as a shadowy figure (clearly a man in a black bodysuit) and has sex with a young woman called Ilona (Inés Morales) who then worms her way into Count Daninsky's confidence, posing as a helpless waif on the road.

In no time at all, Daninsky and Ilona are in bed together and, on Walpurgisnacht (May Eve, a significant date in European paganism), Ilona uses a wolf's skull to bite the slumbering Daninsky, thus turning him a werewolf. She flees the castle but falls afoul of an escaped maniac who is lurking in the woods, providing one of Nashy's infamous red herring subplots.

As bodies start turning up, they are initially put down as victims of the maniac until strange animal tracks are spotted. Meanwhile, a mining engineer (Eduardo Calvo) and his family have moved to the area and soon, Daninsky is at it again with the man's eldest daughter (Naschy writes this stuff, remember).

The makeup, effects and even story aren't much different from what Universal Studios was doing thirty years previously, although Carlos Aured (returning to direct after the success of *Horror Rises from the Tomb*) does his best to keep things lively. There's some good energy whenever Naschy turns into a werewolf, leaping through windows and going for the jugular and the gore factor naturally surpasses anything Universal could have got away with. The movie is let down somewhat by the convoluted plot which can't seem to decide whether the curse is that of Elizabeth Bathory or the gypsy clan or perhaps both and there are far too many elements involved in bringing it to fruition.

The generic Eastern European setting and vague 19th century period dress is reminiscent of Hammer's gothic entries (which the British studio was trying to move away from by 1974) and the movie is well shot with actual night scenes instead of day for night. The orchestral score is also a refreshing touch after the seventies bop of previous entries, making *Curse of the Devil* feel more like a classic horror movie of yesteryear.

LA VENGANZA DE LA MOMIA/THE MUMMY'S REVENGE (1973)

Director: Carlos Aured
Writer: Paul Naschy

Say what you want of Spain's prolific horror movie writer and actor Paul Naschy, he was certainly thorough in dusting off the period gothic of Universal and Hammer and bringing it to modern audiences. As well as his twelve-movie *Hombre Lobo* series about the werewolf count Waldemar Daninsky (which featured appearances from vampires, a Frankenstein's monster and Jekyll and Hyde), 'the Spanish Lon Chaney' also played Dracula in 1973's *Count Dracula's Great Love* and penned several movies about devil worship and occultism set in gloomy castles and mansions (*Horror Rises from the Tomb* and his disowned *Cross of the Devil*). Amongst all this bargain basement gothic nostalgia, Naschy also wrote a single mummy movie in which he characteristically plays several parts.

As is the case with most mummy movies, *The Mummy's Revenge* starts with a prologue set in ancient times. Naschy plays the pharaoh Amenhotep (taking the name of the real-life heretic pharaoh, and possible father of Tutankhamun, who tried to introduce monotheism to Egypt and was nearly scrubbed from history for his efforts). A particularly nasty piece of work, Amenhotep and his consort, Amarna (Rina Ottolina), delight in sacrificing virgins in pursuit of their own immortality. Fed up with their antics, the high priest arranges for Amenhotep to be incapacitated by a potion slipped into his drink while Amarna is murdered in front of him. As punishment for his crimes, Amenhotep is mummified alive.

Centuries later, Egyptologist Professor Nathan Stern (Jack Taylor) and his assistant, Abigail (María Silva who played Elizabeth Bathory in *Curse of the Devil*), discover the tomb and cart Amenhotep's mummy back to London. The sinister Assad Bey (Paul Naschy in his second role) and his assistant Zanufer (Helga Liné, who also played Naschy's witchy consort in *Horror Rises from the Tomb*) turn up and resurrect the mummy using the blood of three unfortunate virgins.

But far from being a mummy under the control of a wicked priest (like Kharis was in so many of Universal's mummy movies), Amenhotep has a mind of his own and demands more sacrifices to restore him fully. Also, the half-Egyptian daughter of the expedition's financier looks just his Amenhotep's love Amarna and, as she is also played by Rina Ottolina, we can safely assume that she is her descendant just as Assad Bey is Amenhotep's. As young women start to go missing in Victorian London, Nathan Stern tries to find a way to dispatch Amenhotep back to the afterlife.

If you've seen any other mummy movies (and I mean *any* of them), there will be a lot that's familiar in *The Mummy's Revenge*. Naschy seems to have plundered every one of them going all the way back to Universal's *The Mummy* (1932) which featured a similar theme of reincarnation and a fez-wearing villain called Ardeth Bey. Its sequels consistently involved mummies being brought back to life by evil sects and used as tools of death. Hammer continued the tradition until its mummy-less mummy movie *Blood from the Mummy's Tomb* which, like this movie, muddled reincarnation, possession and direct decent to a degree where it is unclear which is actually the case (if not, all three).

By trying to ape every mummy movie that came before it, *The Mummy's Revenge* tries to cram too much into its short runtime and, like many of Naschy's movies, suffers a little from too many characters. As a result the 'hero', Nathan Stern, doesn't really get to do a lot. There's also a hint of betrayal and a lesbian subplot involving Zanufer and the reincarnation of Armana which isn't explored much.

Naturally, the mummy make up isn't a patch on the efforts that graced the faces of Boris Karloff and Christopher Lee, but Naschy's mummy is refreshingly more energetic than most shambling reanimated fiends and is able to climb ladders and even talk via telepathy. The movie is decidedly bloodier than anything from Universal or Hammer with stabbings, throat cuttings and head squashings along with gratuitous torture of sacrificial virgins. But aside from the violence, *The Mummy's Revenge* does little different with the classic monster which had grown even staler than Dracula and Frankenstein by the 1970s. The plot is no doubt another of Naschy's homages to the horror movies of his childhood but, despite nice-looking sets and locations, it is in danger of being seen as little more than dull cliché.

The Mummy's Revenge received a short 1973 release in Spain and Mexico before the dubbed version reached US television screens the year later. It enjoyed a second theatrical release in Spain in 1975 leading to some confusion as to when the movie was actually made. It was shot in 1973 as part of a short burst of collaborations between Naschy and director Carlos Aured before the two had a falling out and never worked together again.

BABA YAGA (1973)

Director: Corrado Farina
Writers: Corrado Farina, Guido Crepax and Giulio Berruti

A witch figure from Slavic folklore, Baba Yaga features in this Franch-Italian erotic horror movie by way of Guido Crepax's comic strip series *Valentina*, which depicts the psychedelic, supernatural and erotic escapades of its titular black bob-sporting Milanese photographer. Valentina originated as the girlfriend of the superhero Neutron in the 1965 comic book of the same name, but the series quickly began to focus on her as its main character, changing its name to *Valentina* in 1967.

Italian director Corrado Farina, whose only other movie was the anti-capitalist horror movie *They Have Changed Their Face* (1971), directed a short documentary on Crepax's work called *Freud a fumetti* (1970). With funding from Italian and French production companies, Farina embarked on an adaptation of Crepax's work which became a surreal, stylish and kinky fetish dream layered with the left-wing politics Farina and Crepax evidently shared.

On her way home from a party with her bohemian Marxist friends, Valentina (Isabelle De Funes) rescues a puppy from being run over by a car. The car's owner introduces herself as Baba Yaga (Carroll Baker). Apparently ignorant of Eastern European folklore, this sets no alarm bells ringing with Valentina who is inexplicably drawn to the old eccentric. Baba Yaga steals a clip from Valentina's suspenders, clearly besotted with the young photographer.

That night, Valentina has a surreal dream in which she is forced to jump into a bottomless pit by a bunch of Nazis. That she finds a similar black hole (to Hell?) in

331

the floor of Baba Yaga's house later in the movie, suggests that the old witch has already started exerting some supernatural influence on her. There's a sexual tension between the two but it's unclear how reciprocal it is. The only thing that is clear is that Baba Yaga wants Valentina for herself and will stop at nothing to get her.

For reasons known only to herself, Baba Yaga curses Valentina's favorite camera which kills whoever she photographs with it. She also gives her an alarming doll dressed in bondage gear which seems to have a mind of its own. It's nothing as obvious as Chucky or Annabelle but it refuses to stay where Valentina leaves it and, in one harrowing scene during a power cut, appears to have stabbed one of Valentina's models with a hairpin.

We are given a collection of horror movie tropes in *Baba Yaga* but none of them feel cliché as they are so bizarrely presented that they seem original. The plot's dream logic is a struggle to untangle and probably isn't as important as the movie's visuals which Farina handles excellently, giving us an arthouse horror movie loaded with pop art and high fashion style that has echoes of *Blow-Up* (1966) and *The Eyes of Laura Mars* (1978).

The rundown areas of Milan are beautifully shot and there is an interesting contrast between Valentina's modern, fashionable apartment and Baba Yaga's junk-filled derelict house. Although there is plenty of nudity (at least in the cut Farina restored himself after the studio butchered the movie behind his back), it's never done in an exploitative way. Even the sex scenes are artistically presented in the form of black and white stills shown in the frames of a comic strip (a style called *fumetti*).

A horror movie of the subtlest flavor, *Baba Yaga* is an intriguing oddity that will test the patience of some but for those who enjoy the cinematic surrealism of early-seventies arthouse movies will get a kick out of it.

There are plenty of sequences which might be fever dreams caused by repressed sexual fantasies or the results of Baba Yaga's witchcraft, such as the bondage doll turning into an actual human (Ely Galleani) who then whips Valentina in a bizarre BDSM scene.

HEX (1973)

Director: Leo Garan
Writers: Leo Garen and Stephen Katz

In 1969, two broke writers, Vernon Zimmerman and Doran Cannon, threw together a screenplay for an occult biker movie. Leo Garen, whose career at that point consisted of directing a single episode of *I Dream of Jeannie* bought it and sat on it for a year before rewriting it with Stephen Katz (who would go on to write for *The A-Team, Magnum P.I.* and *Knight Rider*). The result was this absolute oddball of a movie which mixes the biker, western and occult horror genres and plonks them in 1919 Nebraska.

Two sisters live on a ranch and make do after their Native American father and English mother have died. Cristina Raines (using her real name Cristina Herazo) plays the no-nonsense, hard-as-nails eldest sister Oriole, while Hilarie Thompson plays the younger sister Acacia; an innocent hayseed who says things like "Tarnation!" and "Holy Hickory!"

On a supply run to the nearby town of Bingo, the sisters encounter some shaggy-haired bikers who look like they belong in *Easy Rider* (in fact one of them, Robert Walker Jr., *was* in *Easy Rider*). Led by 'Whizzer' (Keith Carradine), these bikers are the usual louts out for kicks that we get in every other biker movie only this time, they are WWI veterans on classic Harleys.

The gang get into an argument with local oaf, Brother Billy (Dan Haggerty, another veteran of *Easy Rider* and half a dozen other biker movies) who drives a ludicrous chopped Model T Ford with a flame paintjob. They have a race down Main Street and then the biker gang are chased out of town.

They seek refuge at the ranch of Oriole and Acacia,

forcing them to be their hosts. One of them, 'Giblets' (Gary Busey), takes a fancy to Acacia and assaults her during the night and is defended by Oriole in an altercation which wakes up the rest of the bikers. Whizzer is none too pleased with Giblets and makes him sleep outside. What happens next is a little ambiguous, but Oriole opens a bedroom window and Gibson is attacked and killed by an owl. Dangerous local wildlife or something more mystic?

They bury Giblets the following day and romance begins to blossom on the ranch. Acacia and kind-hearted kid 'Golly' (Mike Combs) birth a calf and fix a well while Whizzer teaches Oriole all about motorcycles.

None of this feels much like a horror movie and for the first hour, it really isn't. Whizzer's girl, China (Doria Cook) takes exception to his rolling around in the hay with Oriole and breaks things up resulting in fisticuffs with her rival. Oriole is not a woman to be crossed and curses China by sewing up a lock of her hair in a toad's mouth. China then suffers an exceedingly bad trip in which she is attacked by toads, rats and snakes before fleeing into the woods where even the trees have it in for her.

It's clear that Oriole has some mystic powers and now that her ire is raised, things start to look bleak for the rest of the bikers. Whizzer wants to leave but can't until China is found and, as members of his gang are picked off one by one under increasingly strange circumstances, he begins to suspect that the woman he is infatuated with is some sort of witch.

Hex is such a strange movie that 20th Century Fox didn't really know what to do with it. They fiddled around with it for a year, cutting out all the comedic elements and making it a straight horror movie. It was released in 1973 to a poor reception. Leo Garan was given the opportunity to recut the movie but Fox decided against giving it a wide release. It limped out on home video in the nineties under various names such as *Charms* and *The Shrieking*.

Character and drama are the focus rather than the threadbare plot. The use of cheap scares is forgone in place of deepening tension and atmosphere which is helped by the nicely shot isolation of the dusty prairie. But even then, *Hex* barely qualifies as a horror movie, instead landing somewhere in the acid hippie fallout of *Easy Rider*. Once the novelty of the concept has worn off, there isn't a lot about *Hex* to recommend it. The performances on the whole are quite good and it's an impressive cast for such a cinematic outlier. Raines would go on to star in a far better occult horror movie, *The Sentinel*.

SUGAR HILL (1974)

Director: Paul Maslansky
Writers: Tim Kelly and Don Pedro Colley

AIP began to grow concerned in the 1970s that horror was no longer a lucrative option and so began to cross pollinate with other genres. Scoring big hits with *Blacula* (1973) and its sequel *Scream Blacula Scream*, AIP naturally felt that blaxploitation and horror was a winning combination and dusted off the old pre-Romero Voodoo zombie genre for an infusion of funk, soul and large afros.

Marki Bey (in the only starring role of her career) is the titular Diana 'Sugar' Hill, a fashion photographer who is dating flash nightclub owner, Langston (Larry D. Johnson). Unfortunately, gangster Morgan, played by Robert Quarry (Count Yorga himself, here in one of his final movies for AIP), has his sights set on owning Langston's club. When Langston refuses to sell up, Morgan's goons beat him to death in the parking lot.

Sugar is keen for vengeance and goes to local Voodoo practitioner, Mama Maitresse (Zara Cully) who helps her summon Baron Samedi (Don Pedro Colley). In an ambiguous deal with the Voodoo loa, Sugar is given the use of a group of zombies to exact her revenge on Morgan and his thugs. One by one, the men who murdered Langston are done away with in various nasty ways while Sugar's cop ex-boyfriend, Lt. Valentine (Richard Lawson, who played the villain in *Scream Blacula Scream*) tries to get to the bottom of the unusual deaths.

Whatever Sugar has bargained away isn't clear but she's always present when her zombies dispatch the next name on her list, looking fabulous in an afro and white rhinestone pantsuit. The fact that she seems to pop up out of thin air, and always wearing the same getup when exacting her revenge, suggests that this might be a supernatural extension of herself doing her dirty work while she plays innocent elsewhere, namely toying with Morgan who wants to buy the club from her which Langston left to her in his will. She's also a dab hand at Voodoo herself, pricking dolls to torment her victims further, even breaking Lt. Valentine's leg so he will be deterred from pursuing her. This ruthless side to Sugar also suggests a supernatural darkness brought out by her deal with Baron Samedi.

Being a blaxploitation movie about Voodoo, *Sugar Hill* naturally has a few things to say about race politics. The opening Voodoo ceremony which features erratic dancing, chicken sacrifice and snakes to the funky beat of The Originals' 'Supernatural Voodoo Woman' turns out to be a nightclub act for a predominantly white audience. The real Voodoo in the movie is far more subtle, personified by Zara Cully's hermit-like Mama Maitresse who seems to live beyond the sight of the white authorities.

The zombies occasionally drop manacles at the scenes of their crimes, identifying them as former slaves. These perhaps intentional calling cards put the fear of God into the white villains who, even for blaxploitation standards, are hideously racist, right down to Morgan's nasty trophy girlfriend, Celeste (Betty Anne Rees) with whom Sugar has a frantic barroom catfight.

There isn't a whole lot of gore for a zombie movie and it feels more like a blaxploitation vigilante movie along the lines of *Coffy* (1973) and *Foxy Brown* (1974) with occult elements rather than a straight-up horror. And even the blaxploitation staples of violence and nudity are tame enough to warrant a PG rating. But it's a lot of fun nevertheless and one particularly effective scene involves a victim getting a massage, thinking it's

338

from a beautiful woman. Wondering why her hands are so cold, he rolls around to see that he's getting the business from the decayed, dead hands of the zombies right before they strangle him.

There's some slight silliness when one of Morgan's flunkies is attacked by a dismembered chicken's foot but on the whole, *Sugar Hill* is atmospherically creepy. The undead have a unique look with what looks like steel balls in place of their eyes and their bodies matted with cobwebs.

Marki Bey more than holds her own, dealing out sassy and savage putdowns on par with Pam Grier and it's strange she never played the lead in more movies. Don Pedro Colley is also a fine Baron Samedi (his version only a year after James Bond faced off Geoffrey Holder's take on the same character in *Live and Let Die*), putting himself at Sugar's disposal for the duration of the 'contract' and looking like he's enjoying every second of it. With the addition of Robert Quarry as the slimy villain, *Sugar Hill* has a great cast and presents a tight tale of supernatural revenge to make it a solid entry in both the blaxploitation and occult horror arenas.

LES POSSÉDÉES DU DIABLE/LORNA THE EXORCIST (1974)

Director: Jesús Franco
Writers: Jesús Franco, Nicole Guettard and Robert de Nesle

Jess Franco does Faust in this disturbing occult thriller centered on a man's past indiscretions coming back to haunt his family via some nasty erotic horror. *Lorna the Exorcist* is an early collaboration between Franco and his new leading lady, Lina Romay, who would go on to be his lifelong partner and muse, starring in over a hundred of Franco's sexually charged movies.

Lina plays teenager (yikes!) Linda who, on the cusp of her eighteenth birthday, is promised a trip to Rome by her father, Patrick (Guy Delorme). A strange phone call from a mysterious woman changes Patrick's mind and the family head off to Saint-Tropez instead, much to Linda's chagrin. Patrick has been told to come here by the titular Lorna (Pamela Stanford) who he had a fling with nineteen years ago.

We gradually learn that Lorna isn't just some floozy. She helped the down-and-out Patrick win big at the casino table back in the day and promised him much more if he'll hand his yet-to-be conceived firstborn over to her on its eighteenth birthday. His mind on sex and money, Patrick agreed in a heartbeat. The problem is, his decision doesn't seem too clever now nineteen years later when he has a daughter he is very fond of. He tells Lorna to get lost but, as we've already surmised by the erotic dreams of young Linda, the witchy woman has supernatural powers and is already exerting an influence on her prize.

Patrick's wife, Marianne (Jacqueline Laurent)

knows her husband is up to something and is in for a rough time as Lorna clearly wants her out of the way. This results in a bad case of crabs during sex (literal crabs of the seafood variety crawling out of her pubic region). As well as being a gross-out horror moment, it's also a not-so-subtle allegory for a husband's infidelity having unintended consequences on his wife.

Despite its title (clearly conceived to cash in on a certain popular American horror movie that came out the previous year), Lorna is not an exorcist, nor are there any exorcisms in the movie. The narrative hops around a little, skipping between the past and present as well as curious scenes of a mad woman in some sort of sanitorium where Jess Franco himself appears as the doctor. These odd scenes only become relevant in the closing act as Lorna's revenge comes to fruition.

Filmed in the then-new and chic pyramidal architecture of France's La Grande-Motte resort, the backdrop of retro hotel rooms and sterile modernism provides an eerie and alien location for the movie's dreamlike plot. The loneliness of the unfamiliar is conveyed no better than in the scenes towards the end of the movie as Patrick frantically searches the curiously depopulated resort for his missing daughter.

The cast is good with Line Romay the standout, transitioning from wide-eyed innocent to seductive killer as Lorna gradually exerts her control over her. It's her rictus grin in the final scene which lingers with the audience; an unnerving mixture of triumph and horror at what she has become.

The movie is, of course, not without its problems. Franco, director of a hundred-and-seventy-odd movies, was prolific but slapdash. Sloppy editing, curiously long takes and endless sex scenes which drag the movie into the realm of porn plague even his best work and *Lorna the Exorcist* is certainly in that category, being one of his rare movies that offers a solid plot and decent storytelling to go along with the boobs, butts and zoom shots of women's vaginas.

Franco would continue to cash in on the Exorcist craze without delivering any actual exorcisms with 1975's *L'éventreur de Notre-Dame* also known as *Exorcism* about a murderous priest (played by Franco himself) who butchers sexually promiscuous women partaking in fake black masses. A more hardcore cut called *Sexorcism* was released a year later. Franco rehashed the whole thing in 1979, shooting more scenes to add extra characterization, as *El sádico de Notre-Dame* (*The Sadist of Notre Dame*) before a severely cut and clothed version came out on video in the US under the title *Demoniac*.

DIABOLICAMENTE... LETIZIA/SEX, DEMONS AND DEATH (1975)
Director: Salvatore Bugnatelli
Writers: Lorenzo Artale and Salvatore Bugnatelli

Salvatore Bugnatelli's directorial career consisted of a handful of low-rent skin flicks including this 1975 attempt at an occult horror movie with plenty of boobs. His only previous directorial effort was *Scusi eminenza... posso sposarmi?* (*Excuse me, Padre, Are You Horny?*) from that same year and his next movie, shot in 1979, ran out of funds and was rehashed in 1983 as something of a tutorial on how to shoot a pornographic movie titled *Mizzzzica... ma che è proibitissimo?*

Starring Italian stud Gabriele Tinti (also seen in *The House of Exorcism* and *The Eerie Midnight Horror Show*) and Polish actress Magda Konopka as man and wife Marcello and Micaela, *Sex, Demons and Death* is ostensibly a sex-fest which plays on the contemporary theme of young people and their fascination with the occult.

Marcello and Micaela's marriage is struggling. Unable to have children, Micaela suggests that they adopt her teenage niece, Letizia (Franca Gonella) who has been languishing in a boarding school since her parents died. As soon as the stunningly beautiful Letizia arrives, things start to go awry in the Martinozzi household.

Sex, Demons and Death is the kind of movie where every single character is horny and nobody can keep their hands off each other. Marcello and Letizia, Letizia and Michaela, Letizia and the chauffeur, the chauffeur and the maid, the maid and Michaela ... everybody is at it and it's not entirely apparent if this is all down to Letizia's arrival in the household or if this is just

343

business as usual for Gabriele Tinti and his crowd. What's more, somebody is taking black and white snapshots of the sexual shenanigans with a hidden camera, no doubt with blackmail on their mind.

There is also some occult action going on. The first time we realize that Letitia might not be on the up-and-up is when she gives the chauffeur (Gianni Dei) a fright when he walks in on her undressing and she spins around with a snarl, her face a demonic, bearded horror (he actually says "Mamma Mia!" to this before running off). She has telekinetic powers and is able to move ashtrays and pillows about and, in one scene, causes her uncle's friend to miss his mouth while drinking a glass of water, amusingly recalling Robert Hays's 'drinking problem' in *Airplane!*.

Letizia is intent on screwing with (and screwing) everybody in the household. Her attempts to turn the maid (Karin Fiedler) lesbian result in a bizarre scene in which the maid comes on to Michaela who doesn't seem too averse to the idea before recovering her senses and throwing the maid out. The sex scenes, while obviously gratuitous, are tame enough to keep the movie from being classed as hardcore.

As well as the mildness of the titillation factor, *Sex, Demons and Death* is pretty tame on the horror front too with not much in the way of special effects other than some double exposures and a bit of levitating. The only gore to be seen is a vision of a severed head in a bed. Letizia is clearly versed in the occult and uses a Voodoo doll to drive her already hysterical aunt closer to madness but her motivations are left ambiguous until the final act.

There's a nice little mystery buried somewhere in the plot. What is Letizia playing at and where did she get her occult powers? And who is the mustachioed man in a hat played by Xiro Papas who loiters around the

344

villa's grounds, spying on the proceedings? These questions and the interesting twist ending spice up an otherwise fairly dull sexploitation movie that barely qualifies as horror.

THE DEMON LOVER (1976)

Directors: Donald G. Jackson and Jerry Younkins
Writers: Donald G. Jackson and Jerry Younkins

The making of Midwestern Z-grade horror movie *The Demon Lover* has become part of cult movie mythology due to a 16mm home movie shot simultaneously by Joel de Mott, partner of the movie's cinematographer Jeff Krienes. More entertaining (and longer) than the movie in question, it depicts a tumultuous fifteen days during *The Demon Lover*'s making. Titled *The Demon Lover Diary*, this loose 'making-of' received a limited theatrical release in 1980 and is a fascinating insight into independent moviemaking of the lowest order.

It introduces us to Donald G. Jackson and Jerry Younkins, two factory workers who had a dream to make a horror movie. Jerry even severed part of his finger at work to drum up $8,000 in insurance money to finance it. The film shoot has something of the horror movie feel to it as Krienes and de Mott become stranded with a pair of egomaniacal filmmakers who don't have the first clue about making a movie or indeed, health and safety, demonstrated by their insistence on using live rounds in firearms borrowed from rockstar Ted Nugent. After a particularly sour argument, the movie ends with Krienes and de Mott fleeing in their car while gunshots ring out behind them.

The Demon Lover itself focuses on a loose coven of bored teenagers who hang out in a faux castle somewhere in Michigan, partying and conducting black masses. Their leader is one Laval Blessing played by Jerry Younkins under the alias Christmas Robbins (wearing a black glove due to his recently removed digit). He's a bit like an Aleister Crowley of the American Midwest (if Crowley looked like he used to jam with

346

Metallica before they became famous). This gang is everything the post-counterculture obsession with the occult is all about. There are conversations about Vietnam and women's lib as well as breaking free of the chains of the old world and 'tapping the power inside of you', all set against a backdrop of beer-guzzling, enormous moustaches and dreadful dancing as well as a see through 'love-making tent'.

But cracks have started to appear in the coven's enthusiasm, brought to a head by newcomer Pamela (Kyra Nash) who objects to Laval's treatment of the women as sex objects (to be fair, Laval does kick one of his rituals off by saying "The women remove their clothes, and the men form a circle!"). After a huge row, the half-assed cultists split, leaving an enraged Laval alone in his castle.

In vengeance, Laval conjures a naked woman who then turns into a demon which he dispatches to murder Pamela, revealing that she is the victim in the pre-credits massacre sequence. Laval doesn't stop there, however. He wants to rub out every last member of his old coven in a plot reminiscent of M. R. James's *Casting the Runes*.

On the case of the murders is Detective Tom Frazetta (Tom Hutton), the most whiny and ineffectual cop ever. He turns up at the bakery where one of Laval's ex-acolytes works and unsuccessfully tries to get her to talk. When she won't play ball, he childishly pings a rubber band at her before she kicks him out. Fortunately, his wife knows some occult types of the academic variety and he tags along to one of their parties to quiz Professor Peckinpah played by Gunnar Hansen (old Leatherface himself in an astounding cameo).

With names like Frazetta and Peckinpah, it's clear that Jackson and Younkins are having some fun with character names and indeed, there are similar tributes to several comic book artists like Jack Kirby, Neal Adams, Michale Kaluta, Chester Gould and Nestor Redondo as well as other pop culture giants like George A. Romero and Forrest J. Ackerman.

Many of the movies in this book are guilty of a brand of bad acting where people read unconvincingly from cue cards, but then there's the type of acting where actors are given free reign to make up their own lines which can often end up in lots of "ums" and "uhs". *The Demon Lover* falls into the latter category and director Donald G. Jackson would later champion a method of 'zen filmmaking' which basically involves making movies without scripts. It certainly feels like he started early with this one.

With a plot so thin and no real characters, there is naturally plenty of filler like three straight minutes of people practicing judo which is presumably meant to explain how the tubby Laval can handle himself in the barroom brawl in the next scene, none of which has any relevance to the plot. Then there's the three women having a whipped cream fight (not nearly as erotic as it sounds) for no apparent reason before Laval's demon turns up and butchers them all. Incidentally, the spontaneous whipped cream scene nearly caused Jeff Krienes to storm off the set as his camera equipment was endangered.

The violence and agonized screaming of the finale pulls no punches and is lingered on quite a bit resulting in a fairly unsettling end to a movie that is likely to induce laughter for much of its running time. While nothing special on a technical level, the sudden gore manages to shock, in particular when one of the women is slammed against the hood of a car which is seemingly possessed. The rubber demon with red, glowing eyes, on the other hand, is nothing short of hopeless.

Despite a disorganized and tense production of

legendary proportions, *The Demon Lover* made it into theaters by 1977 and then emerged on video in the 1980s under several titles including *Coven*, *The Demon Master* and *Master of Evil*. Donald G. Jackson went on to make many schlocky titles in the eighties and nineties including *Hell Comes to Frog Town* (1987) and a series of movies about futuristic roller-skating warriors inaugurated by *Roller Blade* (1986) which are so campy that one might be tempted to believe his later claims that *The Demon Lover* was intended as a parody all along.

SHADOW OF THE HAWK (1976)

Directors: George McCowan
Writers: Peter Jensen, Lynette Cahill, Herbert Wright and
Norman Thaddeus Vane

Canadian director George McCowan helmed episodes of TV hits like *Charlie's Angels* and *Starsky and Hutch* as well as a couple of feature movies; *The Magnificent Seven Ride!* and *Frogs* (both 1972). Here, he directs a folksy Native American horror on his home turf which has the spirit of a fantasy adventure to go with the chills.

Chief Dan George (an actual chief of the Tsleil-Waututh Nation who is most famous for his roles in 1970's *Little Big Man* and 1976's *The Outlaw Josey Wales*) plays 'Old Man Hawk', a medicine man in a village in the Pacific Northwest. Sensing that he is under attack by an evil sorceress called Dsonoqua, Hawk heads to the big city in search of his estranged grandson whom he hopes to train to defeat his evil nemesis.

Cue Jan-Michael Vincent in his pre-*Airwolf* days as well-to-do womanizing city slicker Mike. Rather unconvincingly, he's supposed to be half Native American, and is the grandson Hawk is looking for. The wicked Dsonoqua is also reaching out to Mike, giving him a fright in the form of a pale, masked specter which appears in his swimming pool and outside his apartment window in the dead of night.

Hawk collapses in the street after Dsonoqua sticks pins in a doll, causing him to be admitted to hospital where he meets reporter Maureen (Marilyn Hassett). Sensing a story, Maureen helps Hawk locate his grandson who is a little miffed at the old man's reappearance in his life and doesn't exactly feel like becoming his protégé. But, seeing a chance to get into

Maureen's good books (and potentially bed her), the shallow Mike agrees to drive Hawk the three-hundred-odd miles back to his home, with Maureen tagging along for the ride.

So begins something of a road movie with the element of the sword and sorcery plot as three mismatched characters head north in a Toyota Land Cruiser while the forces of darkness try to stop them by hurling supernatural obstacles in their path. There's plenty of opportunity for drama and characterization with a man of Native descent rediscovering his heritage and reconnecting with his grandfather for whom he develops a newfound respect. But all of that is only hinted at and never properly explored while Marilyn Hassett unfortunately gets stuck with the damsel in distress schtick and is left in a safehouse for most of the climax.

While never overtly horrific or scary, there's some unsettling imagery, particularly the masked specter summoned by Dsonoqua which bears a similarity to the demon in *Onibaba* (1964) and is used to great effect initially but ends up being overused by the end of the movie, diminishing its creepiness. Other supernatural heavies involve a shapeshifter and, for some reason, zombies. All of this might work if we had a better understanding of what Dsonoqua's deal is and why she wants to kill gramps and Mike, but we never see much of her, let alone find out what she's thinking.

There are some good set pieces however, including a hair-raising trip across a rope bridge and a particularly impressive bit of magic which causes a black sedan to smash into an invisible barrier Hawk has created with some mysterious black powder. These are let down somewhat by a laughable fight with a bear cobbled together from stock footage of different bears along with shots of what is clearly a man in a bear suit.

In all, *Shadow of the Hawk* is entertaining hokum. It never gets dull and keeps things going at a decent pace with TV production talent both behind and in front of the camera.

DARK AUGUST (1976)

Director: Martin Goldman
Writers: J. J. Barry, Martin Goldman and Carolyne Barry

Sal Devito (J. J. Barry) is a man consumed by guilt over his killing of a little girl who ran out in front of his truck shortly after he and his girlfriend, Jackie (Carolyne Barry) moved to a small town in Vermont. Although cleared of wrongdoing, Sal's mental health is struggling, and he fears that the girl's grandfather (William Robertson) has it in for him.

He's not wrong as the grandfather is some sort of occultist who places a curse on Sal during the opening credits. The nature of the curse is ambiguous, but Sal suffers physical symptoms which cause him to collapse in a grocery store. On top of this, he keeps seeing a hooded figure watching him from the woods.

Director Martin Goldman lucked out in getting Kim Hunter (known for her roles as Stella in 1951's *A Streetcar Named Desire* and as the Chimpanzee professor Zira in the Planet of the Apes movies) to star in his low-budget regional horror flick. She plays local 'witch' Adrianna who Sal goes to in search of help. Suspecting that he may be under the influence of black magic, Adrianna works her own brand of white magic (which curiously involves the Lord's Prayer) to save him.

The densely wooded Vermont scenery is nicely shot, contributing to a growing sense of unease which helps *Dark August* explore the seventies phenomenon of folk horror with its constant juxtaposing of city life and country life. Sal's paranoia is exacerbated by the unwelcoming country folk who stand by, glassy-eyed while he has what looks like a heart attack in the grocery store or when he confronts the vindictive grandfather on the street. It's clear that he's the fish out of water and, while falling short of the outright folk horror of *The Wicker Man* or *Deliverance*, *Dark August* does toy with similar motifs to some atmospheric effect.

J. J. Barry is great as the worn-down tough guy, consumed by guilt over the girl's death. A movie dealing with psychological turmoil might go for a more sensitive archetype as its lead, but Barry's depiction of a blue collar Italian American average Joe is a refreshing reminder that anyone's mental health can suffer under such circumstances. Barry does a good job depicting gradual mental collapse and his bedroom scene with real-life wife, Carolyne Barry, in which he attacks her during sex, is particularly unnerving.

There's a certain authenticity to *Dark August* as it eschews occult movie cliches and presents a story that could conceivably happen. The supernatural powers on display are suggestive rather than overt. There are no robed cultists or silly masks, and no special effects or bloodletting. Instead, we get tarot readings, earthy folk magic and prayer which may work or may all be psychological. We don't know for a fact that the old man's curse is causing Sal's symptoms. They could be the effects of his crushing guilt or perhaps the paranoia of a city slicker in the backwoods, all of which makes *Dark August* an interesting character-driven movie amid the less subtle shockers of the period.

As another regional drive-in effort, *Dark August* feels like a TV movie similar to *Hex* and *Shadow of the Hawk* in that it is big on character drama and dialogue and light on horror and action. The electronic and occasionally out of place score along with its leading couple who were primarily TV actors, only adds to this. The movie could have done more with its material, and the ending feels a little tacked on but, if you like your horror of the restrained and more psychological variety, *Dark August* has quite a few things going for it.

La Perversa Caricia de Satán/Devil's Kiss (1976)

Director: Jordi Gigó
Writer: Jordi Gigó

Jordi Gigó's career consisted of a single writing credit for the Paul Naschy-starring possession movie *Exorcism* before he got to write and direct his own movie the following year; this strange and sleazy gothic chiller which blends occultism with mad science. Gigó would only direct a couple more movies, one of them being *Porno Girls* (1977), which was released just as Spain's censorship laws were being relaxed after Franco's death. That tells us roughly what to expect from *The Devil's Kiss*; a much more boring title than the direct translation of the Spanish which is 'The Perverse Caresses of Satan'.

The movie is set almost exclusively at the Château de Haussemont where the Duke de Haussemont (José Nieto) is trying to spice up his parties with a fashion show featuring some ridiculous seventies outfits and some even more ridiculous dancing (the show's presenter is Jordi Gigó himself). Another of the duke's attempts to enliven his gatherings is inviting Claire Grandier (Silvia Solar), a former countess who is now a medium and her companion Professor Gruber (Olivier Mathot), a scientist who also claims to be telepathic.

Claire holds a grudge against the duke as he purchased her late husband's stables for a ruinously low sum, thus making him destitute and driving him to suicide. After giving an apparently convincing séance which causes one of the models to scream and faint in an upstairs bedroom (at what exactly, is never explained), the duke offers Claire and Professor Gruber bed and board in his castle as well as funding for their research if Claire will teach him the secrets of the occult.

Now secured within Château de Haussemont, Claire is free to put her plan of revenge into action. She starts by giving shelter to a dwarf (Ronnie Harp) who apparently assaulted a young girl and recruiting him as her personal 'Igor'.

It's a slow start but builds some interest when the malevolent pair steal a recently buried corpse for use in their experiments. Through a combination of satanic ritual and Gruber's 'animal cell regeneration' research, they are able to resurrect the corpse (Moisés Augusto Rocha) which they control through Gruber's telepathy.

Soon the zombie is rampaging through the castle, killing at the will of its masters. After Duke de Haussemont is murdered in his bed, his nephew, Richard (Daniel Martín), takes over the castle. Richard is a fashion photographer giving Gigó ample opportunity to have more shots of models posing in odd fashion choices (he must have got a deal on a wardrobe of outfits). Richard allows Claire and Professor Gruber to remain in the castle but, as Gruber's health starts to fail, his telepathic control over the zombie begins to wane, which spells trouble for all at Château de Haussemont.

The Devil's Kiss moves at a glacial pace with its characters moving not much faster than its ambling zombie. There are endless shots of people dressing and undressing but only one real sex scene (which is surprising, given the director's later work). It skimps on the horror too with very little blood and most of the kills consisting only of the zombie grabbing the victims by the throat before the camera cuts away.

It's a fairly nice-looking movie, however, with an impressive gothic castle with candle-lit basements juxtaposed with the bright, garish clothes of the mid-seventies. It's all a bit wasted though, as Jordi Gigó fails to shoot anything with a pulse. It's also a little unclear the role Claire's black magic plays in reanimating the corpse as it seems to be a product of Frankenstein-style science and Gruber's telepathy, although it is unable to enter the church in the movie's rather limp climax, indicating some sort of demonic influence. It's an interesting blend of ideas but not explored to any satisfying level.

CRYPT OF DARK SECRETS (1976)

Director: Jack Weis
Writers: Irwin Blaché and Jack Weis

Jack Weis, director of Southern fried sleaze like *Quadroon* (1971) and *Death Brings Roses* (1975) is best known for making the notorious *Mardi Gras Massacre*, a horror movie about a serial killer who sacrifices prostitutes to an Aztec goddess. Some of the ideas in that movie were clearly incubated in his lesser-known half-baked 1976 effort, *Crypt of Dark Secrets*.

The elusive Maureen Ridley (who only had a bit part in one other movie; the 1972 comedy *Private Collection*) plays Damballa, a witch who dwells in the Louisiana swamps. Damballa is a figure plucked from African diaspora religions such as Haitian Vodou. A male figure in the form of a snake, Damballa is supposedly the primordial creator of all life. Needless to say, there is Voodoo aplenty in this swampy supernatural caper, but curiously not a single African American in sight while Damballa is recast as an Aztec goddess, though what an Aztec deity would be doing in Louisiana is anyone's guess.

Ronald Tanet (whose acting career was strictly limited to Jack Weis productions) plays Vietnam vet, Ted, who just wants a quiet retirement. He's moved into a creepy old house on a supposedly haunted island and keeps his sizable pension in a bread bin. He doesn't trust banks, which leads to a highly contrived scene where Ted and a bank teller discuss where he keeps his money right within earshot of a shady type who's just been refused an extension on his mortgage. This shady type (Butch Benit), along with his wife (Barbara Hagerty) and oafish friend (Harry Uher) decide to steal Ted's fortune. They head out to the island and, in a tussle, Ted gets knocked on the head and falls into the bayou where he drowns.

Damballa, who has been spying on things either as a snake or, laughably, by conspicuously peering in through the crooks' window, isn't too pleased. She has taken a liking to Ted and brings him back to life via a sensual dance to invisible bongo drums before straddling his corpse buck naked.

The crooks, meanwhile, have decided to hand themselves in after their ill-gotten loot turns out to be literally blood soaked. But that's not enough for Damballa who recruits the help of a local Voodoo practitioner to hoodwink the thieves into looking for pirate treasure in the bayou before drowning them all with the use of Voodoo dolls. It seems strange that a powerful shapeshifter would need a mere mortal's help or indeed, need to entice the cartoonishly stupid crooks with a lie about buried treasure.

The movie is amateurish tedium entirely lacking in action or scares. There are some nice shots of the Louisiana swamps and Maureen Ridley is quite mesmerizing but even at a paltry seventy minutes, *Crypt of Dark Secrets* stretches its material thin. Every conversation is long and drawn out with characters stating the obvious and shots lasting far longer than necessary. Ted, who should be the one seeking revenge on his murderers, even states that he is uncharacteristically chill about the whole business and does nothing for the rest of the movie other than hand out a few beers to the cops who are understandably confused to find him alive and well.

It's really Damballa's show and her full-frontal nude scenes were undoubtedly the main point of the movie with everything else just filler. Maureen Ridley's strange English accent is probably supposed to be mystical and exotic but we don't learn much about her. There are some flashbacks which present a muddled origin story that doesn't make a lick of sense and neither does the ending. Still, there's boobs and bongo music.

MARDI GRAS MASSACRE (1978)

Director: Jack Weis
Writer: Jack Weis

Jack Weis followed up his questionable 1976 movie, *Crypt of Dark Secrets* with what feels like a loose remake of Hershell Gordon Lewis's notorious *Blood Feast* (1963). While that movie was about a deranged killer who sacrificed his victims to the Egyptian goddess Ishtar (who was, in fact, a Mesopotamian rather than an Egyptian deity), Weis swaps this with an Aztec goddess called Coatl. Weis had namedropped the Aztecs in his previous movie, albeit conflating them with Louisiana Voodoo just as *Blood Feast* reassigned Ishtar to the Ancient Egyptians showing that the general view of the occult in the 1970s was a mishmash of beliefs with various religions and deities seen as pretty much interchangeable.

A serial killer called John (William Metzo) is going around bars in New Orleans, picking up hookers and killing them. He specifically wants 'evil' women, as shown in the hilarious opening scene with dialogue like "Hello, I understand that you are the most evil woman here," and "Listen, honey, I could probably take first prize in any evil contest".

John takes 'evil' prostitute Shirley (February 1975 Playboy Playmate, Laura Misch Owens) back to his apartment where he dons a gold mask, ties her up, cuts her hand and foot and removes her heart before placing it on an altar to his goddess.

Two cops are on the case, played by Curt Dawson and Ronald Tanet. Both had appeared in *Crypt of Dark Secrets* but Tanet (who played the lead in Weis's earlier stinker) takes a back seat to Dawson this time around. Dawson plays Detective Frank who falls for hooker-

361

with-a-heart-of-gold Sherry (Gwen Arment) who saw killer John leave with Shirley the night of her murder. The mawkish romance subplot is explored in montages of New Orleans's seedy nightlife. All this distracts from the plot and distracts Frank from actually pursuing the killer. He needs to hurry up as John is planning his grand opus of three sacrifices on Fat Tuesday.

It shouldn't be necessary to state that this is a bad movie in every sense of the word. The acting is horrendous with wooden deliveries presumably from cue cards. Locals occasionally stare at the camera, no doubt unaware that they're extras in a terrible horror movie. Continuity and editing are all over the place, made particularly apparent in the final chase scene which somehow fails to show any shots of the killer, making it look like the cops are running about with no real aim in mind.

The murders are repetitive with the killer barely altering his M.O. an inch, apparently removing the same heart from the same rubber dummy each time. Of course, there's tons of nudity to go with the gore and the erotic preludes to the sacrifices are greasy and sleazy with the killer oiling his victims up and groping their slippery bodies.

The generic funk soundtrack (which is incessant, even during the murder scenes) by *Black Belt Jones* composers Dennis Coffey and Mike Theodore is at least better than *Crypt of Dark Secrets*' bongo pounding, and, with a fun disco scene (complete with soap bubbles), the movie exudes 1978 trends and makes for an unintentional snapshot of the tacky side of the decade.

The occult angle is superficial and exists only as a motive for the woman-hating killer although the festival of Mardi Gras, while not as essential to the plot as the title suggests, provides a rare opportunity for the killer to mingle with the crowds dressed in his Aztec getup.

Also, an occult expert namedrops the Manson Family, falsely claiming that they were devil worshippers, which goes to show how entwined the idea of devil worship was with fears of the counterculture at the time.

Mardi Gras Massacre received an X rating on release and, like its inspiration, *Blood Feast*, wound up on Britain's video nasty list where it languished until 2022 when Severin Films released it on Blu-ray. It was the last movie for Jack Weis, perhaps unsurprisingly given the level of incompetence shown in his two horror howlers.

TERROR (1978)

Director: Norman J. Warren
Writers: David McGillivray, Les Young and Moira Young

Norman J. Warren, a pioneer of Britain's new wave of horror, returned to the occult (and the well-used country house, Admiral's Walk) after dabbling with sci-fi horror in his 1977 movie *Prey*. But *Terror* is a fairly light-hearted outing in comparison to the wave's nastier entries like *Satan's Slave* and *House of Whipcord* (1974), almost feeling like a metahorror comedy in which Warren may have been lampooning the genre a little.

Opening with a cliché-ridden witch burning in which 'Mad Dolly' (Patti Love) curses the Garrick family line before being executed by Lord Garrick, the words 'The End' abruptly appear on screen which must have confused theater goers in 1978. But of course, it's a movie within a movie, and we are soon out of the realm of Hammer gothic and into the trendy 1970s Britain its new wave of horror was all about.

James Garrick (John Nolan, uncle of director Christopher Nolan) is a movie director and is previewing his latest horror effort (about his nefarious ancestor) to a group of friends. They take it about as seriously as they do the Garrick family curse placed on them by the witch three-hundred years ago. Garrick's pal, Gary (Michael Craze), is a bit of a joker and pretends to hypnotize Garrick's cousin, Ann (Carolyn Courage). The trouble is, it seems to work, and Ann takes a swing at Garrick with a sword which apparently belonged to Mad Dolly, before leaving the house.

While his friends patch Garrick's arm up, blonde bombshell Carol (Glynis Barber) decides to walk home alone, through the woods. That goes about as well as you'd expect in a horror movie and she ends up on the wrong end of a butcher's knife, assailant unseen. A series of other murders take place with Ann the obvious suspect and *Terror* feels very much like a slasher movie, taking its cue from Italy's giallo output interestingly the same year a certain John Carpenter did the same in the US.

Visually, it takes its cues from Dario Argento's *Suspiria*, which Warren had seen before embarking on the project and deliberately set out to homage. The blood is Crayola red, the sets are lit with reds and greens and there are closeups aplenty of eyeballs and knives entering flesh. There's even a group of girls who board together under an eccentric Old Hollywood ham played by Elaine Ives-Cameron who does her best impression of *Sunset Boulevard*'s Norma Desmond as she name drops 'Cecil' and 'Lawrence' while swanning around in her evening dress.

Terror's similarity to *Suspiria* is only aesthetic. Its simple plot is something else entirely and doesn't even make much sense being little more than a series of murder set pieces, many of which involve people who have no connection to the Garret family. A good ten minutes are spent on a red herring in which one of Ann's friends thinks she is being pursued by the killer who turns out to be a helpful mechanic played by Chewbacca himself, Peter Mayhew. But, as the movie races through a series of grisly comeuppances for unpleasant and irrelevant side characters, it's clear that something supernatural is afoot, with the spirit of old Mad Dolly making her appearance in the climax.

Warren is certainly having fun with this one. There are many winks to the audience such as Garrick's office having posters on the wall for other horror movies, including Warren's own *Satan's Slave*. Warren also references his earlier career as a director of soft porn and a running gag throughout the movie is the shooting of the dreadful skin flick *Bathtime with Brenda* on Garrick's set, much to his annoyance.

It's all silly nonsense filmed on a shoestring budget, but Warren still manages to make a fun movie with plenty of humor, gory kills and enough pop culture references of the era to make the nostalgics happy from posters for *Saturday Night Fever* in the club's dressing room to a Led Zepplin album peeking into shot. By using real locations such as Crystal Film Productions' actual office and a grimy BDSM bar, *Terror* has a gritty feel which, when taken with the giallo-esque plot and Argento aesthetics, almost qualifies as a British attempt at giallo.

"This is not a Halloween fable. This is a real-life horror story." – Geraldo Rivera, *Devil Worship: Exposing Satan's Underground.*

On June 17, 1970, the horrifically mutilated body of Florence Nancy Brown was found in a shallow grave near the town of El Cariso in Riverside County, California. She had been stabbed twenty times, one arm had been severed and her heart and lungs were missing. A roving band of drugged up teenagers were arrested and charged by police who tied them to another murder, that of Santa Ana gas station attendant, Jerry Wayne Carlin, who had been hacked to death in the restroom with a hatchet one day before Brown's murder.

The group's leader was one Stephen Craig Hurd, a twenty-year-old self-proclaimed devil worshiper who attracted a gang of misfits and dropouts with whom he drifted around Orange County, sleeping rough, getting high and committing petty crimes. But Hurd was going off the deep end of a satanic trip and had human sacrifice on his mind. On June 4, the devil worshipping drifters had carjacked Florence Nancy Brown's station wagon and taken her to an orange grove in Irvine where they butchered her in a satanic ritual. Hurd returned at a later date to cut out her heart and eat part of it. He claimed that he wanted to use Brown's car to drive to San Francisco and meet the 'head devil', not Anton LaVey apparently, but exactly who he was referring to has remained a mystery.

That these ritualistic murders happened in California so soon after the Manson murders was unnerving to say the least. Unfortunately, they would not be the last occult-connected murders of the decade. The very next month, a hippie hitchhiker called Stanley Dean Baker was arrested in Big Sur, California and was found to have human finger bones in his pocket. These, he admitted, belonged to a man he had murdered in Montana before removing his heart and eating a part of, keeping the fingers for something to chew on. "I have a problem," he told the arresting officers. "I'm a cannibal". Baker claimed he had been part of a satanic 'blood drinking cult' in Wyoming. Then there was the tragic case of nineteen-year-old Arlis Perry whose body was found, violated by a three-foot long altar candle in the Stanford Memorial Church in October 1974, apparently another victim of a ritualistic murder.

Isolated crimes of deranged murderers who happened to have a passing interest in Satanism and the occult, or pieces of a much more sinister puzzle? The fact that drugs (in particular, LSD) had played a part in almost all of these murders might go some way in helping us make sense of their horrific natures, but others were content to focus on their occult aspects instead. Counterculture poet, singer and activist, Ed Sanders, attended the Manson trial and penned a 1971 book called *The Family* full of unsubstantiated accounts from anonymous sources that tied Manson to snuff movies, celebrity drug orgies and child porn rings as well as the deranged crimes of Stephen Hurd and Stanley Dean Baker, claiming it was all part of a nationwide satanic cult called Four Pi which had previously been known as The Process Church of the Final Judgement; that oddball cult who had distributed magazines and owned coffee shops in the late 1960s.

Sanders and his publishers were almost immediately sued for libel by The Process and all references to them were removed from subsequent editions of the book. But the seed had been planted and it would be watered with the blood of over a dozen people between

July 1976 and July 1977. The .44 Caliber Killer, as the press initially dubbed him, terrorized New York in a series of shootings that claimed the lives of six people (wounding several more) as he taunted the police and the press by sending them cryptic letters filled with occult references in which he referred to himself as 'The Son of Sam'. His eventual arrest revealed him to be a mild-mannered postal worker called David Berkowitz who claimed that he had been ordered to kill by a demonically possessed dog owned by his neighbor Sam Carr. He also stated, "There are other Sons out there, God help the world."

The idea that Berkowitz didn't act alone has been argued and contested since the late seventies, given weight by the work of journalist Maury Terry whose newspaper articles and eventual 1987 book, *The Ultimate Evil*, claimed Berkowitz was part of a satanic cult based in Yonkers, with connections in North Dakota. The cult allegedly included the real 'Sons of Sam', John and Michael Carr (sons of Berkowitz's dog-owning neighbor, Sam Carr), both of whom died mysteriously within two years of Berkowitz's arrest, Michael in a car accident and John by suicide in North Dakota.

Berkowitz, embarking on six consecutive life sentences, was keen to play ball from his prison cell, scrawling cryptic notes in a copy of Peter Haining's 1974 book *Anatomy of Witchcraft* which he smuggled out of prison to one of Terry's associates. His 'clues' were always too vague to be of much use but tantalizing enough to keep Terry on the case, much of them in line with Ed Sanders's wild theories, suggesting that Berkowitz had read that book too. One chilling footnote even alluded to the stalking and murder of Arlis Perry who, interestingly, hailed from North Dakota. In 1993, Maury Terry interviewed Berkowitz for *Inside Edition*

369

and the killer confirmed that there *were* multiple shooters but remained characteristically reluctant to elaborate or implicate anybody else.

While the theatres and drive-ins of the 1970s churned out movies about satanic cults, demonic possession, and black magic, it was clear that there was a darker side to the decade's seemingly fathomless interest in the satanic and the question must be asked; was art imitating life or was it the other way around? Berkowitz claimed that he was 'obsessed' with *Rosemary's Baby*(7) and ten years later, fellow serial killer Richard Ramirez scrawled pentagrams at the scenes of his crimes and made some of his victims pray to Satan before he killed them. 'The devil made me do it' is an excuse that rarely receives anything other than derision but, as the 1980s dawned, some believed that the satanic pop culture of the seventies hadn't been a fad at all but a symptom of a society under the influence of an actual satanic cult that had infiltrated America to its highest echelons.

The panic had been incubating throughout the seventies. A year after Ed Saunders's sensationalist book, evangelist Mike Warnke claimed in his own book, *The Satan Seller*, that he had been the high priest of a satanic cult in the 1960s involved in drug dealing and murder and had attended a satanic ritual in 1966 at which Charles Manson had been present. That Manson was still in prison when this supposed meeting took place didn't dissuade some that every word was true and the book became a bestseller, but it wouldn't be until the publication of *Michelle Remembers* in 1980 that the true 'Satanic Panic' hit its stride.

Cowritten by Michelle Smith and her therapist (and eventual husband) Lawrence Pazder, *Michelle Remembers* is a purported account of the sessions between Smith and Pazder during which repressed memories were recovered concerning Smith's abuse at the hands of a satanic cult in the 1950s. Smith claimed that from the age of five, she was tortured, locked in cages, sexually assaulted and forced to partake in satanic rituals which involved smearing the blood of sacrificed babies on her body.

Satan, as it is often said, sells and similar tales of satanic ritual abuse (SRA) began popping up, often accompanied by lucrative publishing deals, describing things far more sickening than anything to be found in an occult horror movie of the previous decade. The panic reached its most notorious point in a series of trials from 1987 to 1990 in which several members of the McMartin family who operated a preschool in Manhattan Beach, California, were accused of sexually abusing children in their care. The first allegations were made by Judy Johnson, the mother of a two-year-old boy at the preschool, who accused one member of staff of molesting her son as part of a satanic ritual. Other children were interviewed via techniques which were highly coercive and full of leading questions resulting in hundreds of bizarre stories of flying witches, satanic cults, pedophilia, animal sacrifice and a warren of secret rooms and tunnels beneath the preschool.

The McMartin Preschool Abuse Trial (the longest and most expensive criminal trial in American history) resulted in all charges being dropped against the defendants, although one of them had spent five years in jail as a result of the accusations. Judy Johnson was revealed to be a diagnosed paranoid schizophrenic who drank herself to death before the first trial began and no evidence of any secret rooms or tunnels beneath the McMartin preschool has ever been found.

Accusations of cannibalism and child murder have often been levelled at religious minorities and other outsider groups, either real groups like Jews or invented ones like witches, and, as the satanic ritual abuse scare took off, it seemed like the old 'blood libel' myth of the Middle Ages had resurfaced for a new age. As claims of satanic conspiracies were becoming more numerous and far-fetched, the environment of the early eighties seemed tailormade to accept them. The rise of Christian fundamentalism and the creation of the Moral Majority organization in 1979 by Baptist minister Jerry Falwell Sr. saw a mobilization of conservative Christians against what they saw as the moral decay of modern America. The election of Ronald Regan as president in 1980 (whom the Moral Majority had lobbied) signified an alliance between evangelical America and the White House.

Nobody encapsulates the conservative crusading mentality of the era better than comic book artist Jack Chick. Rabidly anti-Catholic, anti-communist, anti-feminist, anti-gay and anti-rock and roll, Chick's fundamentalist tracts and comic books spread conspiracy theories and tried to save the souls of America from damnation. The occult and satanic boom offered Chick a plethora of new targets and his 1978 *Spellbound?* comic used the conspiracy theorist (and alleged 'ex-grand Druid priest') John Todd as a basis for its character Lance Collins who warned Christians about the dangers of the role-playing game Dungeons & Dragons.

Released in 1974, D&D as it is commonly known, quickly came under fire from Christian conservatives who were worried that it encouraged devil worship and witchcraft. In 1979, sixteen-year-old James Dallas Egbert III vanished from the campus of Michigan State University, leaving behind a suicide note. After a failed attempt to kill himself in the steam tunnels below the university, Egbert went on the run, and it took a private investigator to find him. In the interim, wild stories began to circulate in the media once the PI had learned that Egbert had played Dungeons & Dragons.

Egbert was returned to his family but took his own life a year later, most likely due to mental health issues and may only have had a mild interest in the game in the first place. That didn't stop Dungeons & Dragons becoming part and parcel of the Satanic Panic, inspiring Rona Jaffe's 1981 novel *Mazes and Monsters* and its TV adaptation (starring a young Tom Hanks) the following year. Another tragic suicide of a troubled teen was linked to Dungeons & Dragons in 1982. Seventeen-year-old Irving Lee Pulling II, a keen player of the game, shot himself in the chest hours after a 'curse' had been placed on him by fellow players. Despite his reported social problems and unhappiness at school, Pulling's mother was convinced that the game was responsible for her son's death and founded the public advocacy group B.A.D.D. (Bothered About Dungeons & Dragons).

In fact, groups were popping up left, right and center in the 1980s, made up of parents and politicians who were concerned about the youth's apparent indoctrination into the occult. And there were plenty of targets besides role-playing games. Rock music has long been associated with the devil from the Faustian story of blues legend Robert Johnson selling his soul to the devil for mastery of the guitar to the occult pretensions of the Rolling Stones and Led Zepplin. In the seventies, Black Sabbath, AC/DC and Kiss took rock music into more overtly satanic territory and, by the mid-eighties, artists like Mötley Crüe and Ozzy Osbourne were cheerfully emblazoning their album covers with pentagrams and devils.

In 1985, the Parents Music Resource Center (PMRC) was founded by a group of 'Washington Wives' including Tipper Gore. Their goal was to introduce a rating system warning parents of records containing offensive content such as occultism. They compiled a list of songs known as the 'Filthy Fifteen' which wagged their finger at heavy metal bands Venom for their song "Possessed" and Merciful Fate for "Into the Coven". It wasn't just the occult the PMRC were concerned about. Prince, Madonna and Cyndi Lauper also made the list for their sexually explicit lyrics.

A 'porn rock' Senate hearing resulted in the now commonplace 'parental advisory' sticker which quickly became a fashionable t-shirt and poster logo, but Christian conservatism wasn't done with heavy metal just yet. One of the PMRC's allegations was that some bands were using 'backmasking'; the recording of lyrics backwards on a track containing a hidden message which can be heard when played in reverse. The Beatles had fooled around with backmasking on their 1966 album *Revolver*, fueling the bizarre conspiracy theory that Paul McCartney had died and was replaced by a body double and that the band were putting subtle allusions to this in their records.

The now-debunked idea that these subliminal messages could reach the subconscious and alter behavior appealed to Christian fundamentalists who insisted that a satanic conspiracy was using backmasking to recruit teenagers or even drive them to suicide. Led Zepplin's song "Stairway to Heaven" was accused of containing satanic messages such as 'Here's to my sweet Satan', and, despite claims of pareidolia (the brain's tendency to see patterns where there are none) and the observer-expectancy effect, there were many heated debates and church organized record burnings. Yet more suicides of troubled teens were blamed on occult pop culture resulting in court cases in 1990 and 1991 against Judas Priest and Ozzy Osbourne respectively, both of whom were accused of including subliminal messages on their records encouraging suicide. Both cases were dismissed and the backmasking myth began to die out in the face of consistent scientific reports indicating that even intentional subliminal messages would not be picked up by the brain when heard in reverse.

As the satanic panic grew, the claims and conspiracy theories became ever more ludicrous. Rock band Kiss stood for 'Knights in Satan's Service'. The *Smurfs* cartoon promoted sorcery. There was even a rumor that the logo for consumer goods corporation Proctor and Gamble (a man in the moon looking at thirteen stars) was an indication of their satanic allegiance. Police departments hired self-proclaimed 'occult experts' who pointed at graffitied pentagrams as sure signs that satanic cults were operating in their jurisdictions. Credibility was lent to the incredible by the supposed voices of reason. Geraldo Rivera presented a sensationalist television special for NBC in 1988 which interviewed 'ex-Satanists' and claimed the breeding of babies for use in satanic sacrifices "may really be happening" while Oprah Winfrey hosted both Michelle Smith and Lauren Stratford (author of a similar 'recovered memory' book, *Satan's Underground*) on a 1989 episode of her show.

The validity of *Michelle Remembers*, the most prominent instigator of the Satanic Panic has since been contested by many sources and, in the early nineties, *Cornerstone* magazine (an evangelical publication, no less) debunked both *The Satan Seller* and *Satan's Underground*, revealing the author of the latter to be a con artist called Laurel Rose Wilson who would also falsely claim to be a Holocaust survivor. As for the satanic murders of the 1970s, that decade saw a drastic rise in serial murders in general with many explanations ranging from rapid urbanization and increased hitchhiking to a generation of boomers who had grown up in violent homes due to returning war veteran fathers with undiagnosed PTSD. While plenty of serial killers of the seventies and eighties like Ted Bundy and John Wayne Gacy had no occult connections, it is perhaps to be expected that at least a portion of them would have some interest in the occult as the occult has always attracted the loners and the misfits. If they weren't killing for Satan, then they would quite possibly be killing for some other cause.

And the prospect of life behind bars encourages many killers to place a portion of the blame for their crimes on either satanic cults or the devil himself. David Berkowitz may well have been part of some sort of occult group that also involved John and Michael Carr but so far, nothing conclusively ties them to the killings or proves that Berkowitz didn't act alone. No support of his claim that he had inside knowledge of the murder of Arlis Perry has been found and in fact, a key suspect, Stephen Crawford (the security guard who found her body), shot himself when police tried to apprehend him in 2018 after finding new evidence implicating him in the murder.

It's one thing for serial killers to take inspiration from horror movies, but when seemingly rational people believe that movies like *Rosemary's Baby* and *Race with the Devil* have some basis in reality, the end result can be just as destructive. The Satanic Panic of the 1980s petered out in the nineties, but it had claimed many victims in the form of ruined careers and false imprisonments. As late as 1994, three teenagers known as the West Memphis Three were convicted for the horrific murders of three eight-year-old boys whose bodies were found naked and hogtied in a water-filled ditch. The prosecution rested on the confession of one of them (who had a reported IQ of 72) after he had been picked up by the police and grilled without legal representation for twelve hours of which, curiously, only forty-six minutes had been recorded. The usual claptrap was spouted by 'occult experts' at their trials to support the idea that the murders were part of a satanic ritual. The defendants were loners, wore black, listened to heavy metal, had a mild interest in the occult and one of them, in a particularly weak argument, read Stephen King novels. The three teenagers spent eighteen years behind bars before new evidence allowed them to accept a deal in 2011 and finally walk free.

Witch hunts, moral panics and demonizing of the unknown have always been with us and are seemingly as indelibly a part of our collective mentality as our thirst for secret knowledge and command of the natural world. Recent years have shown that conservative fears of societal change which can snowball into accusations of devil worship and pedophilia have gone nowhere. In 2016, a twenty-eight-year-old man opened fire with a semi-automatic rifle at a Washington D.C. pizzeria, thinking he was rescuing children from a child sex ring linked to members of the Democratic party. This conspiracy theory, known as 'Pizzagate', had gained widespread attention online during the 2016 presidential election and was later sucked into the much larger 'QAnon' conspiracy theory. Originating as a series of posts on the website 4chan by an anonymous 'Q', the theory claimed that the Trump administration was secretly battling a cabal of Satanists including high profile Democratic politicians and Hollywood celebrities who are operating a global child sex ring (which also involves cannibalism, naturally).

The internet and social media have ushered in an age of misinformation where any crackpot conspiracy theory can gain as much exposure as mainstream news articles. The tailoring of posts and media to individuals based on their interests and political opinions has created online echo chambers where reason, facts and logic cannot compete with confirmation bias and neotribalism. The Satanic Panic of the 1980s, like the Red Scare of the 1950s, the witch hunts of the 17th century and the blood libel of the Middle Ages, should serve as a warning to us. Isolation and fear of things we don't understand can cause hysteria and hypervigilance leading to false allegations of some imagined threat. And what is the most precious thing in our society to be threatened but our children?

The occult horror movies of the 1970s look positively tame compared to the allegations so many people accepted as factual in *Michelle Remembers*, the McMartin preschool trial and QAnon's posts. Unconstrained by such things as taste, our own imaginations, it seems, can conjure things far worse than what we would dare conceive of as fiction. The devil has always served as the root of all evil, the very worst thing to align enemies with. He is a tool, both religious and political, the evil behind any crime, no matter how heinous. To declare a person or group to be in league with him, is to put them in league with pedophilia, kidnapping, cannibalism and human sacrifice. It's a lazy way to quite literally demonize somebody. Nothing is easier. Don't like somebody? Claim they are a devil worshipper. To quote the title of Maury Terry's book, he is the Ultimate Evil.

With the lessons of the Satanic Panic in mind and the steady normalization of conspiracy theories by normal, young people on social media, where baseless accusations can go viral and anonymous harassment is all too easy, it is perhaps more important than ever that Satan remains a fictional monster. Rather than inspiring serial killers or recruiting young people into the occult, satanic horror movies serve to put Satan in the same box as vampires and werewolves, reducing him to a stock monster of trashy pop culture and, essentially, robbing him of his power. Maybe it is best that Satan is left in the celluloid.

REFERENCES

1. https://www.theguardian.com/books/2015/oct/2
   7/the-occult-kind-of-awakening-colin-wilson
2. https://www.cielodrive.com/archive/movie-lot-
   satan-portent-of-death/
3. https://www.therialtoreport.com/2016/04/24/jos
   eph-mawra/
4. Graham, Billy "Billy Graham Tells Why He's
   Afraid to See The Exorcist: An Exclusive Interview." National Enquirer, March. 3, 1974
5. Mubarki, Meraj. (2013). Mapping the Hindi Horror Genre: Ghosts in the Service of Ideology.
   History and Sociology of South Asia, 7. (1) 39-60.
6. Collier, Kevin Scott. *The Life and Cinema of Ted
   V. Mikels.* Kevin Scott Collier, 2017
7. Fishman, Steve. "The Devil in Serial Killer David
   'Son of Sam' Berkowitz." New York Magazine,
   Sept.   8,   2006.
   https://nymag.com/news/crimelaw/20327/

Made in United States
Troutdale, OR
12/03/2024

25827327R00235